TEXAS BLOOD

*Herman Ehrenberg's Odyssey
in the Texas Revolution*

Texas Blood

Herman Ehrenberg's Odyssey in the Texas Revolution

By Herman Ehrenberg

Mockingbird Books
Boerne, Texas

Originally published in 1845 as
Fahrten und Schicksale eines Deutschen in Texas.
Based on a 1925 translation by Edgar William Bartholomae.
This edition copyright 2016, Mockingbird Books.
All rights reserved.

ISBN 9781932801361

Mockingbird Books
Boerne, Texas
mockingbirdbooks.com

Table of Contents

Introduction v
Mexico Before 1835 1
New Orleans 9
Nacogdoches 17
The Coffeehouse 23
The Banquet 31
The March to San Antonio 35
The Prairie Fire 41
The Camp of the Militia 53
The Storming of San Antonio 69
San Antonio 89
Departure for Matamoras 99
Fannin's Landing 115
The Campaign of 1836 Begins 123
Independence 129
The Fall of the Alamo 139
The Battle of Coleto 145
The Imprisonment 163
The Murder of the Prisoners 175
Fannin's Death 185
My Flight through the Wilderness 189

TABLE OF CONTENTS

The Colonies	199
Urrea's Camp	209
Old Sam	227
On the Colorado	235
The Amnesty	241
The March to Matagorda	247
Matagorda	251
San Jacinto	259
The Retreat	269
Away from the Free and Sovereign Prairie	285
The Capture of the Rhine-Prussian	295
Santa Anna	301
Santa Anna's Attempted Flight	307
Conclusion	315

Introduction

Herman Ehrenberg left his native Prussia for New York City in 1834, at the age of 17. The autumn of 1835 found him in New Orleans, where he enlisted with the New Orleans Greys to fight in the Texas Revolution.

Ehrenberg and the Greys fought with Benjamin R. Milam in the 1835 siege of the Alamo. After occupying the Alamo, they ended up under the command of Colonel James W. Fannin, bringing Ehrenberg into the frustrating and confused events that culminated in the Battle of Coleto and the Goliad Massacre. Ehrenberg was one of the few to escape the massacre, struggling cross-country to find sanctuary. Attempting to pass himself off as an American non-combatant, he ended up a prisoner of Mexican General Jose de Urrea.

During the latter stages of the revolution, Ehrenberg was a captive of the Mexican army at Matagorda under the command of Lieutenant Colonel Juan Jose (Johann Josef) Holzinger, who took Ehrenberg with him on an attempt to flee to Matamoros on flat-bottomed boats after the defeat of General Antonio Lopez de Santa Anna at San Jacinto.

Ehrenberg's first-person account of his epic adventures is remarkable, but his chronicle is also valuable for his inclusion of second-hand accounts gathered from contemporaries. These episodes provide windows into the Battle of the Alamo, the Battle of San Jacinto and other conflicts as they were known at the time, before journalists and historians began contesting the facts.

Just as importantly, Ehrenberg gives us rich images of life among the settlers and soldiers of the period. His descriptions of farms, plantations, towns, rivers, bays, prairies and life on the frontier provide a fascinating sense of what Texas was in the late 1830s.

It would be a mistake to read Ehrenberg without recognizing that he added doses of romanticism and adventure for his German audience. It is entirely possible that some of his episodes are invented or embellished. And the young Ehrenberg's memory is not perfect—his account contains some simple mistakes of fact. There is no dispute, however, about whether Ehrenberg was there, on the battlefields of the Texas Revolution.

Ehrenberg's book was printed in German in three editions, each of which was substantially identical but bore a separate title: *Texas und seine Revolution* (1843), *Der Freiheitskampf in Texas im Jahre 1836* (1844) and *Fahrten und Schicksale eines Deutschen in Texas* (1845). This English translation is based on the 1845 German edition, and is derived from a 1925 translation that Edgar W. Bartholomae produced as a thesis in support of his Master's Degree in History from the University of Texas. The Bartholomae translation was placed in the thesis collection of the university, but was never published as a book and has remained unknown to all but the most diligent scholars.

INTRODUCTION

Another translation of Ehrenberg's account was performed by Charlotte Churchill; that version was heavily edited and sanitized by Henry Nash Smith to be suitable for Texas school children and was published in 1935 under the title *With Milam and Fannin: Adventures of a German Boy in Texas' Revolution*.

The Bartholomae translation is not without its critics. Professor James E. Crisp of North Carolina State University is the most prominent authority on Ehrenberg and Bartholomae's translation; together with Professor Louis E. Brister of Southwest Texas State University, he has long been working on an improved and annotated translation of Ehrenberg's work, combined with an Ehrenberg biography. That edition has not yet been published; this edition takes into account corrections to the Bartholomae translation that have been flagged by Crisp in the *Southwestern Historical Quarterly*.[1]

This edition has edited the Bartholomae translation to modernize some language, refine some inside-out German syntax, improve word choices and re-translate some obviously erroneous phrases.

---

[1] James E. Crisp, "Sam Houston's Speechwriters: The Grad Student, the Teenager, the Editors and the Historians," *SWHQ* 97 (October 1993): 203; Crisp, "In Pursuit of Herman Ehrenberg: A Research Adventure," *SWHQ* 102 (April 1999): 423.

Mexico Before 1835

UNTIL THE MEXICAN WAR OF INDEPENDENCE, the permanently established Spanish officers as well as the aristocracy had done everything within the range of human power to fetter the respect and independence of the Mexicans through fraud and bloody executions. Slaves, yes worse than slaves, dogs, were the peoples of the particularly beautiful plateaus and mountains of Anahuac. Yet these bloodsuckers were not the greatest enemies with which the nation had to battle; another and far greater enemy, working hand in hand with the former, had drawn its terrible weapons against the inhabitants.

The disciples of Loyola had, with the aid of the rack and the funeral pyre, forced a spirit-killing form of religion upon the once peaceful people. These servants of God began with demoralization to convert the Indians to Christianity; and splendidly, yea splendidly, did they succeed in this holy work. Here they displayed their masterwork, and not one step did they remain behind their brothers in South America. The gaze of the North American free states wanders with horror from their borders down over the south. Splendid, incomparable lands spread themselves out here; but all these fruitful stretches are flecked with murder and debauchery.

The indescribable misery of Mexico had reached that state where further endurance was beyond human power. Furiously, frantically arose the ragged peoples and, poorly armed or armed not at all, they threw themselves into the struggle. To war! To war! sounded to the hills of Tenochtitlan and the echo multiplied a thousand times, rebounded like thunder to the south and east, north and west. Down with the *Gachupins*! Down with the dogs! Mexico be free! Free! *Viva Mexico*!

For eleven long years the opposing parties battled and murdered; and in rags, not unlike robbers, if in reality they were not such, wandered about the land. Blood, blood was the rallying words from all sides. The one faction, the Spaniards, carried the sword of murder for greediness and for slavery; the other one, the Mexicans, for vengeance against its oppressors who for several hundred years wielded the whip over their heads.

The year 1821 approached and with it the last stand of Spanish despotism. The vice-regal government was compelled to recognize the independence of Mexico. After protracted disputes among the patriot leaders, Iturbide succeeded in establishing himself at the helm of the shattered machine of state. Iturbide became emperor.

Putting aside its form, the government might have worked worthily for the welfare of its country, but, suspecting treason, Iturbide devoted most of his attention to enslaving the newly liberated people again. A large number of envious Mexicans, watching his movements with distrust, seized this opportunity to dethrone him, and after a single year of rule the imperial government was destroyed. Iturbide vanished and in 1824 a most liberal constitution, with the exception of a few articles corresponding with that of the United States of North America, was adopted.

Had the people of that time only had sufficient consciousness of political freedom, they would have played practically as important a role in the world theater as the neighboring republic. But the indolent slaves of the priests delegated to them and to a few ambitious important soldiers the political field and the reins of the government without taking advantage of their rights won through struggle and victory.

The Spaniards were banished from power; Mexico's glowing hatred subsided. And again the people fell into a condition not far removed from that of animals. Sensuous pleasure and a life without work was all that they desired. Several political parties sprang up but their efforts were mainly directed toward securing control of the government. Their various courses, however, crossed one another; and they arose one against the other as enemies. Through misrepresentations and appeals of the priests, the ignorant people were incited bulldog-like one against the other, without knowing why they should shoulder the musket.

Thus it was until the year 1832 that this garden of the new world was the scene of dark deeds. In this year, however, Santa Anna announced his support of the liberal constitution of 1824. He offered himself as leader of the liberal party for the purpose of overthrowing the despotic government of Bustamante. He succeeded, and again Mexico began to show its incomparable sluggishness. Again the nation resigned itself to its dear repose and, with the exception of the inhabitants of Zacatecas, trusted the duplicitous victor, Santa Anna.

It was a favorable moment for him and he used it. The just-promised restoration of the legal constitution was again refused; the edicts of the dictator were put into execution at the point of the bayonets of the raw soldiers—Indians—and all states that arose against this forcible overthrow and their own annihilation were suppressed by their own troops. A centralized government was to be established, the sovereign states were to be converted into plain provinces and the whole nation was to be placed under military guardianship.

Now the northeast province, Texas, appears in the foreground and few words are necessary in order to understand the following.

Until the Mexican War of Independence, Texas had only a small Mexican population, which lived in the towns of San Antonio, La Bahia, Nacogdoches and a few mission establishments where they were by virtue of their numbers protected against the Comanches and other prairie Indians.

The reason why such a land as Texas should contain no more than six thousand inhabitants lay on the one hand in the jealousy of the Spaniards of the neighboring states from whose liberal institutions they had everything to fear, and on the other in that the Indians made all culture and all intercourse of the land unusually difficult. Their hordes swarmed about in the border provinces and penetrated ever deeper into the remaining states. In Texas the Mexicans paid tribute to the Comanche authorities; and when one of the red chiefs honored San Antonio with a visit, the commander of the troops was obliged to obediently hold horse and stirrup for him.

In order to stop these Indian raids, the Spanish government shortly before its fall accepted a plan of an American, Moses Austin, who proposed founding a colony of his countrymen in Texas to protect the frontier. Moses Austin died soon after he had laid the foundation of the colony; his son, Stephen F. Austin, continued the work. Hundreds of families from the states swarmed over. The Mexican war broke out, independence was won, and another policy friendlier to the colonies was adopted by the government. Their former rights were approved, new ones arranged for, and a constitution especially fitted for the Americans was given them. From year to year the colonies grew larger, and new ones were laid out with the approval of the general government.

Conditions of life for the colonies became increasingly safe on the plantations, and soon the Indians didn't dare to trifle with the determined vigorous North Americans as they were in the custom of doing with the Mexicans. The attention of the Texans was also fixed on Mexico. And only too clearly did they recognize the weaknesses of the various governments that so rapidly succeeded one another. Texas was too remote from the theater of war to cooperate effectively, but on their own soil the Texans always contended for the constitution of 1824, though it was distressingly mutilated in Mexico.

Up to the year 1832 several undesirable laws had seriously affected the welfare of the colonies. The colonists felt affronted in the highest degree, and they obtained justice on a few points only after determined protests to the weak authorities.

The keen spirits of North America looked down with indignation and contempt upon the sinful nation with which they were to associate — with a people which did not cast a single glance beyond the present and which promised to remain the tools of deceitful priests. With this race of negro, Indian and Spanish blood, which could not comprehend its freedom, and which was not conscious of its own rights, the liberal colonists could not possibly intermingle. Nevertheless, the colonists still hoped for the best from the future.

Already several disquieting movements had taken place in Texas, and a part of the citizens were under arms against several garrisons because of their unjust actions, when suddenly the glad tidings were received in the colonies that

Santa Anna had placed himself at the head of the liberal party. And here also was the corresponding banner raised at once and the garrisons were obliged to yield to it.

Santa Anna, as previously mentioned, became untrue to his political pretentions, and his government came to be viewed by the colonies in Texas with greater suspicion than any previous one had been. The petition of the Texans to the general government for separate statehood in the Union, for which they were ready and to which they were constitutionally entitled, remained without result. Their representative, Stephen F. Austin, was imprisoned in the city of Mexico and was held a long time without trial. Peaceful citizens were arrested without cause and on barest suspicion, and other excesses were committed.

In the summer of 1835 Austin returned after two years' detention in Mexico, and he was received with rejoicing by the offended colonists. Lorenzo de Zavala, a Mexican and hero of the revolution who had opposed Santa Anna's violent and illegal measures, was compelled to leave Mexico and he placed himself under the protection of the Texans.

Ugartechea, then the political chief at San Antonio, received instructions to march into the colonies from San Antonio to put Zavala forcibly into chains. Soon after him General Cos from Matamoras appeared with reinforcements to take command in the colonies. With him appeared a number of senseless laws for the Texans of which I will mention only the following two.

All the arms of the Texans were to be handed over, and as evidence of special consideration the inhabitants of each five plantations were to be allowed one gun. The colonies were further forbidden to build churches. All other mandates of the Mexicans were also beyond the possibility of execution. How unreasonable and spiteful was the first law in a land like Texas at that time surrounded on all sides by marauding Indians, and how unworthy of justice was the other. Thus are all the others. It is barely necessary for me to explain all of them; I believe that I have said enough to show by what right the colonies were justified in bringing force into service against force. And now to the revolution.

New Orleans

"PUBLIC MEETING"—projected in letters two feet high on corners of the unusually straight streets of New Orleans—"great public meeting tonight at eight o'clock in the Arcade. Liberty is at stake, the sovereignty of a people in whose veins flows the blood of the Anglo-Saxons—Texas, the prairie land, has arisen in order to oppose with arms the tyrant Santa Anna and the greedy and imperious priests of Mexico. The liberal citizens of the Union are being besought for aid. We have therefore instituted a general meeting of the inhabitants of our city and we hope to see our citizens in large numbers at the place."
"The Committee for Texas."

The numerous periodicals of the city hastened to advise the public of the new happenings in Texas. The sympathy was general, and the avowed organs of the Whigs as well as those of the Democrats and the smaller neutral blades united in their support of brethren beyond the Sabine; and united they thundered their weighty voice among people of the United Free-States of North America.

Independent journals privileged to convey the truth to the people are the main support of the state; they hinder the retrogression of civilization and inspire the citizens to noble deeds. They exchange views and protect against intrigues of Jesuits of all ilks whose aim has always been the tyrannization of the world. Here, too, they inflamed the spirits. Americans as well as Europeans, Protestants as well as Catholics, armed themselves in order to make sacrifices on the holy altar of liberty.

Portentously the bells struck eight in the cathedral, and a Mississippi River composed of people flowed toward the gigantic coffeehouse, the Arcade. Already thousands stood under the high colonnades and shoulder to shoulder formed lines in the crowded galleries.

Speaker after speaker ascended the tribune. The unrestricted noise of the mass ceased and the stillness of the desert settled over the audience. Vigorous speeches that purposed to convey to the public the causes of the national uprising of the Texans were held. Others contained the pleadings of the colonists to the inhabitants of the Free States for support against the usurper, Santa Anna, who in conjunction with the priests had destroyed the constitution of 1824. The speeches of the citizens touched the hearts of the masses that crowded close around the speakers' stand, and happy was he who could speak to the people that day. Even though his speech organs were not of the best, the cause for which he raised his voice was much in his favor; and at every pause the public thundered its applause for the struggle for the prolific prairie.

The enthusiastic citizens crowded around the subscription list lying on the speaker's table, and even before the assemblage had left the colonnades, ten thousand dollars had been subscribed. Another list was opened for volunteers who desired to support their former countrymen in the struggle. A six-foot Kentuckian now ascended the speakers' platform and signed up at the top under the thundering applause of the, enthusiastic mass that surrounded him. "Old Kentucky" was, as always, the first to seize the rifle when it was necessary to go into the field to struggle for the right. The meeting was closed and the lists posted in the same building for further participation in them in the morning.

Squire Stern, the representative of the Texans and a native German, was highly elated over the result. On the next morning, October 12, 1835, the *Washita* had already steered up the Mississippi with the first Texas volunteers, the first company of Greys, who desired to make the journey overland. All of us had speedily purchased grey uniforms, which we found ready-made in the numerous magazines, and from which the name of our company had its origin. Our weapons were the rifle, pistols and to the Indian fighters the well-known Bowie knife. We also received on board several cannon from the Texas committee that were to make the journey with us. A day after our departure a second company of Greys left New Orleans, going, however, through the Gulf of Mexico to Texas; and the next expedition to be fitted out was the Tampico Blues, whose destination, however, was not Texas but, as the name indicates, the Mexican city of Tampico. It was composed of Americans, Britons, Frenchmen, and a few Germans. Our two companies, the Greys, numbered six Germans.

The *Washita* soon left the mighty waters of the Mississippi and turned into the narrow but deep Red River. Here it was that we first tried our rifles, and it was on the countless strongly armored alligators that were lying on the numerous old tree trunks with which all streams in the primeval forests are bordered. They sunned themselves and were in the habit of paying no attention to the passing Greys until a few bullets from us threw them down into their miry element. Very seldom did the residence of a planter appear on the damp, impenetrably forested banks; and first near Alexandria, a little village on the right bank of the Red River, appeared a few settlements. The arrival of the Greys was already expected here, and soon the whole militia was on its feet to entertain the champions of liberty. Our impatience to enter the war zone did not permit us a very long stay; but after we had emptied a glass of real Holland or a few, more tasty champagnes on the welfare of the colonies, we marched in pompous parade back to the panting *Washita*. And as the last sound of the signal bell had resounded in the forest, the boat was roaring upstream through the thick, turbid waters. Before we had reached Natchitoches we were through with the election of officers. Breese was elected captain without opposition.

In Natchitoches we were received in the same manner as in Alexandria; and as we had to wait here for a few articles, our camp was pitched for the first time under the primitive trees of the stately forest. The open-hearted citizens immediately sent us out a wagon-load of provisions of all kinds; and when we walked through the streets we were invited to friendly meals from all sides. On account of inactivity, dissatisfaction broke out in the company on the second day after our arrival in spite of the pleasant living. It was the highest time when Captain Breese appeared in camp near two o'clock and issued orders for immediate breaking of camp. The important news that the colonists aimed to make an early attack on San Antonio had just arrived. We therefore had little time to spare if we would have a share in this glorious undertaking.

Hardly had a half hour passed before we were already hastily marching through the meanderings of the forest that abounded in game, and by nine o'clock in the evening we had already covered a distance of forty-two miles. On the next day we had to circumvent a fort occupied by Uncle Sam's troops which stood on the boundary to protect the American settlers from attacks of the wild Indian tribes. The fort's commanding officer could not allow us to march through to the Mexican, now Texan, boundary if the friendly relations between the Union and Mexico were to remain undisturbed; consequently, we proceeded cautiously.

A few miles beyond the line of observation we encamped for the night with a gentleman named Thomas, and from there we reached the mirror-bright Sabine, a part of which borders the United States, on the following day. Silvery waters, more welcoming than the thick, loamy waters of the Red River, rolled softly toward the Gulf, and on the opposite bank—Texas—we were received by men of the region who had remained behind to protect the homeland and the families.

The tender hand of a fair Texan gave us in the name of a number of beauties of the land a splendid blue silk flag on which the following inscription appeared: "To the first company of Texan Volunteers from New Orleans."

After we had kissed the soil, received the holy ordinance of citizenship, and Captain Breese had to some extent expressed to the ladies our inexpressible thanks, we marched enthusiastically on, and on the second day following we reached the new little town of San Augustine.

Barely had we left the forest that surrounds the same when the excellent militia marched out to meet us with the deep roll of the drum, out of which the drummer, in harmony with his own steps, drew forth the most dismal sounds. Regularly his strokes fell on the flabby hide, and the echo rumbled back out of the dark forest like the voice of a spirit. But this kind of music is well adapted to stimulate sentimental thoughts, and these didn't at all agree with those of the enthusiastic Greys. Consequently, our drummer began to roll the lively "Beer in the Mug" march, which occasioned a complete change in mood. The good music had its effect, and our ears suffered little more from the death march of the now closely approaching militia.

On command of the citizen captain his drummer was quiet, and the tones of our drum died away just in time for us to hear the hurrahs of the worthy backwoodsmen. The tri-colored flag flew past us in a rustle, and again the deep-toned drum accompanied the gravitated march of the militia that paraded by us two men deep and then joined our column to march, the old citizens and the new ones, widely spaced to avoid keeping step, into the marketplace of San Augustine. Three small cannon roared us a welcome, but what truly pleased us the most were the truly gigantic beef-steaks and roast beefs which were awaiting our arrival in the mammoth chimneys, to be immediately devoured by us on mirror-clean china plates and white tables. Large glasses of milk and sparkling water stood at each splendid cover, so that full consideration had been made for all the patrons of temperance societies. But for those for whom an affiliation of this kind is a picture of terror stood the nicely ground bottles of cognac and Holland gin in the center of the table, and the simple laconic "Help Yourselves" of our hosts constituted the only ceremony that we had with the eating.

After nightfall four companions and I, together with our host and his sons, sat about a brightly flickering fireplace, and the first northwest storm of the season swept down from the far distant Rocky Mountains through the woods of northeast Texas. Inwardly happy, we sat comfortably in the inviting home of the old colonist who delighted us with fiery anecdotes out of the American War of Independence. We sat motionless in wide circle about the singeing heat with the stern inhabitants of the West, except that the old gray-headed planter, who sat on the right side of the corner, and whose sharp features were overcast with a glowing hue that gave him a scary appearance, was constantly in motion. With the poker in his right hand, he constantly stirred the fire from one side to the other; he would barely lay the logs in such favorable position that the flames could break forth brightly through the intervening spaces, when the skillful hand in a few moments brought everything into a new position with the iron again; and disregarding the disturbance, the flames soon crackled forth anew. Meanwhile, we newcomers in the wilderness listened with delight to the spirited accounts of the planter and marveled at his tireless industry and skill while his eighteen- and twenty-year-old scions amused themselves, as it seemed, by whittling neat little figures out of wood. But barely were these created before these artists called forth countless alterations with their sharp little pocket knives, and ever shorter did the stick become until finally the last figure flew into the fire and another piece was brought forth for the shortening of the evening. Out of all of these evidences we would have at once recognized the planter as an immigrant from hospitable Kentucky even if his accounts of the triumph of his countrymen over the British at New Orleans had not indicated that he was one of those excellent marksmen whom "Old Hickory," as General Jackson was called because of his unyielding disposition, had commanded not to fire on the charging enemy until they could see the whites of the eyes of the British; the order was strictly obeyed, the first line of the British fell, and after a short but terrible contest the remainder fled in great confusion over the marshy ground of the region back to their fleet. But the six-miles-away New Orleans and the independence of the Union were saved, and all hopes of the British crown to re-subjugate the transatlantic colonies had vanished forever.

From time to time good advice for us and his sons flowed in laconic form from his lips. He could not strongly enough recommend economy with the powder because every mis-hit from our side would inspire the enemy with new courage, whereas a sparing but telling fire would occasion fear and confusion.

It was about eleven o'clock when we threw ourselves on a pile of bear and buffalo skins in order to break camp by sun the next morning for Nacogdoches. This town was two days' journey, however, from where we expected to begin our large 490-mile journey to San Antonio on horseback.

The signal for the breakup sounded, and after an invigorating breakfast prepared by the kind and beautiful hostesses, we marched away; a salute from a little cannon wished us good luck on our journey, and the echo of the forest conveyed to the friendly people of San Augustine our hearty thanks.

A few weeks later we saw the men again; the gallant men of San Augustine did not want to be found missing in the struggle for freedom, and another time the old planter seized the bright rifle which since 1815 had been unfriendly only to the beasts of the forest. With youthful spirit he stepped again into the ranks of fighters, and, united with his slender sons, he was always to be found where the enemy bullets flew thickest.

Nacogdoches

WE PLANNED TO ARRIVE AT NACOGDOCHES on the second day after our departure from San Augustine, but approaching frosty night found us still scattered in the different parts of the forests, and most of us spent the night in the scattered plantations that lay from five to six miles apart along the road. The nearer at that time that a person approached the town, the less often did he find the homes of the white man, notwithstanding the fact that this was the most thickly settled part of the land.

Already quite a while had passed since the last rays of the sun had disappeared, when several of us in company began anxiously to look around for the abode of a planter; we looked about in vain in the dense forest enveloped with darkness and were thinking of throwing up our quarters in the open. Suddenly we espied an open treeless region that we at first took for the fields of several planters; we soon convinced ourselves, however, that it was a prairie, the first of importance that we had struck on our journey.

Not far away several dogs began to bark, and soon a low blockhouse stood before us out of whose little windows bright rays of light shone forth. The inhabitants, a small family, were seated about the fire and, busy with themselves, they took little notice of the disturbance occasioned by the loud barking of the dogs.

A slender vigorous man of the Virginian stamp stood with his rifle on the dark side of the door and looked keenly at us as we came nearer. However, as he noticed our color he lowered the rifle and in a friendly manner invited us into the house, to the beckoning fire and an invigorating cup of coffee. After we had informed the host that we were volunteers from New Orleans, he again shook our hands vigorously, whereupon he explained to us his cautious position in front of the house. He had only recently moved across the Sabine and intended to settle here with his family, but as the Cherokees and the Cuschottes occasionally frequented these parts, and as one could not really trust them, on our approach he had gone out to determine what kind of wanderers were making their way so late through the lonesome prairie. Of course, he added, pointing to the blooming hostess, I always have the satisfaction of being laughed at by my old woman on my return, but I think a little precaution is better than a little thoughtlessness. We laughed also, but agreed with him, especially as he was a newcomer in the land.

Since we were informed that Nacogdoches was only six miles away, we decided shortly to make that two hours' march and, disregarding the persuasions of the host and his pretty family, we stormed out another time into the darkness; not, however, before we helped to devour a frugal supper of ham and eggs and the beefsteak that seldom failed to appear on the American table.

Strengthened by this meal, we soon reached the end of the prairie, and again the forest, which continued from here to the town without interruption, received us. At last after a march that seemed forever the dark figures of the homes of Nacogdoches arose about us. Unnoticed, we found ourselves in the southeast quarter of the little town.

Thoroughly tired, we knocked at a two-story house, the outside of which, like the others, did not betray any signs of being inhabited. Still, it was not necessary for us to go further, as an old negro opened the door and with a friendly light in his hand bade the first Greys of New Orleans welcome in the name of his master.

We found ourselves in the house of Squire Stern, who had already made all preparations for our reception, and in a few minutes an inviting supper steamed on the table. After the march of two hours we were again in a condition to execute wonders in our attacks on the mighty roast beefs and excellent roast venison and other game.

While we were executing our work in this festive manner, no one spoke except the old negro, who from time to time gave us the benefit of a few flourishes of his Gumbo-English. And we were just laughing heartily as our host, well pleased with our arrival, entered. He also had just returned from the Queen of the Mississippi and had been expecting us for a few days; besides, he was rejoiced to find a few native Germans among us.

"Bob," he called to the old negro, "Bob, four of the long, slender ones out of the corner on the stand, do you understand?"

"Bob understands, Massa," replied the old Guinea negro, as he departed to obey.

"How," continued the squire as he took a seat, "how do you like Texas?"

"Heavenly, Squire," replied Peter Mattern, "and the people are all so hospitable and truly gallant that I would not like to be back at Frankfurt for the present, especially as I hope that Santa Anna will chase a cloud of his creatures on our necks."

"There will be work enough for all of us," said the Squire, "every honest white skin will have to shoulder the musket to protect his family and property from the vultures of the enemy; but we will compel no one—no one, gentlemen. Everyone must go voluntarily and courageously to the struggle, because it is an honorable, a just cause that is calling our nation to the struggle. It is for our religion, our God, that we are fighting, and for the freedom of our children that we are whetting the Bowie knife."

"And therefore," interrupted George Curtman, "do we wish that our bullets will hit, and as a citizen of the new state I pledge you my last drop of human blood for the new republic—"

"Halt, my countryman, pst! pst! Do we wish to stir up the whole of Mexico against us? even the liberal party? No! Another time, pst! We are yet too weak to stand alone, and only by combination with the liberal party can we overthrow Santa Anna. Possibly in later times when many more of our brethren are clearing out the forests on this side of the Sabine and are defending the land with guns and strong arms, then can we unfold the banner of independence, and only then first, only then, let us proclaim the freedom of the prairies."

"Does the honorable squire mean to say," I interrupted him, "that we came to Texas to bow anew under absolutism after we had barely gotten acquainted with the living of a free people? Does the worthy gentleman mean that the Greys entered the prairies to clear out the primeval forests under Santa Anna or any other copper-faced slave driver, in order to break the land for their priests, or to raise large herds so that when that clique should once have a desire to do so, they might do to us even as the archenemy is now doing, swinging the dagger of despotism over the head of Mexico? Ho—we beg to be excused, squire. We will not remain standing halfway on the road. We are going the 'whole hog' as our friends in the states are accustomed to say. My countrymen need not be afraid now, the long anticipated time has arrived. Old Kentucky, true to its character, will not now look on leisurely, and I wager ten to one that even now the cry to arms is resounding through the hills of this hospitable state: 'for your brothers in Texas!— for the liberty of America!' And shortly the whole southern states will send their aid, if independence is at stake. Do you desire that the tri-colored flag of Mexico shall continue to wave over Texas, these colors that are now shot into a terrible oneness because they were not true, the colors which from day to day seem to assume more and more the appearance of those with which the whole herd of Jesuits and their minions would so gladly darken the whole world? Under those conditions this great nation through whose domains the mighty Mississippi wends, whose shores are bounded by the waves of the Gulf, the still waters of the Atlantic and the great seas of the north, will not sympathize with the inhabitants of the Mexican province of Texas. If she will at once energetically shake off the yoke, immediately raise up a flag whose colors will glow in the glitter of the southern sun, only then will the South and the West send its youths across the Sabine to aid the new republic that is just now springing into life. Therefore, another time, squire—the Republic!"

"Halt, young man, here comes Bob, may we strengthen the word with the grape juice of the Fatherland." Bob, who entered with four bottles, placed them on the table and the squire filled the glasses to the brim, and as a German scion he cried out: "This sparkling glass of worthy old Rhine, may its fluid soon flow only through that land of a single, a great free, nation."

"The old German Rhine!" repeated the chorus composed of many nations, and the flowing gold of the first glass rolled over our tongues.

"And now, squire," said Peter Mattern, filling anew, "The Republic of Texas! May the Rio del Norte be the boundary against Mexico; with Uncle Sam we will probably be able to get along."

"Gentlemen, I drink this toast with pleasure; you wish our arms to be successful, so bury it deep in your system. Spies are abiding among us. Santa Anna and the gold of the priests work in the dark, in order to make us to be hated by the whole nation, and it is still not, as I remarked a while ago, the time to throw off the mask; that would incite the nine million Mexicans against the prairies and forests; but the day will soon come when we can act as freemen, and then will the people declare the republic en masse, and then will I shout: the free and independent State of Texas! and for this let us empty our glasses."

"For that time!" we chimed in emptying our glasses, and another time we emptied our tumblers for the Father of Texas, Stephen F, Austin.

Stern's suggestion, although it was past eleven o'clock and the beds were awaiting us—namely, to go to the Mexican coffeehouse—was willingly approved. Here we found the Mexican people of Nacogdoches, which consisted of nearly one half of the whole population, in colorful confusion. A mass of men, women, and girls were forcing their way through the room filled to smothering with fumes as we stepped in.

The Coffeehouse

ABOMINABLE EXPRESSIONS IN BROKEN ENGLISH issued from a group of people resembling a band of Gypsies. With every fourth word one could hear either a damn or a Spanish *carajo* emanating from a being in the center of the room accompanied by loud applause from those standing around. The squire, who had for many years seen scenes of this kind, pushed his way through the spectators, who, filled with curiosity, made room for us as we approached.

"Now," said the squire, "the Greys shall see the kind of an enemy that we have to deal with. As you here see the Mexicans, so is the whole nation with the possible exception of a few of Spanish descent, which represent the Mexican nobility. But in moral aspects they are all alike. A murder on the conscience of one of them does not weigh much. While the rich, the so-called cultured classes, absolve themselves of their own sins, the padre in Sail Antonio forgives the poorer, uncultured classes their minor transgressions for a few pesos, and a good well-trained mustang for his reverence, the apostle of Rome in the West, will overbalance all criminal cases and soothe the conscience completely as well as release the souls from purgatory where we heretics must languish and suffer without mercy.

By this time, we had penetrated the inner side of a circle of people, where we discovered a little four and three-quarter foot high man jumping about in graceful movements, if the movements of such a clumsy figure could be called graceful, around a not larger Mexican donna. The vulgar speech and suggestive positions of each filled us with amazement.

The donna understood the dance in all of its completeness and kept time to a miserable English translation of a Mexican song that her almost transparent companion screeched out to us in the cawing voice of a raven. He was in fact a most interesting object to look at. His long, coal-black hair flounced in wild twirls about his comparatively large head so that we could get only an occasional glimpse of his copper-colored, wild, emaciated features and his wide-open mouth.

An old fiddler, also a descendent of the Montezumas, stood in frightful enthusiasm at the edge of the circle, and as his brown bow screeched across the three strings of his musical contrivance, his little time-stamping foot moved with amazing rapidity and followed the not-languishing movements of the Señora.

The Señor was smoking a real Havana and the Señora a lovely little *cigarrito*, which was very becoming to her neat mouth, pretty enough to kiss, and to her whole person. The Mexican, Ol' Bull with his fiddle, stood enveloped in terrible fumes, and a grey mass of smoke hovered over the heads of the circle of very respectable dons and donnas.

"Squire," said I, "this is sufficient, abundantly sufficient, for one evening's entertainment; let us seek fresh air. This coffeehouse is a highly interesting place, but what a prodigious difference there is between the fandango here and the fandango on the floor of the St. Charles in New Orleans!"

The squire replied, laughing, that he always amused himself very much whenever he came to this place. "However," he added, "we have not seen everything yet. Step through this door and you will find nothing less interesting in this black chamber." The black chamber was really a black apartment. The smoke of 100,000 cigars had settled on the once-white walls and formed a complete covering for it. Black as if covered with velvet were the floors, the walls, the ceilings, the window frames, the chairs, the cabinets, and the shriveled-up inhabitants; even a few rather pretty little Mexican Amazons appeared to have been darkened by this playhouse atmosphere. Most noteworthy was the furrowed face of an old matron. The rising vapors encircled her drooping Roman nose in mottled, encircling cloudlets, and one cup of coffee after another rolled down her thin, long throat. Her grey head was constantly in motion when she was not busy with her coffee or concerned with the sale of coffee, grog, or other articles; and as the master fiddler with his three strings lured forth the most melting sounds, her mossy head waved back and forth now fast, now slow, over her ever constantly empty yet ever filled cup.

The table was clean, because its constant use, the endless rubbing of the arms, had wiped the smoke away. Every place on the benches was occupied and piles of silver were stacked up on the table. The center of the one side was decorated with a crafty, one-eyed, gaunt creole from Louisiana guarded by two professional gamblers, former, but now banished inhabitants of the undesirable section of Neches. They had barely escaped the Manila ropes of the citizens of that place. Their precipitate departure from the country had saved them from the fate of their blackleg companions who were suspended in the air of Vicksburg to dance to the howling of the winds and the cawing of the crows. These three gentlemen, this noble trio, migrated with mile-boots over the Sabine to flee from that terrible country where they attach perfectly honest people of their type to limbs of oak trees for decorative purposes as a matter-of-fact routine procedure.

Now they were here to give a few demonstrations of their black art in return for the Mexican dollars, and the silver stack behind the black table grew from minute to minute. With every hand that the creole drew, the knights of the white metal inconsiderately wiped in the gains without even noticing the agony with which the loss of the last peso was drawing the chest of the despairing one together. Without saying a word, the greedy eyes of the player rested on the disappearing money.

The brown, very pretty features of a girl dressed in black contracted cramp-like. An unnatural column of smoke, coming as from a crater, rose from her cigar into the supercharged atmosphere; her dark eyes hung lifeless on the card that concealed the fate of her last dollar; the hellish one-eye led off and with mechanical precision the three noble companions of leeches brought down the last dollar of the unfortunate girl. Enraged, she sprang up, struck the table with her doubled fist and burning torch with such force that even the last sparks died out and rushed out of the door in order to—after the air had somewhat refreshed her—win back her lost money tomorrow night, the Lord permitting. The little black forest clock that hung in this hell struck twelve as these revelers of the night decided to lock the bank and close for the day, not because they had already won enough but because they had won all there was. The Mexicans with grate-iron-like faces sailed slowly without ballast through the black chamber.

"Señora," yelled the creole to the napping sybil, "____damn it, Señora, grog, grog! Doesn't the old lady see that we are thirsty? Damn your eyes! Here with your brew! The

Señoritas are warm and the cold norther is blowing on the outside. The pretty ones will take a deathly cold if they do not immediately take an invigorating glass of your rum concoction. Also quickly, old lady, quickly!"

"How many glasses," crowed the old lady, "did the Señor order?" "Damn you", the creole broke loose again, "two, three, four glasses for everyone, as many as my worthy friends wish to drink; do you think, old cab-horse, when Sam Johnson treats that he will act niggardly over ten, fifteen, or twenty dollars? No, never, damn his soul! If he were such a skinflint, he would not deserve to be called the son of his noble father, damn it, how often have hundreds of dollars flown forth from me, but Sam Johnson is still Sam Johnson."

"It is easy for you to speak that way," mumbled the old lady, "You rake the pesos together with such easiness that one is almost persuaded to believe that you were in league with"—She made three crosses—"Mother Maria, keep us in the fold."

"Shut up, you old wrinkle, and hurry to get your hellish drinks ready instead of making unseemly and wicked accusations, lest my good friend old Patrick and I shall serve the sustenance."

The magic strains of the fiddler in the other room had ceased and the dancers had disappeared. A few of the victims of the gambling table still sat in half despair in the black room to drown their sorrow with the fiery stupefying drink that the old witch of Nacogdoches had brewed in her smoky corner. We left soon, telling the squire of our surprise to find the cunning thieves here that had been driven out of Neches some time ago. They had come to Texas to begin a new period among the Mexicans with their lowdown business, "That will continue only for a short time," replied the squire, "Soon the last dollar will have disappeared from the pockets of the Mexicans, and Sam Johnson and Company with nothing more to do will follow our army to San Antonio. I see no difference between the effect of a bullet from a respectable planter and that from a respectable pickpocket—both respectable gentlemen in the presence of the enemy, assuming that each does his duty."

"What, Squire?" responded I, surprised, "do you believe these all-consuming, all-destroying fellows will ever have the courage to step out in front of the enemy? There the honorable squire is most assuredly mistaken. At the sound of the first gun you will see such a hasty departure of this thieving gentry that you will be amused to see them march off in all their glory to the Rio Grande to gamble for Mexican silver at Matamoras or other places."

"Well, good also," replied the squire indifferently, "It will be all the same how we get them across the border. If they do not wish to fight—well—then they may run. If they do not want to run—well—then they will have to dance."

"What—dance, squire? How do you now get on the dancing? Please, how do you mean that?"

"Psah," continued the squire, "I mean that the noble lads whom we are discussing will be permitted to dance. Sam Johnson understands the highland fling in all of its completeness. Once he may be allowed to dance to our whistle,"

"Squire, you are an unsolvable riddle. I must beseech you, and if you hold the Greys worthy of confidence, to draw the veil from those meaningful words."

"Why shouldn't I?" mumbled the thoughtful Texan. "Well," he continued, paused a while and began anew. "I mean if they do not wish to fight, they will, like a superfluous garment on the nail, be hung on the first convenient sycamore."

We were startled with surprise. "The squire is not speaking in seriousness," said Curtman. "To hang people, sir, is no small matter."

"Just because, sir, it isn't a small matter we will have to bring it into service. What do these gentry care for small matters?" continued the squire.

"But," responded I, "have the Texans a right to put their countrymen out of the world this way if they have committed no crime within the border of Texas?"

"Why—I don't know—concerns, me little—we do it just the same," answered the squire.

"Why," interjected Peter Mattern, involuntary imitating the squire, "Why we do it—that is said easy enough, but what right do you have to do so?"

"What right?" continued the squire, "what right have the States to chase a bunch of pilfering thieves over here to us? Who allows this thieving rabble to disgrace our prairies by their presence—especially since Mexico has seen to it 'til now that the hated province, Texas, always had a good apportionment of this article on hand. But things will have to change. Soon, soon shall they march, pack and bundle, to their soul-comforter over the Rio Grande, or to him in hell. Away they must, and the province, must be free of these vagabonds within a year. Run, fight or hang—from those they may choose—we want a free land, unstained by such thieving birds; and with our independence a strict rule of justice must enter. The laws must be respected. But pardon for him who will forsake the old paths. It will be the last time that a hand will be extended them to draw a curtain over a black past, the last time, gentlemen."

"Squire, you are terrible but just," I added, "yet it would he agreeable to me if we could win our freedom without the aid of these defeated gentlemen; it is such a sacred matter for them to take part in."

"Wild imaginings; when the victory is won, it will make little difference to us who did it. It is better for the deer to fall than the faithful cow—better for the last cock than for the brooding hen. If one of the gamblers fall, a good act is done the world. On the contrary, if a colonist falls, we lose a good citizen and have a distressed family in the land. A fourth of a load of lead in the gun of the former might have saved his life. No, gentlemen, no one is so despicable that he could not be used somewhere in helping us roll back the Central Colossus from our El Dorado. Ever projecting points will offer themselves as fulcrums for the levers, and the resulting force will roll back the colossus over the Rio Grande. And thereafter will be the time for us to set our internal affairs in order."

We now found ourselves at our stopping place and, tired, we wished each other a good night's rest.

The Banquet

"THE VOLUNTEERS FROM THE STATES!" cried a large, strong man who sat at the head of the 150-foot-long board table. "The Greys!" he cried and poured down the foaming champagne as he gave the toast. The two rows on the sides of the heavily loaded table raised their glasses at the same time and eighty dollars' worth of the precious beverage disappeared on the welfare of the Greys.

In the center of the table, amid festive decorations, stood Mr. Petz, a large black bear, hide and bones, meat and claws, and between his grim teeth he held the flag of the constitution of 1824. The remainder of the table was occupied by raccoons, squirrels, and turkeys. But two large nicely roasted hindquarters and the backbone of an ox decorated the table also. As the satellites stand around their planets so stood the foaming champagne and the sparkling Rhine around the cooked wild animals.

Hopping Johnson arose to make a few remarks, although I must here observe that he was not the notorious Sam Johnson. He was a gentleman-squatter who had conquered the world hopping three times, and at that on his left leg. He also carried the nicknames the Typesetter[2] or the Great Hopper. But in general he was known as Hopping Johnson. The

---

[2] *Setzer*, which does not translate meaningfully. Bartholomae chose "the Supposer."

Cornbreaker's nature[3] radiated from all of his features; the blood that flowed in his veins was completely Virginian. From the day that the old Johnson, the great-grandfather of our Hopper, had set foot on the new continent in order to become a Virginian squatter (at that time the Alleghenies were still called the backbone of the colonies and Old Virginia was a wild disorderly land frequented by Indians) none of the Johnsons had ever gone beyond the boundaries of the state, which seldom happens among the people of Uncle Sam's territory. But our young Hopper had left the good old land against the will of his father and traveled for many years through the states with several exceedingly fine thoroughbred race horses that his father, who was a breeder of thoroughbred stock, had raised. He became well known for his excellent fast horses. Later on he settled in Texas.

"Gentlemen," sounded his clear voice from the center of the table. "Gentlemen, the men of Nacogdoches have prepared a banquet for the Greys of New Orleans, and the ladies have taken charge of the work of the kitchen. Vain patriotism, gentlemen; the red Cherokee has tracked the opossum and laid low with his gun the raccoon, the young warriors have furnished our table with guineas and squirrels, but Sam Johnson has searched the primeval forests for three days, living on the game of the chase, that he might sacrifice this gentleman here—pointing to the bear before him—at the feast of liberty. Long did he quietly track after him and only on the third day did he discover him growling in a dense thicket. The ball dropped him. Sam returned victorious to the village to get more help to bring Petz home. Petz, gentlemen, was brought

---

[3] *Cornbräckernatur*, which refuses to translate meaningfully. In a footnote, Ehrenberg says that it is a nickname for Virginians.

in and now stands in our midst. Nicely roasted he wishes us a good appetite."

He drew a deep breath, wiped his brow and continued, "Your white plates, gentlemen, surround the noble juice of the Rhine and that of the Champagne. With these are polished crystal glasses. You will miss the knives and forks"—which in reality were missing. Sam Johnson was appointed by the patriotic ladies' committee to explain their absence. "Hear—hear—gentlemen, Sam Johnson has never concerned himself about the kitchen department. If he had his steaks and cornbread together with a little glass of Kentucky wine[4] at mealtimes, he did not ask for anything else. For the simple reason that the ladies in their haste could not secure sufficient of these instruments of destruction, or at least not without an additional amount of trouble, gentlemen, there will be nothing left for us to do—drawing his Bowie knife—but to imitate the red warrior, who fells his enemy with his tomahawk and shortens his existence with his scalping knife or who similarly kills the doe and prepares the meat for his nourishment. So, my hopeful soldiers of the prairie, out with your Bowie knives and away with the well-roasted slices of Mr. Petz, Opossum, Coon and Company's fat carcasses. Pitch, in! Pitch in!"

"Long live Sam Johnson, the Hopper, the tireless bearhunter!" cried the occupants of the table and emptied a glass on his welfare.

The Hopper took a deep breath, expressed his thanks and drew the skin of Mr. Petz to the side, and the otherwise black gentleman in death made a more tempting appearance than he ever was able to do in life. The two-foot-long knives issued from their scabbards and wrought destruction on Mr.

---

[4] Corn whiskey.

Petz and the rest. Toast was drunk on toast, political speeches were made, the causes of the war were discussed, inflammatory appeals resounded, thought was also taken of the squatter women as they sat at their hearths, and it was already very late when the feast was over. One after another with revolution in his mind and boundless courage in his heart had quietly left his seat to look up his quarters, and prophetic figures stood in unending forms before the enthusiastic spirits. In the morning our horses were driven up, and that evening we galloped out of the streets of the little town.

The cheers of the inhabitants followed the delighted cavalry troop of Greys until they disappeared in the dark forest.

The March to San Antonio

THE JOURNEY DID NOT PROGRESS AS RAPIDLY as we had expected, but we came a little nearer our destination every day. The colonists along the road received us with great joy, and the best in their homes was put at our service. In several places they aimed to give us a banquet as they had done at Nacogdoches, but the Greys had no more time to spare. Forward! was our motto, in order that we might arrive at San Antonio before the militia there executed a major stroke. We hastened forward over the rushing Angelina. The majestic Trinidad with its incomparably rich lands and broadly forested banks soon lay a few days' journey behind us. Before us in a long, black line lay the forests of the Rio del Brazos. The innumerable changing colors of the many kinds of trees, the vines and air-plants added to the heavenly scenery an inexpressible charm. The autumn, the most beautiful season of the year on the new continent, was unfolding its festive colors in these magnificent landscapes.

We tarried for a few days in the then-new Washington. Several hundred new dwellings were going up in the forest, which resounded with the friendly echo of the energetic immigrant's art. Hourly the splendid oaks and the majestic pecans and hickories fell; many a noble persimmon had its almost ripe, pretty, reddish yellow fruit scattered about on the ground by the crashing fall. Large piles of brush, crooked limbs and tree trunks were burning in every direction to clear the ground and only since recently did the sun send its warmth down to the damp, fruitful, dark brown earth below. The place contained several coffeehouses, a lodging house, a grocery and general merchandising establishment containing readymade articles, dress goods and all other necessities for the backwoodsman. We also found a good billiard room and, as everywhere in America, a courthouse, and finally, the never-failing gunsmith shop.

A few miles from this place the prairie regions begin and extend clear down to the coast. For days now we trotted through a constantly changing park and, disregarding the cold northwest wind, nature here displayed an indescribable fullness and splendor.

The prairies here are not like those immense stretches between the Guadalupe and the San Antonio that reach clear up to the mountains or that enormous grass ocean of Tamaulipas that extends in varying widths of a hundred miles or more from the Gulf to and over the Rocky Mountains to those practically unknown treeless regions further north, but rather an open country, here and there ornamented with groups and mottes of trees, lies before the traveler. To the right and left one always sees at great distance the horizon bordered with dark forests and, near the traveler, small forest areas alternate with open meadows. Occasionally a little brook, whose course is marked with a string of trees, winds its way down from the mountains. Again the scenes change. Now the post oaks stand in regular rows around meadows that resemble the meadow regions of the Old World. They differ only from these in that the meadows of Europe are encircled with willows and poplars while the little prairies are surrounded with oaks. Everything is so systematic that one is almost persuaded to believe that human hands had part in the planting of the trees.

The March to San Antonio

In the vicinity of Bastrop, approximately one hundred miles from San Antonio, the country becomes somewhat hilly; and, agreeably surprised, we found ourselves again in dense resin-wood forests, the first that we had struck since our departure from Nacogdoches. We rode through the gigantic needle-wood forest and momentarily expected to enter a little prairie or to see the long sought little town of Bastrop. The sun passed behind the pinnacles of the gigantic pine trees and it was beginning to get dusky. We still saw for a long time the golden hue that spread itself out over the majestic treetops, but it finally disappeared, too. We rode on slowly, step-for-step through the night that enveloped us in its darkness. The sign of the road was the open stripe over our heads that permitted us to gaze on the starless deep-blue heavens.

The horses stepped cautiously forward and searched for a way that was invisible to the human eye, while we peered ahead to keep from being torn from our horses by the long pine limbs that at times reached far out over the road. It must have been near midnight, and we would have pitched camp long ago, but no forest brooklet or spring flowed across our path where we could water our faithful horses, nor could we find a suitable place to graze them. We had to keep on. Suddenly the leading horses nickered lustily into the thus far uninterrupted night, a sign that something to them agreeable was near. We spied about and discovered several lights of the little town in a deep depression to our right. The road shortly led us down the steep hill and soon we were passing through the streets to the waters of the Guadalupe[5] to water our horses. The residents, however, took charge of this matter, and as we

---

[5] Ehrenberg errs; it was the Colorado River.

had been expected for some time, we could at once take an invigorating supper with the several colonists.

After we had finished, we stepped out into the broad streets, where the inhabitants had started a number of large fires. From eight to ten tree-trunks had been laid in layers on each pile and their flames lit up the dark carpet over our heads.

It was late when we rolled ourselves up in blankets and laid down around the fires, disregarding the wishes of the people that we sleep in their houses for the night. We had so accustomed ourselves to camping in the open that we declined the invitations with thanks. As we wished all a last good night we drew the covers over our heads and slept for the last time among the colonies. Tomorrow our journey over the one-hundred-mile prairie to San Antonio was to continue. Since we had nothing to fear of the redskins in the center of the town, we slept without sentries.

It was the fourth day after we had left Bastrop. Up to this time we had not come upon the home of a single colonist in this charming wilderness, and from time to time the bent-over bleached grass, in places man-high, indicated traces of a Comanche troop that had probably just come down from the mountains.

We now kept ourselves closer together than we had while riding through the colonies. Our muskets were always loaded, partly to kill the necessary game for our support, and partly because we were now passing through a level stretch of country that the unfriendly Indians often frequented in large numbers during this season of the year. Woe to the erring hunter if he should fall into the barbaric hands of his red colleagues; a terrible death would be his lot. Terrible is the character of these people of the chase; like the brown inhabitants of Mexico they are characterized by their cowardice.

The Comanches have sworn eternal enmity to the world. Their five thousand to six thousand red warriors chase about in troops of from one to four hundred men, together with women and children, over the regions of the Guadalupe and San Saba mountains. Formerly they even came down into the lower regions of Texas. At times they swoop down like a thunder cloud on the Mexican side of the Rio Grande and return again to their valleys with large herds of stolen stock.

All male Mexicans are scalped and the women and children usually are led away as slaves to be released again only on payment of a heavy ransom.

Their cowardly nature, however, does not permit them to come down any more among the settlements of the Texans, except under the guise of friendship. At such times, especially in the spring, they exchange furs and silver bars for lead and woolen blankets. Spirituous liquors are repulsive to them, contrary to all other brown hunters of the West. They characterize themselves by wearing little scrubby beards which the red brethren prevent growing by tearing out the roots during early youth. They are constantly on horseback, hunt on horseback and attack the enemy only on the prairie where they can make use of their skilled horsemanship. They sit in council on horseback and, armed with lances and buffalo shields, they invade the lands of other Indians. The weaker side is destroyed without mercy, but not very often do these terrible hunters of the prairies suffer appreciable losses in these massacres because that nation whose territory includes both the prairie and the primeval forests is stronger and more daring than the others.

On the western horizon black clouds, whose purpose for being there we could not understand, just now began to appear. Our aim for today was a little shady island ahead of us. Splendid live oaks spread out their enormous branches and formed the most attractive arcades, incomparable with any that we had ever seen. From the evergreen pyramids hung silver grey garlands, the so-called Spanish moss, almost down to the ground, giving the group a melancholy appearance. On our arrival the horses were unsaddled, a nice place for the campfire selected, the food brought forth, and preparations for supper made, and soon we could enjoy the heavenly evening in comfort.

The Prairie Fire

PURPLE, MORE BEAUTIFUL THAN ON THE DARK WAVES of the roaring sea, did the sun glow as it sank appear behind the unknown mountains of clouds in the west, and terrible black masses rolled up like gigantic dragons against the clear starless horizon. Anxiously we gazed at them, hoping to discover an explanation. Our thoughts floated to San Antonio; we saw a sea of fire destroying the town, heard the battle cry of the combatants, and here were we without any prospect of getting any further during the night, without being able to take part in this fateful event. We listened with keenest attention toward the lightly blowing wind to catch the possible distant sound of the deep thunder of the cannon, but all was in vain.

Brightly flickered the fires around which we were lying. Silently we roasted huge pieces of beef and quarters of venison on the frying spits. They meanwhile assumed a friendly appearance, from which the grease trickled down. The company first cut pieces from the surface of the roasted or done side, while the other side was being roasted. After we were through with the one side we turned the roast over and ate sedately from the other. We reflected deeply upon the peculiar lot of mankind and of these quarters that an hour ago were the parts of living beings and now were the best tasting fry that had ever gladdened our tastes and stomachs.

Depressed, we looked into the flickering fire where a mighty iron kettle was boiling the brown fluid—as that was to serve as refreshment and aid to digestion after our delicious meal. I shall never forget how excellently the coffee tasted. I had never drunk any better. I must give our cook pro tem credit for knowing how to cook this invigorating beverage, regardless of whether it is for old dames or for hunters in the wilderness. Everyone sat still and observed his proceedings. Suddenly he cried out: "Bill, where is the coffee? Here into this boiling water that it will mix quickly. The water is boiling up!" A sudden stillness set in, a quietness such as precedes an earthquake. The cover began to rise, a cover of ground coffee that had formed a crust over the water. As the earth cracks apart so this cover split in twain. Seething, the precious fluid boiled forth. An instant and the coffee was ready.

An oppressive stillness lay over the immense region. A faint glow had somewhat reddened the clouds. Our guards were lying at their posts, as it is more expedient to lie on guard duty in the prairie than either to stand or walk. Every visible object is noticed by the marksmen of the forests at amazing distances and the careless one will soon fall a victim to their skill and cunningness. Even the mustangs were crowding around the dying campfires; moved by secret misgivings of the mysterious stillness, they pressed in friendly manner near their masters as if anticipating danger.

All of a sudden the shrill barking of a dog sounded sharp and cutting through the stillness of the night, now tapering off as a death howl, soon again so penetrating that the ears rang and an apprehensive shudder ran over the body. Without moving, we stared into the dark night as a second and slightly deeper voice chimed in, and a few moments more a third, then a fourth, a deep base. A few moments more and thousands upon thousands entered the great chorus. This music of hell of the coyotes[6] was intermixed with the frightful howling of the great black wolves that live in company with them. That deep sound that issued from the depth of the throat as from a cavern and that can be compared only to the howls uttered by a number of dogs on hearing the sounds of to them unpleasant musical instruments, is in itself terrible; then think of the howling of a thousand voices.

We were still standing in amazement, then, quick as lightning, everything was quiet. Still as the grave was the night. Only the monotone calls of the whippoorwill and his mate penetrated through the darkness. Sadly he calls his name and the little wife answers in the same manner.

One is agreeably surprised. With pleasure he listens to the melancholy duet, their tender calls, as if they were exiled spirits in the splendid expanses of the West. There again we heard the terrible yelling sound as before, the second, the third, the fourth, and then the whole chorus.

Rudely awakened, my comrades sprang up, seized their guns and peered into the darkness for the hellish spirits that had interrupted the quietness of the night with their tumult threatening trouble. Barely had we recovered from our amazement, when another pack of these spirits of hell in the opposite direction raised their horrible voices. At first we could distinguish the howling of the two parties, but soon it melted into one immense deafening din. Thousands upon thousands of shrill tones like the awful war-whoop of the redskins pierced the air. Then again one could perceive the difference between the two parties for a few moments. Now the noise became weaker from moment to moment and, after a

---

[6] Ehrenberg says *Präriehunde*, literally "prairie dogs."

few minutes more, only a few long, drawn-out sounds like weeping and moaning cries came across to us. The wolves and the packs of dogs had made short shrift of the sad duet of the whippoorwills. But immensely more frightful was that of the former. The echoes now resounded, faint across the lonesome prairie, like the groans on a battlefield at night after the bloody work of the day before. But the inhabitants of the country, accustomed to such nightly confusion, did not let the bluster disturb them in their quiet sweet slumber.

And now only the winged ruler of the night, the owl, cried his terrible farewell song at his nightly companions in his hollow tones, as from the grave.

With the exception of the guards we again stretched ourselves out around the fires to seek slumber under the covers. The horses also began to move out on the prolific mesquite grass to graze. Today was the fourth day that we were in the region of the mesquite prairies. This beautiful nourishing growth, which resembled a ripe field and was from three to four feet high, concealed the tender young blades from the gaze of the casual human observer, but not from the horses. Greedily they plucked the delicacy, to them until now unknown, which yearly draws down millions of buffalo from the Rocky Mountains to graze here during the winter when the cold northwest wind takes their food in the higher altitudes,

"Who's there? Relief! The Release!" sounded in monotones through the now softened nature as the corporal released the several posts. "The corporal let me wait a long time," mumbled Bill. "I have been here at least three hours because the pale star there stood high as I came on duty and in three or four minutes now it will disappear behind yonder advancing hills."

The Prairie Fire

"Exactly two by the watch," was the answer, "but is there nothing to report?"

"Hmm, do not know, many a sly wolf led me into temptation to use my gun, and the canaille of huhuhuhu, or the hangman as she cried it, comes perfectly independently by here—never moving a joint—flies around me and yells her huhuhuhu into my ears. At first I thought that it was the spirit of old Mother Fizkins, my honored grandmother, who was surprised to see her grandson, Bill, shoulder the musket. Thought that she was laughing at me. If a nation ...."

"Forward, march!"

"Halt!" cried the interrupted one. "Halt, corporal, a moment—comrade, look out—I believe the sun is coming back because that cloud in the west looks like the vain rosy hue of morning."

Truly the black cloud, which had gradually taken in the half of the horizon, was illuminated with a purple glow similar to the northern aurora. Ever bloodier did the heavens become. Awakened for the second time, we newcomers in the prairie marveled at the bright illumination.

"The prairie is on fire—the redskins are near," at last said Bill, "they were hunting today; many a poor deer, to escape the fire, no doubt ran into the deadly musket of the brown hunters. We must ...."

Suddenly, like an army in a storm, the wildly lashing flames charged over a slight elevation about a mile away and raced with the wind down upon us. We sprang up and rushed our horses, which were already looking wildly at the fire, into the little island that, like an oasis in the desert, marked the freshly green and damp spots in the prairie. Here the burning rays of the sun could not penetrate through the densely growing moss-covered oaks to dry up the grass. Consequently, we were secure from the flames in this retreat, although there was no real danger as one could jump through the flames. The horses, however, if left to themselves, would, like the wild animals, have taken to flight in the opposite direction to run as long as the flames followed them. On this condition the drive hunts of the prairie Indians depend. They use the fire as driver and conceal themselves in favored places in front of the flames. The game falls in spite of the poor guns.

The Comanche, like all sons of the wilderness, never shoot more game than their needs require. He regards the deer and buffalo of his territory as his property. The prairie Comanche divide into groups of several hundred. Each migrates northward during the spring from year to year with the immense herds of buffalo, but the winter drives them back to these bald but productive regions. In company with the buffalo and other game, they prefer the southern climate to the northern winters. This is the time for the squatters and the rangers of the far west to be on the lookout for their horses and stock. As long as the red man can live on tame cattle he will never kill one of his friends, the deer or the buffalo.

Expectantly we saw the bankless sea of fire rolling forward; nearer and nearer crackled the flames. Black clouds rose up and rolled slowly along over the flames, when suddenly as far as the eye could reach the whole line went out. Only for a moment single flames here and there flickered up, then everything was over, nothing but the smell and the still-rising black smoke remained.

The dew was now falling as thick as fine rain, and it alone is what preserves the vegetation, as it often does not rain for months. The singeing rays of the sun would burn up everything if it were not for the refreshing dew. The lonely wanderer who pitches his camp in the open will draw up the cover

The Prairie Fire

after nightfall and at times over his head because it gets fresh, cold and, as just mentioned, the dew falls in such quantities that it gradually smothers the fire unless it is a very strong one.

Nothing interrupted the latter part of the night. During these few remaining hours we slept undisturbed, but by five o'clock everybody was awake with the first shimmer of the rising sun.

Merrily flickered our watch fires, but ever paler in the same degree that the sun rose higher. Finally, she stood there in her full splendor, and the blue mists that were lying low on the prairies fled like clouds from the fiery god and soon disappeared completely. But how different was the view today from that of yesterday! Yesterday waving fields, similar to ripe grain, today what awful appearance. From our feet to the distant rim of the horizon was one continuous black shroud, no tree, no twig, nothing but a black ocean.

Lively sounded the bugle for the breakup. The quartermaster and a few others trotted out on the black floor. I soon followed on my little Cherokee, well-pleased with the continuous good weather and full of hopes of arriving in San Antonio at the right time to satisfy my wish to participate in the first stroke for the freedom of the prairies.

In spirit I already saw the city with her solid, proud walls, her stately domes and churches and the formidable fortress, the Alamo with the tri-colored standard of Mexico or better, the standard of Santa Anna, over it, as he was the nation, and his will must come to pass.

The wind blew black clouds of ashes toward us. This was highly unpleasant as it filled our noses, mouths and eyes to such an extent that we could barely see. Toward noon we, the first four, arrived at the high rock bluffs of the Cibolo, one of those remarkable streams of Texas that, when the stream is low, disappears in places for ten miles or more in the bed of the stream and flows along underground in the same channel, and then again appears on the surface at different points in considerable strength. The bed of the Cibolo is about a half mile broad and grown up in some places with oaks and in others with mesquites. However, the larger part is covered with immense pieces of chalk rock against which the rays of the sun shatter themselves with increased heat and brightness. No breeze blew in this section. The high, white bluffs obstructed the easy northwest wind, which, when the Gulf breeze did not blow, constantly streamed down out of the rocky hills through the endless succession of open prairies.

For a long time we searched in vain for water for ourselves and our thirsty horses. Finally, behind a large chalk rock, we discovered a considerable pool of clear fresh water with many fish in it.

Today, too, it was our lot not to arrive at the longed-for San Antonio. However, the surrounding country had changed. More timber, many herds of deer, wild turkeys and flocks of other birds that were frequently seen put us in good humor. We camped for the night on the Salado, six miles from San Antonio. Strong guards stood all around the camp, but nothing disturbed us and nothing interrupted the stillness of the night except the calling, far and near, of the many whippoorwills. The whole forest seemed to be alive; but as the pale moon set towards twelve o'clock, the sad notes of these inhabitants of the forests died away also.

Only the relieving of the guards was heard from time to time. Dreary flickered the fires and hour after hour hastened by.

It was the last watch before the break of day, which I could barely await as I sat dreaming before the fire and gazing into the flames, when—listen—the winged morning wind wafted the muffled thunder of the cannon of the Alamo over to us. It was a sign that the first fiery stripe in the east was announcing the coming day. In a moment everybody was on his feet, breakfast was prepared, coffee was cooked, horses were saddled and everything was ready. But a leader was lacking, as no one knew the way, much less the location, of the camp of our friends. On the Salado, it was said, we should wait, and thus it happened too. The sun had disappeared again when at last two persons, a Mexican and an American, came in sight and led us to the main army. It was late in the night when we arrived at the camp.

Our drummer, an Englishman, had carelessly led out troops and had lost the right way. Nelson, the Briton, marched cursing along the road in the opinion that he had already gone too far, in which his tired horse fully agreed with him; and only under protest did it follow the knight of freedom, who was pulling with all his might. He blasphemed first the long road, then his mount, and then again the Texas horse-miles when one had to go on foot. A salvo of not very tender expressions rolled from his lips to his protesting saddle pony when several bold *"quien vive!"* were called out to him.

"O ho, what kind of gibberish is that, all Turkish for me, but my faithful nag, farewell, and farewell, my gentlemen *quien vives*. Will answer tomorrow, must first learn Spanish."

But the gentlemen *quien vives*, for whom the answer was not sufficient, sent something Mexican in the form of musket bullets after him, of which one put an end to his innocent horse while another lost itself in his side, which he, however, since he was in a considerable hurry, did not notice until he fell head over heels into a pond several hundred yards away from the sentinels. He did not notice the pond in the darkness.

Here he lay unpursued until next morning when some of our people found him and brought him into camp, which was nearby.

Our drummer also had his troubles. A cutting hunger and burning thirst plagued him considerably. His drum hanging limp in front of him, leading his faithful horse, which did not exceed Nelson's mare much in slenderness, by a line thrown over his shoulder, he went slowly forward. By the way, I must mention that the five-hundred-mile trip had cost our horses a good piece of flesh. Several times hunger drew the stomach of our drummer together so angrily that he was about to beat the alarm. Now he stood still to reflect on what should be done in such despairing situation. He didn't lag the Briton Nelson in good wishes for the people who really were not his particular friends, such as the Mexicans, and also for his highly indispensable mare. He, however, had the advantage over Nelson in that he was master of three languages, and an ocean of French, Spanish and English words of endearment rushed forth and no doubt would have continued for a long time—because the creole was inexhaustible—if a strange voice had not addressed him with a *buenas noche*. The cunning drummer, a creole from Louisiana, had his mind made up quickly when he found himself among the Mexicans and told them in Spanish that he was a parley officer. A parley officer with such a horse and out here in the dark appeared a little too blue for the Mexicans; but when he added that four thousand volunteers from the States were on the way to destroy all the descendants of Montezuma in Texas, the matter became a little more serious for them. He was taken to the Alamo as a highly dangerous and embarrassing fellow where, after a hearing, he was informed in perfect order that he would he shot in a few days. A good consolation, but the Louisianan did not lose his spirits; did not Uncle Sam's boys stand before the fortress, and was the old fellow ever beaten!

The Camp of the Militia

THE AUTUMN SUN, WHICH HAD JUST RISEN above the constantly clear southern horizon and spread its fiery rays over the already stirring camp of the backwoodsmen, showed the Greys, after the greeting from the Alamo and the reveille had died away, a camp that differed radically from anything that had been seen before. In spite of our active imagination and the descriptions and accounts of the War of Independence in the States that we had read and heard, we had not pictured after this manner an army composed of volunteers and militia fighting for freedom. Practically all of us had seen the shifting trappers along the western border of the States, and several of us had participated in their excursions through the prairies. We had also wandered through the camps of the Indians in the forests of the States and on their invitation not only smoked the peace pipe with them but also helped to devour their captured game. Yes, even a few of us equipped with gun and beaver traps formerly traveled through the regions of the Rocky Mountains. Thousands of miles from civilization they once marched through the domains of the Blackfeet, the Flatheads and the Crows. But never did a view offer itself such as the encircling camp of the Texans.

To our left flowed the warm San Antonio River, which had its source only a few miles from here. It already had a depth of from six to eight feet and a width of from eighteen to twenty yards. It formed a respectable stream and flowed, forming a peninsula on the way, down toward the enemy. On the upper outside edge of the bend lay our camp. On the opposite lower bank, however, and on the right bank of the stream, lay the old, honored San Antonio, which was concealed from our view at the camp by the trees that border all the Texas streams. Between us and the town lay a cornfield, which extended for about an English mile along the river, but it was now barren. On the opposite treeless bank, and only separated from the town by the river, stood the main fortress of the former province of Texas, the previously mentioned Alamo, about three-quarters of an English mile from our camp. Immediately around us on a flat at least a half mile wide lay the camp of the citizens of Texas. On the other sides it was surrounded partly by large cornfields and partly by prairies, overgrown in places by running mesquite and by enormous groups of the gigantic cactus species. Among these the horses and cattle of the troops grazed peacefully in the tall grass. When one would go across the fields, millions of blackbirds would darken the sky. Stirred up, they would rise like a black cloud, swarm around in circles a few times and settle down again a short distance away to look for food on the ground. But the field where the cattle were butchered, which was not small, had its inhabitants also. Great flocks of vultures of various kinds hunted their food on this slaughter place, and was to be had in abundance, or they sat with outspread wings and open beaks on the dry limbs of the nearby pecan trees and warmed themselves (a true picture of the Mexicans) in the pleasant rays of the sun. A few large wolves and coyotes also wandered, as if they belonged to the army, among the heads,

The Camp of the Militia

skins, and other refuse of the slaughtered cattle and had their breakfast as composedly as we.

The roll of the drum now sounded through the camp, the muster rolls of the companies that had pitched their tents and huts promiscuously here and there without any regard to order were read one by one. In order to give a true picture of the organization of the army it is necessary only to select any one company of those patriots against whom guns and valor, all discipline, and even the overpowering numbers of the enemy could not avail.

It was similar to the protection of the human rights in the colonies of the States under the great Washington. The result of their arms is known to the world: that proud Britannia was compelled by land and sea to strike her colors before the Yankees, and so were the Mexicans before the colonists of Texas, even when these were without all accessories and with a population of twenty-seven thousand had to battle against eight million.

The company that lay opposite was, like the others, called out of its pleasant occupation of roasting its meat on the spits furnished by nature. But soon a row of partly clad warriors stood in front of their sergeant, who was waiting for the arrival of the others with the list in his hand. They were without firearms and most of them had in the one hand a friendly wooden frying spit ornamented with a smoking fry and in the other the famous Bowie knife. Several did not fall into line, as their partially roasted meat did not permit them to leave it to its own fate, or possibly the threatening condition of the coffee did not allow them to take their places. These certainly were important reasons, and the sergeant decided to begin even if all the company were not together. Alternating, now from the ranks then from the fires sounded the stentorian voice of a backwoodsman. Even one time a muffled "Here!" broke forth from under a bundle of woolen blankets in a tent, followed by a general laughing of the company. The sergeant, although a little provoked, passed it up as nothing unusual. After he had finished reading the names, it was not necessary for him to give the dismissal order as every one, as soon as he had answered to his name, returned again to his former place at the fire. The last one to stand in line carried a smoking coffee can in his hand.

We looked at each other, especially we Europeans, and didn't know whether we should laugh at what had just happened or at the seriousness with which it was executed. It is true that the European soldiers possessed a little more discipline than prevailed here—with them at least the form existed. If there were no necessary detentions, they appeared in mass. But with us the roll was never called in the morning. We had no formalities after the signal to arise had been given. We raked up the fire, prepared the breakfast, and then broke into small groups, if there was nothing to fear from the Indians, or large groups, and galloped away as we pleased. Only in one respect were we very strict: on the journey the quartermaster with two or three men always rode several hours ahead to let the people know of the approach of the Greys, who then prepared everything for our reception.

Everyone had to do his part of the work; there was bread to be baked, corn to be ground, coffee and tea to be cooked, steers to be butchered and other similar necessary things. If things were not as we wished them to be and the quartermaster was to blame, he was immediately removed from office; similarly, other officers shared the same fate and had to take their places in the ranks as common soldiers. But I must say that we were never obliged to depose our captains, as Captain Breese of our Company and Captain Cook of the other company of Greys knew how to command respect, and the latter particularly was well liked.

Toward nine o'clock we went out into the cornfield that lay between our camp and the town to enter a small entrenchment that had been thrown up mainly by Captain Cook's men. It was fortified with only two small cannon with which my comrades thundered on the old Alamo. We could in fact see pieces of the old walls roll down from time to time. The whole thing was being done for amusement and every effective shot was accompanied with loud applause from the Greys. Neither was the enemy lazy, and his grapeshot from eight or nine pieces secluded in several canyons swept the field around us, tore up the ground in every direction and chased clouds of dust toward our camp. It was no easy matter to get into the entrenchment from the camp as one had first to cross from six hundred to eight hundred yards of the open field, and the artillery of the enemy was being used far more than ours. But this latter circumstance made us a lot of fun as the cartouches put some of our men into close quarters as they ran across the field to the entrenchment. It was pure curiosity that drove us across, because we had no orders and no other purpose than to see the Alamo, which, from here, offered an imposing view and to join in the applause with the others when part of the masonry of the old building or of the deserted old church tumbled together.

Eight men, among them myself, set out together to cross the desolate field, while the enemy, as if he had directed all the cannon of the fort against us, enveloped us with his grapeshot like a heavy rain. We were obliged for a moment to seek shelter under a large pecan tree. After we had taken place here, we looked at each other and laughed at ourselves, eight men standing behind a single tree while the malicious laughter of our comrades, those in trench as well as those in the camp, accompanied every full load that struck our faithful pecan tree and rattled down dry limbs.

"This is, then, what they call waging war," said one of our future heroes, Thomas Camp. "And this," replied another as a swarm of iron mosquitoes flew past us, "we Americans call the variation of Yankee Doodle." "Yes, and we call it," interjected another, "the last groaning of Santa Anna with his, till now, all overthrowing central government," "And we," as the dry limbs rattled down, "wish that you disappear at once," which address, however, we did not hear to the end as the next second saw us on the way to the trench. The limbs of the pecan tree covered the ground where we had stood.

Everything was lively in the trench. They all stood around the cannon, and first one and then another had the pleasure of taking a shot at the old walls. Not a little betting went on. Before firing every man was first required to indicate which part of the Alamo he intended to demolish and the bets were placed accordingly,

"A hundred ready-made bullets against twenty!" one was heard to call out, "that I will hit between the third and the fourth window of the barracks."

"Accepted!" cried three or four voices simultaneously; the gunner fired, and he had to pour bullets all of the following day.

"My pistols, the best on the ground," cried a new candidate, who was about to fire, "against the poorest ones in the trench!"

"Well! Sir, reckon I can risk it," said a backwoodsman in a greenish pea jacket, whose pistols, although not quite as good as the others, were at least the next best after them. Away flew the ball and the lost pistols of the gunner wandered over into the belt of the man with the pea jacket, who magnanimously drew his and handed them over to the poor artilleryman.

"Well, in order to give you revenge, comrade, I will take a shot also. If this child doesn't hit, either—well, comrade, you may have your pistols back again." After he had, with the aid of a few of the Greys, loaded the cannon and gotten it into position, he looked down over the barrel for a long time. With one eye shut as if he had a rifle before him, his face presented a mathematical problem while his right hand drew a number of geometrical figures in the air.

The noise about, which he could not hear by nature, did not disturb him. Only the cannon only could speak clearly to him—none of the human voices were audible.

At last he was ready. Another time he cast a hasty glance over the cannon and reached for the torch. Driven by the mighty load of powder, the destroying ball flew towards its mark. The rattling of the stones indicated to us that he had hit his mark before the smoke had cleared away. After the smoke had disappeared we searched in vain for the third and fourth windows. As one voice a hurrah went up for old Deaf Smith, as they called him, the most gallant Texan that ever chased across the prairie and who later rendered such fine service with his scout corps on the Mexican border between the Nueces and the Rio Grande. The figure of a backwoodsman in the real sense of the word stood before us.

Dangerous it was for the enemy that got within the range of this man's gun, as he never missed his mark; on the chase he never shot his game other than in the head. For that reason, he looked down with such disdain on the Mexicans, with whom it was a pure accident if the bullets of their muskets reached their aim.

While we were thus engaged with the demolishing of the Alamo, several shots were fired from the tall grass and bushes on the opposite bank, which made it inadvisable for us to look out over our breastworks.

Indignant at the impudence of the enemy we decided to drive them away and proceeded to put a plan into immediate execution. Thirty to thirty-five men of the Greys with their rifles took position in the woods on this side of the river's bank, where we were protected from the artillery fire of the Alamo. Through effective shooting we soon silenced the guns of the enemy and probably some of the enemies besides.

Becoming excited through the continuous firing, and being some distance away from our camp, we as one man attacked, without previous council, the outposts of the city, which, although they were stronger than we, immediately cleared the field for us, whereupon we followed in triumph. This the enemy seems not to have expected at this time, and all inhabitants and soldiers fled toward the center of the town, which was very strongly defended; all the streets could be swept with artillery from there. Triumphantly we entered the captured houses and brought forth much-needed cooking utensils. While a part thus loaded itself down, the rest of us fought with the appreciably increased guard. From the center the bugles sounded the alarm and the roll of the drums called the carefree enemy to arms. The cannonading of our trench ceased, but our cannons still continued from time to time to send their smashing balls to the Alamo. We pressed forward energetically from house to house and from street to street while the enemy in proportion to his superior strength defended himself comparatively weakly and fled out of the

The Camp of the Militia

working circle of our excellent guns. After we had penetrated a small part of the town in this manner and, drunk with victory, were loaded down with booty for the kitchen, we thought of retreating, because we would soon have the whole Mexican array on our necks if we didn't. But it was too late. Before we could begin, Mexican grapeshot fire from the right, where they had almost surrounded us, pierced the air over our heads. At the same time two four-pounders on the roof of the church in the center slung their balls right in among us, but they usually bounced off and whistled away over our heads. Instinctively our men made submissive bows to the disappearing balls. They were obliged to yield to necessity even if the deep bowing is in bad taste with a free republican. A full volley down the street from the center also accelerated our retreat. We directed a few shots to the artillery to the rear, which now, since we had retreated, was to the left of us. We were compelled to leave the cannon, but we could neither spike it nor take it with us, as the Mexican bluecoats were swarming out of the streets like bees. It was the highest time for us to return to our comrades, from where the rolling of the general march sounded over to us.

Barely had we left the captured cannon before the Mexicans returned and followed us with its balls. However, since we could feel the vibration of the air and hear the report of the fire a little earlier, we did as before: bowed, and the swarm of copper pills that General Cos, the commander of San Antonio, had intended for our benefit rattled away over us. But when we came within the range of the cannon of the church and of the Alamo, from which we had been protected by the banks and woods of the river, we were embarrassed because we could not tell which way we were supposed to bow.

Soon the whole cornfield from the town to within a short distance from where we were was covered with the infantry of the enemy, and we were saved only because the soldiers did not take definite aim at the objects at which they were shooting. They held their heads far away because their muskets were more dangerous for the men behind them than for the men before them. A single shot will change the color of a white man's face in a moment and make it look like the color of the southern sky. And the bullet, instead of hitting its aim, whistles away twenty to thirty feet over it. So it was here. Bullets that were intended for us flew a quarter of a mile further and fell to the ground near our companions. Hard pressed and in danger of being accidentally hit and wounded, we hurried to a group of trees which reached out about one hundred and fifty steps from the river and lay across our path. Here we took a definite stand and sent our bullets effectively among the enemies. Conscious of their enormously overwhelming numbers, they would not let themselves be held back, and with a wild mixture of blowing bugles they pressed forward to surround us. There was nothing left for us to do except to flee under most dangerous circumstances; but suddenly, imagine our pleasure! the old strains of Yankee Doodle chimed merrily over to us and around a projection of the forest came the backwoodsmen and the remaining companies in order, as they said, to help the Greys out of a pinch. In marked contrast with the quiet, cool bearing of the soldiers, the fearless scout of the army, Deaf Smith, rode with wild gesticulations in front of the army from the left wing to the right. In his left hand he carried the staff from which the tri-color fluttered briskly, in his right the never-failing gun. The bullets that tore his flag did not bother him nor did the deafening noise of the bugles and

The Camp of the Militia

drums of the enemy. The Texans now awoke from their lethargy, and went into battle against Santa Anna's soldiers under Cos. Smith had for the longest urged an attack, but he could never induce the officers to undertake one. They consoled him by waiting for reinforcements. He replied that he could take fort and city with half of the troops already present.

But again he was to be disappointed. Barely had the Mexican soldiers seen the army of Texans, barely had they heard Yankee Doodle, familiar to the British, before they fled behind the protecting walls of the town, and the backwoodsmen didn't even have an opportunity to fire off their guns.

We were led back in triumph to our camp together with our welcome kitchen utensils, which no one had thrown away. After that the Greys rose powerfully in the esteem of the brave Deaf Smith, and he was accustomed to call us by no other name than his boys.

Several days passed again without anything of interest happening, aside from a few brushes between the enemy outposts and our restless volunteers; also a fight was offered the Mexicans with Smith's co-operation. It was the well-known Grass Fight, where the Texas militia took a number of prisoners — about 160 men, whom, however, we liberated again during the night because they made us extra trouble and had to be fed from our provisions. A few would not leave because they liked it better with us than with their countrymen.

From day to day we insisted on storming the fort and town, but couldn't induce the commander of the militia, of which the larger part of the army was composed, to do so until Colonel Grant, who formerly was an officer in the Scotch Highlanders but now for a number of years a citizen of Mexico, succeeded in arranging for a general meeting of the troops, where General E. Burleson, the commander of the army, purposed to disclose his plans. If they should be approved, it was agreed to put them into execution the next morning.

With new life the drums sounded through the whole camp, and the happy expectations of a decisive battle smiled on every feature. With pleasure we threw our gun over the shoulder and hurried to the place of meeting where we, in perfect formation, awaited the arrival of Burleson. Not a man, a few wounded excepted, was missing.

At last the commander appeared in company with several other officers. He immediately stepped to the front, and, sickly as he appeared, he addressed the army as follows:

"Citizens!

"In response to the general demand to bring about a decisive turn in our war for independence, in response to demands from all sides to know whether we will in the future be permitted to reside on the soil of Texas which we have just made arable by our perspiration while in the first epochs of the colonization the muskets could not leave our sides to keep the Comanches from our new hearths, to do justice to these demands I have given the matter ripe consideration and have sought the advice of Major Morris and Colonel Johnson. It is my opinion as well as that of the Colonel's that, in view of the unfavorable season, we should withdraw behind the Guadalupe until spring, enter comfortable quarters, await reinforcements from the States and undertake a sudden attack with renewed strength on San Antonio in February or March without entering quarters here as now."

Cries of disapproval ran through the lines; and even Grant, the gallant Scott, shared our views.

"If we withdraw," said a captain of the Greys, "the boundaries of Texas will be our destination, and barely will the Greys lie quiet and idle for five or six months. The spring would not find them in the army. No, now is the time, now to San Antonio—or never."

From all sides applause was accorded the captain, and Burleson continued:

"As I notice, gentlemen, you are not of the same opinion with me—a matter that I had anticipated—and I have worked out a plan for this case also. If the troops find this one good and workable, I am of the opinion that it should be executed tomorrow morning before the break of day."

A hurrah from our midst, and he continued:

"We will divide the troops into three divisions of which the first, under Colonel Milam, will attack the center of the city from the river on the northwest; the second, under Major Morris, will simultaneously storm the center from the west, and Mr. Smith, who has lived a long time in the town, will serve the second as guide; the third I will command in person and with it remain back to protect the camp and in case of accident cover the retreat."

The anger that had possessed the army soon changed itself into contemptuous laughter, and, one by one, the militia left the ranks. Burleson, who had nothing better to submit, advised those that still remained that the present attitude of the army made a retreat imperatively necessary and that we would have to take advantage of an opportune time to drive the central army under Cos out of Texas.

But against this the Greys protested vigorously, especially Captain Cook. He asserted that should he leave the present camp and postpone the attack until the spring, he and his companions would not withdraw behind the distant Guadalupe but would camp during the winter a few miles from here in one of the fortified missions now in ruins on the San Antonio river.

Burleson permitted us to do as we thought best and, full of anger, we returned to our huts that we had left so joyfully.

The fires flickered forsaken in the camp; and in front of the huts and tents everybody was busy saddling the horses and packing up. Some of the militia were already riding off to the colonies, as there was no hope for a successful attack under such leadership.

A short time had passed and possibly half of the militia was already on the way to the Guadalupe. The Greys were downcast and still undecided what to do. What could one hundred and thirty men do against nearly fifteen times that many? Nothing but sacrifice themselves; on the other hand, should they languish in the colonies for three or four months?

That was not the purpose for which they had come to Texas. Why did they renounce the brilliant positions and prospects that were offered them in New Orleans? Why did many leave the parental hearth? Not honor, and not to become a soldier, because the regular soldier is an object of contempt to the industrious citizens of the States; only seldom does one find the sons of Uncle Sam among them; they are mainly whiskey-loving foreigners.

No, it was for the rights of their kinsmen, for the rights of every man that they entered the field without any prospect of remuneration, that they left the safe haven to plunge out into the raging sea.

But they were not to grieve long. Suddenly five horsemen came riding down the river on the side on which the

The Camp of the Militia

camp was located. The leader, a little lean man, wore the uniform of a Mexican lieutenant, which he in reality was. A white flag fluttered in his left hand.

He asked hastily for the commander, where, after we had led him thither, he pledged himself to lead our troops unobserved near the center of the town. Yes, he even said that, if a part of the troops would follow him, he would lead them under the window of General Cos.

His offer, however, was not accepted, as we were afraid to trust him. Too many circumstances spoke against him. In the first place he was a traitor, secondly he was a Mexican, and thirdly some Comanche blood flowered in his veins.

All of these made Smith's warning to be careful unnecessary; but his advice to attack the city, as he had suggested, was accepted after some encouragement from Smith.

With new life the Greys shouted through the half-deserted camp. The militia did not agree with this plan and considered an attack now as foolhardy. Half of our troops had left us and we could not muster more than four hundred men. Nevertheless, we frankly declared it our intention to try the attack, even if the volunteers would have to make it alone. I said "volunteers" because the slender volunteers from Mississippi had just as large part in this work as the companies from New Orleans.

A call for volunteers to storm the town next morning was issued. A list was passed from man to man, which everyone in favor signed. When the last had signed, the names of two hundred and thirty men stood on the paper. The names of only a few of our company were missing—the wounded.

The plan for the attack was this. A part of the troops, which were to remain behind to guard the camp, went up a short distance soon after midnight, crossed the river and under cover of the night planted several pieces of artillery quite remote from the Alamo. They then waited until near four o'clock and made a feigned attack on the fort to draw the attention of the enemy and most of the troops in their direction. Meanwhile we marched, double quick, in two columns down two streets paralleling the river toward the center of the city. In the vicinity of the latter we purposed to take position in a group of stone buildings whose walls were three feet thick. There we were to wait for day, survey the surroundings, and make further arrangements.

In spite of the approach of the fateful day, we slept excellently. Wrapped in our blankets from head to foot, we lay around the fires with our guns near us and the saddles for pillows. In this position the northwest wind that blows down so lonely from the Rocky Mountains through the southern plains during the winter could not disturb us. In the early spring it often causes the death of sugar cane, and even at times cotton and corn. Often the thermometer drops to forty degrees Fahrenheit during the night and by noon of the next day reaches the same high reading as the day before. Although a northerner whose blood has not been thinned by a southern summer may not find this climate disagreeable, it is just as severe on the regular inhabitants of these broad plains and more unpleasant than the cold January is to the inhabitants of the north.

The Storming of San Antonio

A NORTHER LIKE THE ONE MENTIONED in the previous chapter was piercing the prairie during the night of December 4 to 5, 1835. Tents and huts were blown down and the last sparks of the fire blown away, but we lay quietly under our covers and dreamt of the adventures of the coming day. It was just two o'clock as the guards, who had been relieved, stepped from tent to tent to quietly awaken the sleepers. They started up out of their dreams but dropped back just as quickly when the icy breath of the storm whistled around their warm joints.

But soon we stood in line with our faithful guns on our shoulders. We were wrapped in our blankets and awaited the signal to march.

It was, however, a little too early to work simultaneously with the troops that were to make the feigned attack. Consequently, we were obliged to wait a while longer. During this time, since we had started no fires, we froze terribly and waited anxiously for the time to march. At last Major Morris stepped among us and read out our names another time.

Only two hundred and ten men were on the meeting place to answer to their names. The night had removed many heroic thoughts, and the storm had blown away many weak spirits that last night glowed in the hearts like the last sparks of the fire. But this had no influence on the others, whose motto was: "The fewer the number the greater the glory." We believed that those who could not face the enemy with courage and love for the cause would do more harm by their example than good.

At last it was past three o'clock and we hurried quietly across the cornfield toward the city. Carefree, the numerous enemy posts cried their *"centinela alerta!"* into the night. Aside from these long drawn-out words and the howling of the norther there was not the slightest noise. Soon we paid no further attention to the unfriendly breath of the Rocky Mountains, but warm from our running and the expectancy of soon seeing the enemy, our woolen blankets flew to the right and the left on the road. Without reducing our speed, the watchword "Bexar" ran from man to man.

We were about halfway across the field when a thunder different from that of the norther indicated to us that our friends fulfilled their duty and were attacking the Alamo.

Instantly the enemy drums began to roll and the bugles pealed in motley confusion. From the fort there was an incessant booming to the place from where our people with their little guns challenged the whole Mexican army. The glances of our leader, the Mexican lieutenant, hung constantly on the Alamo, which we could see to our left as a black colossus.

He peered uneasily through the darkness as if he feared that our purposes had been betrayed. At last he broke his long silence and said, pointing to the Alamo, where several rockets were just rising:

"The way is clear; we are safe. Yonder sparkling, artistic stars are calling a part of the troops of the town to help the Alamo. Now briskly ahead that we may reach the town within ten minutes. Do you see yonder outposts at the fire? Let them run away unnoticed. Our shooting would kill a few but would bring the whole garrison down on us. However, quickly after them so that we will get to the plaza at the same time with them. The further ahead we get this morning the more stone buildings will fall into our hands."

We were within twenty steps of the fire before the sentinels noticed us, and without uttering a sound, they fled, some even without their muskets.

Unobstructed, we rushed, as stated before, in two columns into the city. The first column, with Breese's Greys in the lead, was to follow the street next to the river. But for reasons of safety we hurried along on the left side of it through the little Mexican gardens and over banks of the San Antonio, in places treeless, toward the plaza.

As already stated all the streets were commanded by Mexican artillery. Well was it for us. When we were within almost two hundred steps of our destination, the first load of grapeshot of the enemy swept along the street. And soon, just as the day began to dawn in the east, we were obliged to take a position in an enemy guard house, a substantial stone structure.

We viewed with interest the dark outlines of the quadrangle that surrounded us. We had never seen buildings of this kind before. They were generally one story high and built in the form of a long chest. Toward the yard, the structure that served as our refuge had two doors but no windows, whereas there were four of medium size on the opposite side next to the street. The roof was flat and surrounded with a stone wall two feet high. At the lower end of the house and parallel with the center ran a wall three feet thick and six feet high to a small outbuilding. From there another one of the same kind ran parallel with the river, exposing itself and the front of the dwelling to the fire of the Alamo, which was about two thousand yards away. The other side of our little fort was shut off with a few small buildings. All the dwellings of the well-to-do Mexicans are in form of little fortresses. The walls, on an average as thick as those described, are very practical for this climate; they are cool in the summer and warm during the winter storms. Consequently, one seldom sees any fire in the chimneys. Elegant furniture is nowhere to be found.

In the yard an enormous steer tied to a stake by his horns was lowing discontentedly. He came in very willingly when we ran short of food. In the house we found a few opened barrels of Missouri cornmeal and a few remnants of sugar, coffee and cacao.

Disregarding the fact that it was still night when we arrived, the enemy soon revealed his location to us by his murderous fire. The whole plaza was a flashing line. The firing was an irregular, uninterrupted infantry fire, intermixed with the groaning of all of the Mexican cannon, of which twelve to sixteen six-pounders were directed against the little fort of the first division. One of them stood within eighty steps of us and was playing against the lower wall, behind which we were just busy setting up a nice, long six-pounder.

The balls sang us a morning song of a singular kind. In countless tones from soprano down to bass like those of the harp of Aeolus they vibrated over our heads. Several of our men, who had taken position on the flat roof behind the wall, were compelled to keep themselves very quiet; they had never experienced a shooting of this kind before. Even behind the walls they were not safe as the guns of the church, which reached high up above all other buildings of the town, commanded our roof also. Consequently, shortly after daybreak they were obliged to jump down in the greatest haste and had the pleasure of being given the laugh for their dexterity.

By eight o'clock we still did not know where our second division was. It was said that they were nearby, but where, no one could say. We finally discovered it by an unfortunate accident: from stone buildings to our right and a little to the rear little smoke clouds issued from time to time. From the light fire we concluded that not very many enemies could be in the buildings. Consequently, as a quickly conceived plan to take the buildings and put them in communication with us was about to be executed, several shots from there indicated to us that they were our own people, who were mistaking us for their enemies. One of the bullets struck a Mississippian by the name of Moore, which, fortunately enough, glanced off from two dollars that he had in the vest pocket. A second laid low another, the tall Mississippian. The bullet tore the brain out of its cavity and spattered it on the walls and over us who stood near him. His colossal body twitched convulsively for hours in the thick clotted blood that flowed out of the wound. It showed us novices the battle of the body with the parting life.

The clear crack of the shot and the small bullet that glanced off from the money supported the belief of a few that they were our own people who were firing out of the buildings. And several offered themselves as volunteers to Colonel Milam, who now commanded us, to jump over and inform them of their error. The offer was accepted and immediately executed, but not until another one was sacrificed. It was this time a German, William Thomas, who had just taken aim to fire on the plaza. A gun cracked, smoke issued from out the building of friends, and momentarily the gun of the heavily wounded German dropped to the ground. The wounded man, driven by a mighty force, made an involuntary movement, a puff of wind blew past him and a stream of blood issued from his sleeve.

Pale as marble he looked about, clapped his hand on his left shoulder and remarked that he must be wounded, although he felt no pain. The terrible pain came later. Later the shattered shoulder bones caused the surgeon more trouble than all the other wounded together.

After the second division was advised of our presence, leaving nothing to be feared from this side, a door was broken through the thick rock walls and a ditch to our people was thrown up as the safest and most convenient means of communicating with each other. Running across the street was highly unsafe. As soon as the enemy got a glimpse of us, which was only after a few seconds, they would send past us a large quantity of lead and copper paradise apples, but would hit only seldom.

The eighty-yard-distant cannon that, together with those of the Alamo, constantly raged against our walls, doing considerable damage, was now the main object of our attention. It was silenced in a short time as the backwoodsmen and the Greys, through little holes dug through the walls, laid out every bluecoat that approached it. It, therefore, could not be loaded much less be directed at us. On the other hand, our long, bright six-pounder now played effectively on the row of buildings opposite us. We were, however, obliged to use our balls sparingly as we did not have an oversupply of them.

In the afternoon we began to experience a little thirst. As there was no well in the house, we alternately jumped down to the one-hundred-and-fifty-yard distant San Antonio, dipped our vessels into the water and rushed back to our companions under a rain of enemy bullets. This finally became too dangerous, as constantly increasing numbers of bluecoats posted themselves opposite this position. Soon the price of water rose from three dollars to four dollars per bucket. Finally, no one was willing to risk dipping out of the crystal waters at even a higher price.

A Mexican woman who was in the house when we arrived, and who at once cooked and baked bread for us in a friendly manner, offered to go to the stream and get water for all of us since she, as a woman, would have nothing to fear. This we, and especially Colonel Grant, roundly forbade her to do as we were apprehensive that the bluecoats would fire on her just as soon as on us. She insisted, nevertheless, and said laughingly that we knew only very little about the female-of-the-species-loving Mexicans. And before we were aware of it, she was on her way to the stream. Hastily she filled her buckets and was on the point of returning when a swarm of bullets swept by, and, pierced with four bullets, she fell lifeless on the green turf. Our men gazed with horror over the wall. Only a few seconds passed before several men rushed out to bring in the unfortunate, good-hearted woman. All the enemies had discharged their muskets and the dead body was brought in without a single shot being fired. Others of the Greys taking advantage of the impotence of the Mexicans, sprang down to the bank, filled their vessels and returned safely, much to the chagrin of the bluecoats.

Toward evening a call was issued in our division for volunteers to take a stone house which stood to the right of us and a little nearer to the plaza. There was rather brisk firing through the open spaces of the palisaded windows, which, on account of its nearness, did not occasion us any great pleasure. Partly on that account did we wish to take the building and partly because its possession would put us appreciably nearer the enemy magazines. The first company of the Greys under Breese was determined to take the building without other help, as another one had already been handed over by the enemy to the other division. But we came too late. As we sprang through the windows and rushed forward without wrecking bars, there were the six-foot-high namesakes of the mighty Father of Waters whose wrecking irons, put in motion by their powerful muscles, were tearing the thick stone walls down. Barely had ten minutes passed before the first stone fell inward. Instantly we sent the contents of our guns through the little opening into the darkness within.

A terrible crying of women and children from within indicated to us that the building was full of people who were now plaintively pleading for mercy.

At once our not-joking guns were silent. But the walls were crumpling again and soon the Mississippians had broken in a powerful door from which a long stream of women, children and men now issued forth. The latter surrendered their guns and expected us to imprison them. But the tall victors, who had nothing to eat themselves, explained to them that it was far from us to wage war against the citizens of Mexico and that they need not be concerned about their property. With that they gave them permission to leave there, which the prisoners did not have to be told a second time to do. They went under full wind and sail to the empty houses that lay between us and our camp.

Cook's men had also taken possession of another long building, and with the capture of a third one the next morning they intended to supply all of us with fresh water as at a little distance from them a canal had been built through the city.

The dawn of the next, still stormy, day revealed to us a blood red flag on the pinnacle of the church steeple, a mirror that truly reflected all the dark places and folds of Santa Anna's heart. We laughed at Cos's purpose to frighten us with that color. In fact, it was gratifying to us in one respect as we alone were now fighting under the tri-color and the enemy under the standard that carried despotism in all its folds and promised death to all rebels who opposed the ambitious plans of Santa Anna and who, in the uninhabited savannas of Texas, dared to take up arms when the mighty states of the Confederation had bowed humbly under his sword.

During the previous night our long twelve-pounder had arrived, the largest caliber that thundered in the valley of the San Antonio, and we proceeded at once to throw up breastworks. A number of buildings fell into our hands today, and several mesquite hedges that lay between us and the enemy were set on fire. By four o'clock they were in full flames, and by eight o'clock the cover under which the enemy might have approached us unnoticed lay as a large still-glowing ash field before us. The groups of houses that we occupied were completely connected up with trenches during the second day.

During the night the enemy kept up an incessant fire, and in the darkness he also used the cannon standing opposite us. In spite of the constant firing we slept as well as if we were lying in the peaceful closely settled regions of the States.

On the third day the battle was opened by us in grand style. We gazed with satisfaction on our twelve-pounder as she slung her thunderbolts out of her new parapet and defiantly bellowed forth her war whoop to the old church tower from which the enemy molested us with their muskets. With the third shot that the Brunswicker named Langenheim sent off, part of the dome caved in, a warning to the enemy to quit this point for the future. In order to spare the venerable old ruin, we discontinued our fire with this. But we directed all of our artillery on a few buildings that we shortly intended to take. Our artillery, however, suffered severely. Soon all the men, with the exception of the long Brunswicker, as we called him, were wounded. He, an attractive man six feet high, miraculously remained uninjured, although he constantly exposed his full length to the bluecoats in adjusting and firing the cannon.

We enjoyed ourselves today at the expense of our enemies. Our people found great sport in putting their caps on ramrods and holding them above the wall. I had just returned from a round when I saw several of these punctured caps and hats on perfectly sound heads. This seemed strange to me, but the riddle soon explained itself. Just then a Grey held his head covering slightly above the wall, and barely had it projected above the rim of the wall when twenty to thirty bullets swarmed around the place. With loud cries of applause from the enemies, who believed that they had laid flat another heretic, the cap sank slowly back behind the wall. A pause set in, at least from our side. But the bluecoats continued to fire incessantly and it must have been much the same to them whether they fired into the sky or at us as their bullets sang away over the buildings even when no one thought of shooting over or through the punctured walls. After a while another cap appears boldly over the wall, and as expected the bluecoats cry out a good morning to it. But the hail of bullets could not scare the wounded. Unafraid, they maintained their position while the enemy troops fired their bullets lengthwise and crosswise, over and under, the position. Soon their anger was converted into consternation. They stared over to our walls and they as well as their muskets were silent. Then sounded the loud laughter of our men, who were showing the enemy the cap in all of its terrible condition.

With this, however, our fun came to an end. Following this event, the enemy would not fire on our caps, nor on the broad-brimmed hats of the backwoodsmen, nor even at our real heads unless we contributed a part of the body also. After a while, however, they fired as briskly again as ever, but not at our caps and hats but at the gourds that our people had decorated with their own headpieces and let look over the wall. This had the result that the enemy shot his powder away and occasionally exposed himself to the eyes of the backwoodsmen or the Greys when, if he did not drop himself, he dropped his musket with a shattered arm.

We had a serious loss today: a good artillery man, an Englishman named Cook, was killed. Formerly he had been gunner in the English fleet and in Texas he had immediately taken his place with the artillery. He was the first one to be killed in operating the twelve-pounder.

Another incomparably greater loss we had in the death of our gallant Colonel Milam, who fell lifeless to the ground with a musket ball in his forehead in the center of the yard where the first division lay. During the evening they were both quietly buried by us while the enemy artillery sounded taps for them. But when they were lowered into the graves all of our artillery in the town as well as that in the camp gave evidence of our grief and our esteem.

For the remainder of the siege we were without a definite leader, and all expeditions against the enemy were executed by calling for volunteer troops. The only authorities that were present were Major Morris and the two captains of the Greys. But I must observe in fact that I never heard a single order during the whole siege. Our own consciousness of being able to do something against despotism under the flag of the Union kept order and discipline in our ranks.

On the fourth day five hundred reinforcements under Colonel Guardechi, who had come from the other side of the Rio Grande and had missed the eyes of our rangers in their march from Tamaulipas through the wild prairies, moved in. But we had little fear of these as most of them were required to serve because of murder or robbery or because they had taken part in uprisings against the usurper that had occurred in all of the states of Mexico. They were chained together in pairs, and disregarding the fact that many of them wished death for us infamous heretics, it is easy for one to imagine how little there was to be feared from such rabble. They, therefore, did not frighten us in the least, and we vigorously continued our plans to conquer one part of the city after another. In fact, we purposed soon to undertake a coup de main.

At five o'clock in the evening volunteers were called for to take several buildings that were filled with bluecoats. More than were necessary pressed forward to have a share in this major stroke, and even before the sun sank into the waters of the peaceful ocean we stood about in irregular groups equipped with arms and tools at the buildings to be stormed. The militia was armed with wrecking bars to tear down the walls. Although the soft stones rolled out quickly, it seemed to take a long time because the enemy was firing unpleasantly at us from a little trench that had been thrown up across the river opposite the first division.

Meanwhile it wasn't very long before the masonry fell inward into the building, and soon thereafter the contents of our guns followed. The openings were enlarged as soon as we had reloaded, and we fired in another salvo. But the bullets of the enemy also whistled, although without effect, through the ever-enlarging holes. The militia prudently did not expose anything but the wrecking bars. Finally, the openings were large enough to admit a man at a time, and another volley from our guns cleaned the apartment of the bluecoats who, as we pressed in, had withdrawn to more distant and safe atmosphere.

The door to the next room was strongly barricaded and we were obliged to proceed with our axes, which, however, had to be done with the greatest caution as the enemies were shooting through like wild and two men already were slightly wounded.

As soon as the sun had disappeared behind the western horizon, the night, as in all southern regions, settled down over prairie and town with amazing rapidity and already black, impenetrable darkness prevailed in the conquered room when the door to the next room crashed together. This room had also been evacuated, and we felt about on the walls in the darkness without being able to see the least or to find an exit. In the adjoining room shot thundered upon shot, but, as it seemed, also without aim. Only from an opening near the ceiling flashed the fire of the burning powder, and the bullets that were fired against the ceiling fell at our feet accompanied by the limestone that they knocked loose.

At last we found a door, also barricaded, but it also soon lay in splinters. The room was, like the other one, vacated by the enemy.

This gave us possession of the building and we were now only about thirty to forty yards from the plaza. Nothing now remained but to eat a link out of the chain of buildings that surrounded the large quadrant, the center of the city, in order to put us in possession of the magazine in the church which stood in the center of the plaza, and, I might say, to put us in possession of the whole city. But we had done enough for today and another day was designated for that purpose.

"Glory enough for one day!" cried the backwoodsmen and rolled themselves up in their blankets to sleep.

The fifth morning sun broke forth in full bloody autumn splendor and sent down her warming rays from the deep-blue vaulted skies. The whole divine nature lay soft and quiet around the scene of battle. The howlings of the norther had ceased and that indescribable charm that pervades the wilderness on such a day lay on the western prairie that stretches westward from San Antonio as an enormous carpet to the Rocky Mountains. The waving mesquite fields were not fresh and green but bleached, like the ripe meadows of Europe. The sea of grass in the unlimited distance blended with the dark clouds above us.

But in terrible contrast the deserted streets lay about us and the desolate field, the burnt-off mesquite hedges and a few buildings before us, while the buildings around us looked more like broken rock heaps than human habitations. Again, more active than ever before, the artillery of the enemy without interruption jarred the trembling, partly fallen-together walls of the Free Corps; and without aim, as before, the shower of copper bullets rolled uninterruptedly from the outranked Tower muskets of the enemy. General Cos, like the chameleon, had again changed his color, and unpardonable hatred waved from the steeple of the town instead of the blood red flag; the black standard of death hung limply down from its high staff. Powerless, its folded form threatened the winning force of besiegers from whose headquarters the splendid tri-color was displayed with enthusiasm.

Devastation raged from our artillery as well as from that of the enemy, and the heavy fire of our old faithful twelve-pounder laid in ruins the walls of the building that we expected to take during the evening. But the balls for our six-pounders had been shot away, and they would have remained silent for the remainder of the siege if the enemy had not occasionally supplied us with the needed article. Whenever a ball would hit our walls, our people would hastily jump over after it, quickly load into our cannon and fire it back at the enemy with our compliments, for which he usually thanked us with eight or ten others. At the most two or three of them would hit our building.

Toward three o'clock in the afternoon we saw and heard for the first time the pomp of Mexican attack. A division of bluecoats from five hundred to six hundred men strong streamed forth from the walls of the Alamo. As if they intended to attack our practically deserted camp, they marched in that direction toward the river with the sound of their bugles, but were driven back by a few volleys from our companions. This, however, was only a sham attack and was executed for the purpose of drawing the larger part of our men out of the town, whereupon Cos would have attacked the few remaining with his superior forces. We, however, saw through that gentleman's plans, and neither he nor his many confusedly blowing buglers could draw a sign of fear from us. We sat quiet and expectantly, like the fox in the kettle, in our stone houses. If he attacked our camp, the guards might be able to defend it; if they could not, they were told to turn it over to the enemy and come to us into the town inasmuch as we would need all the men and guns the following night so that we could together deliver our final attack and ultimately free the prairies of the legions of the central government.

After they had, at a very respectful distance, paraded around in all their splendor for a time and toward the end had received a few loads from our artillery, they very quietly and without ostentation marched back to the Alamo, and found that their ruse was in vain.

We of the first division determined to take an important position in the plaza this evening in which the second division of Greys, although located in another building, intended to support us; but at about nine o'clock, just as we were making our preparations, the enemy made a ferocious general attack on the first division. All the cracking and thundering that we had heard up to now was only pretense in comparison with this attack. Every moment we expected to see the hordes of bluecoats on our walls that were in places now practicably shot down to the level of the earth, and whose ruins were serving as a breastwork for our men lying behind them. We lay man alongside of man with our hammers cocked, ready to drill through the first one who would be foolhardy enough to set foot on the breastworks; and at the little holes they had broken through the walls stood the backwoodsmen. Every bullet that left their guns laid one of the enemy on the ground. The Mexicans, as usual, considered it expedient, however, not to come too near our guns and remained at a respectful distance. This finally became too lonesome for us and about twenty of our Greys determined to attack the enemy in the flank. Without fear, although we were being attacked by from six hundred to eight hundred men, we rushed through a little bypath and attacked the four walls of a former blockhouse. The darkness was in our favor, and before the enemy was aware of it, we were among his murderously firing hordes. The discharge of our guns and all of our pistols instantly caused a wild confused retreat of the bluecoats behind the walls and buildings of the plaza, where they, however, continued incessant firing, especially at our roofless conquest. It also thundered like wild from the second division, and it seemed that they had to stand a harder fight than we ourselves. The bugles whirred wildly out of the plaza and the drums rolled for battle. The profanity of the enemy and the incessant musket fire was completely drowned by the cannon of the Alamo, which now in short intervals thundered through the darkness. But there was something inspiring in this powerful roaring through the night. A similar feeling took possession of me as in those days when I for the first time saw the powerful towboat that panted up the Mississippi with a fleet of ships, frigates and schooners. With a muffled, hollow thunder the white smoke issued at regular intervals from within the lighted-up behemoth. Long after it had passed out of sight we could still hear the puffing of the boat.

After eleven o'clock the tumult died away in every direction and we left the four walls to see how it stood with our attack on the plaza. But imagine our surprise when we found all of the buildings of the second division empty. We were still standing about unable to explain the cause of their absence when a wounded man lying in the corner gave us the information. Immediately after the enemy's attack on the first division, everybody hurried away to unexpectedly storm the designated position from a different direction. And the plan succeeded completely. In a short time, they had driven the Mexicans out of two of the largest buildings and spiked the cannon, so dangerous for us, eighty yards away.

It may appear to many a one that we proceeded very carelessly without planning, which conclusion could especially be justified by the fact that the second division not only left us without any assistance but also even left their position to undertake a charge while we were being attacked violently. I cannot justify this with anything except that we considered ourselves invincible, a conclusion that later caused us deep wounds and almost caused the destruction of the new republic.

The fifth day was thus closed gloriously and we were looking eagerly for the sixth, the tenth of December. The fire of the enemy had died down, and only occasionally a shot was fired from the little trench on the other side of the river whose ball, like a lost wanderer, carelessly hurried through the darkness and crossed that space where, for five days and practically four nights, thousands had crossed each other. The thundering roar of the artillery had died away and the quivering earth had quieted down. Only the groaning of the wounded reminded us of the bloody sacrifice that was made for freedom. Nor did we know how much more blood it would require. But the Gods do not require blood when justice is done in peaceful manner; immeasurably more acceptable to them is the victory won through the noble feelings of the heart. If these are destroyed, if the understanding is blinded, then the oppressed hand must swing the bloody sword for the right.

Lighter and lighter did the east become, and the dark shadows of the night were disappearing before the fiery December sun that was to reveal the fall of the enemy. The humble white flag of submission was waving from the ruins of the Alamo. The black flag of death had disappeared from the high dome whose pinnacle was now ornamented only with its own dignity.

The capitulation was agreed upon by nine o'clock. The Mexicans were to be allowed to march away unmolested. As a protection against the Comanches they were allowed one hundred and fifty guns, a little powder and lead and a four-pounder.

The officers were obliged to give their word of honor never again to fight against Texas. The officers and troops

The Storming of San Antonio

were to leave the town at once, the Alamo on the 12th of December, and to evacuate the whole country on this side of the Rio Grande as speedily as possible.

On the designated day, Cos marched away with his troops, and by virtue of conquest we took possession of the magazine and the Alamo. Forty-eight cannon, approximately four thousand muskets, a considerable amount of powder, ready-made cartouches, and a large supply of cannon and musket bullets fell into our hands. We also found a large number of enemy uniforms in the magazine, which was located in the rear part of the church, but they were not of the slightest service to us as, although they were new, every Texan would rather have made himself, like the brown inhabitants of the prairie, a hunting shirt and a pair of moccasins out of the skin of the slain deer than to have worn the suits of the contemptible soldiers.

The loss of the Mexicans ran up to seven hundred and twenty-odd killed, and a small number of slightly wounded who left with General Cos, while a large number of the seriously wounded were taken under the treatment of our physicians with the same carefulness that was accorded our own wounded.

Our loss was six killed and twenty-nine wounded, who were lying in the military hospital, together with a few slightly wounded who took up quarters in the town. This proportion of the enemy's loss is so infinitely large that it appears almost unbelievable. But practically all battles between these two powers show that the number of Texans killed multiplied by one hundred will generally give approximately that of the Mexicans.

Our treatment of the enemy was good, as was our treatment of the inhabitants of San Antonio, although they united with Cos and opposed us. We still regarded Texas and Mexico as a large whole. Consequently, now, as formerly, the tri-color of Mexico waved over the church. And we hoped that fame on its mighty wings would soon spread the result of our contest against the usurper's troops over the sister states of the republic and that it would call forth a renewed uprising of the whole people to throw off the yoke of the central government.

San Antonio

SOON AFTER THE DEPARTURE OF THE MEXICAN TROOPS, most of us moved into the ruins of the Alamo, and each one, according to his own pleasure, searched out a favorite retreat for protection against the cold and storm of the winter. A little detachment of nine men, among whom was the Virginian Paw,[7] who had now become lieutenant, selected the rather well-preserved church, which had been robbed of all ornaments, as their quarters. There were several large arches at the front entrance under which it appeared dangerous to tarry long. The outer side was provided with several figures of the saints chiseled out of sandstone, in front of which the Mexican women regularly every morning knelt down without being disturbed in the least by the passing in and out of the volunteers. It was said that the sandstone saints were being visited more now than ever before, and I have often wondered whether the black-eyed Señoras became so pious because they were now in such close contact with us heretics, or whether it was the presence of the heretics themselves that drew them into these desolate ruins.

---

[7] Probably John J. Baugh, who would become a captain and adjutant of the Alamo garrison.

After everything had gotten quiet again in the town, and the country around only occasionally resounded with the discharge of our guns when a deer or a turkey was being killed for the table, the inhabitants of the town at last returned in large numbers. Most of them had left their walls during the siege and quietly awaited the result of the battle on their ranches that lay from six to eight miles down the river. The homes of the rich and the blockhouses of the poor soon filled up again, and the streets were alive with Mexicans and Texans moving back and forth. Through the broad streets glided many a neat Señora, even if not as elegant and as elastic as the pretty New York ladies as they flutter by the hundreds through the magnificent Broadway, yet endowed with that charm and courtesy for which their nation is known and which so cuttingly repels the rougher manners and customs of the inhabitants of the north.

The Mexicans are great lovers of pleasure; they dance, ride, eat, drink and sleep their lives away. We frequently visited different families. If we came between ten o'clock in the morning and five o'clock in the afternoon, we would usually find all the members of the household sitting on a carpet that was spread out on the floor of the room. Apparently everything was happy. The dons very pleasantly chatted their time away with the brown beauties, or talked about horses and cracked pecans, while the whole party smoked their *cigarritos*. After five o'clock, when the rays of the sun are not burning so hot on the prairie and the evening wind is blowing refreshingly cool from the mountains, the masculine world drives the horses home. The brown Amazons of the west mount their favorite steeds and away they race with the men in a flying gallop through the streets to the prairies where they chase about until seven or eight o'clock. Then, however, they return to close the night in the dance halls with the music of the fandango.

The first days passed in intoxicating pleasures as it appeared that we were welcome everywhere. Aside from the conversations composed of sign-language and a combination of English and Spanish words, everything went briskly forward. And not infrequently did the peculiar combinations occasion loud laughter. But after a week, as this pastime regularly repeated itself from day to day, the charm of the newness began to disappear. Our restlessness rose again and demanded other nourishment than the endless and at last lonesome fandangos and the still more lonesome association with the inhabitants of San Antonio.

The hunting in the vicinity also wasn't good any more, as first the siege and then the constant hunting had frightened practically all the game away. 'Tis true that the prairies were covered with herds of deer, but to hunt them was tiresome and a worthless pleasure, especially as we preferred flesh of the cattle that we had in abundance to that of the deer.

We had to undertake something else. Consequently, Joseph Spohn, a creole from Louisiana, Thomas Camp, an Englishman, and I rode several miles down the stream on a pretty day, the ninth since our entrance into the Alamo, to view the old partly decayed missions that the Spaniards had erected here in pretty style during the eighteenth century. All the buildings together with the church stood on one end of a flat quadrant from eight to twelve hundred feet across which was protected on all sides by high walls. Along these walls the Mexicans of San Antonio had lined up their corn bins.

We aimed to go to the station of San Jose and, well armed, heavily loaded, and with a lunch of several fried ox ribs buckled behind our saddle, we proceeded on our journey.

About a mile from the Alamo we saw the yet comparatively well-preserved church, Concepción, in whose vicinity Colonel Bowie and Captain Fannin with eighty men had a battle with four hundred of the enemy a few days before the arrival of the Greys. Here the militia captured that pretty six-pounder that the first division put into such good service against its former owners.

On the other side of the old church we had to cross the strong current of the San Antonio, which was no small matter for our horses as they had to go into the water up to their bodies. Two miles further on the right bank, however, lay the second mission to which we directed our horses. For quite a while we saw the steeple of the high dome projecting above the dense and dark magnolia and pecan forest; but not before we came to a large cornfield did we see the weather-beaten old buildings. It was an interesting sight to see a ruin here in the middle of a primeval forest, which reminded me of the Thuringian ruins of my fatherland. The dignity of a greater age than it really possessed sat enthroned on the grey stonework. The rough northwest storms had accomplished in a short time what would require hundreds of years of the German climate; in the hot south, also, everything ripens and dies sooner than in the cold sedate north. The high arched door through which we just entered was the only entrance for horsemen; various cactus species covered every horizontal part of the walls; Several round, slender horses and fat calves grazed in the center of the quadrant, but not a human being was to be seen on the whole place. We unsaddled in the center of the plot and left it to our horses to choose whether they would take their noon meal with the rest of them or rest in the shade of the buildings.

As we entered one of the wretched Mexican huts, we found the whole company. There were probably fifteen persons seated on the ground and busy with a mighty pile of pecans, in the opening of which they showed great dexterity.

In a dark corner sat several very old grey-headed men whiling the time away playing cards; their constituent parts consisted of a wrinkled skin and a human skeleton. The drying atmosphere of the highland of Texas, it seemed, had not missed its influence on them, and they appeared to justify the old saying of the Texans that the inhabitants of San Antonio never die, but gradually shrivel up and, feather light, are finally blown away by the wind. There are, in fact, some very old people here on whose faces one can barely discover the features of a human being for the wrinkles, but I am not quite willing to vouch for the blowing away part.

As we were very thirsty, we asked for a little milk, which was, apparently unwillingly, handed us. After we had bought a quantity of pecans, we set out for the church and the old cloister in the expectation of finding supplies of arms and food there. We purposed to make a close examination.

From the top of the dome, to which a step made of several hewn tree trunks led up, we had a charming view; about us lay the forest out of which two other steeples at a little distance projected; before us lay the already-described quadrant; to the left rolled the San Antonio; behind us was that large cornfield; and to the right the green savannah rolled away to the southwest. Everything except the prairie was encircled with the forests of the San Antonio. The prairie reached out over the distant rolling hills, and only occasional low mesquite trees stood on the plain, among which grazed the herds of the inhabitants of the mission. No watch against the Comanches was kept, although these unwelcome visitors from time to time drove off some of their stock.

A few bats and even a screech owl flew away as we approached their retreats and fluttered about in the cool, dark, high room of the church hall. In the desolate cloister building, which stood in immediate communication with the former, also lived the just-mentioned denizens of the night. Everywhere the floor was dug up and eaten through by destructive mice. In one of the rooms stood a large, black oak table at which the good monks must have emptied many a goblet on the well-being of the Indians whom they were to convert. A small dark room that we now entered showed the traces of devastation in a higher degree than the other parts of the ruin. The floor was overspread with lime and stones that had dropped down from the walls and ceiling. This appeared suspicious to us, and after a little scraping we discovered a loosened plate, which, on taking it away, permitted us to look through a narrow opening into a dark room, but we could not see the least thing.

The sound of the stones that we dropped in indicated to us that it was not very deep; and I decided to jump down while Tom got a rope from our horses with which to draw me out again. After I had let myself down through the small opening as far as my arms permitted, I jumped down the rest of the way on good luck into the unfamiliar apartment. Brilliantly were our expectations fulfilled. After about a ten-foot drop I landed on from twelve to fifteen wagon loads of corn that the Mexicans had concealed here. And although it by far exceeded their needs, they would have let it rot here rather than to help support our army with it, notwithstanding the fact that we usually paid enormous prices.

After I had very carefully searched through every nook and had discovered nothing beside the corn, except a little exit that was barricaded with stones and through which a few rays of light penetrated, my companions drew me back to the light of day. The stone plate was put back in its former position and we covered it over again like the remainder of the floor with lime and rubbish. And over it all we threw a layer of dust. Hereupon we left the buildings, saddled our horses and hurried with the parting sun toward the town; but the fire god had long disappeared when we rode through the long, dark door into the Alamo.

We immediately informed the general-quartermaster of our discovery. He did not neglect such a welcome treasure as this one when provisions were so short. Early next morning six wagons under the guidance of myself and assistants to the quartermaster were on the way to San Jose to get a part of the corn. Soon we were in sight of the old ruin; and as our wagons drove through the high door to the small entrance that had been so artfully concealed from the outside by a pile of stones, the Mexicans, who were so sullen yesterday, came out and tried to bribe my companions and me with a pair of pretty horses that we had admired yesterday. But as this inclined me against them rather than for them, a quarter of a hundred women and children came and succeeded by their lamentations to induce us to suspend the loading of the corn. They maintained that this was all that the families had to live on until the next harvest.

As we volunteers knew well enough how much was necessary for one meal but did not know how much would be needed for eight or nine, I decided to ride to headquarters with one of the Mexicans to speak with the officers themselves about the matter, while the wagons were to wait for my return.

As it was getting late, we rode rapidly toward the town, and as darkness was about to set in, our horses were foaming in front of the quarters of our officers. My companion presented his case with Mexican cunning and the officers were already inclined to believe him and to issue orders not to disturb the corn, when an old Mexican and Deaf Smith stepped forward and said that the present inhabitants of the mission had always been the most bitter enemies of the Americans and that San Jose concealed a proportionately larger amount of corn than was necessary for the families, as they had sold large quantities in San Antonio every year and that their present conduct was pure hatred for the army.

After both sides had spoken, I received instructions to take only three loads thereof and to leave the remainder with the families.

The Mexican was overjoyed to get off so easily and to receive such a reasonable price for the three loads. He was so elated that he spent the night at the fandango. I, however, mounted my horse and, with my gun before me, trotted off toward the mission. Since Comanche signs had been seen several times during the last few days, I cautiously watched in all directions; I distinctly cherished no desire to let myself be scalped. While my whole attention was thus centered on the various objects as they appeared from time to time, I rode forward on a wrong road, which, although the distance seemed long, I did not notice until I was frightened by a powerful noise caused by thousands of cranes flying up from a pond just as I rode out of the prairie into the forests along the banks of the San Antonio. The flapping of their wings and their loud, repulsive, confused calling caused such an uproar that my usually gentle horse made a violent jump to the side. Trembling all over and snorting intermittently, it stretched its head forward to determine the cause of the nocturnal disturbance

Evidently I was on the wrong road and, therefore, obliged to turn back. After I had returned to the prairie I decided, after wandering around a while, to pitch camp for the night in the tall grass. After I had hobbled the forefeet of my horse, as usual, and had spread out one of the blankets on the grass, I threw the other one over me and my faithful gun to protect us from the heavy nightly dew; the pistols and the saddle served as pillow. But barely had I wrapped myself up so comfortably, when several shots at no very great distance caused me to spring up again. Speedily my warhorse was saddled, and cautiously I rode off in the direction where just then another shot had fallen.

I might have been barely a hundred yards away from my camp when a dark object that I soon recognized as the dome of San Jose rose above the forest before me. In a few minutes I was with my companions, who were much concerned for me and who, since I had promised to be back with them before midnight, had given me the signals.

Next morning, we entered San Antonio with our welcome provisions, where all the troops, reinforced with a new company from Mobile, Alabama, also called Greys, were holding a grand parade at which Major Morris was commanding officer.

At the same time, it was decided today to march off to Matamoras on the 30th of December, and everyone who was disposed to take part in the expedition was instructed to be in readiness by that time.

Half of our company and a smaller part of the others remained back for the protection of the fort in San Antonio, and the rest of us, included four Germans, united ourselves with the Mobile-Greys under Captain Burk's command as a quiet soldier life did not please us at all.

Departure for Matamoras

THE THIRTIETH OF DECEMBER APPEARED and we took leave of our friends who were to remain here, never suspecting that they would fight sooner than we and that this would probably be the last time that the Greys would exchange brotherly handshakes.

The cannon thundered a last farewell after us, as we camped for the first night on the Salado only six miles from the Alamo. It was the same place where General Cos and his troops and a few days later a troop of Comanches had camped.

On the second day we marched through the deep, densely forested valley of the Cibolo, and again, as further up where we had crossed it the first time, practically the whole stream had disappeared, and only a little brooklet wormed its dwindling way down the channel. That night we camped at Seguin's plantation that lay on the approximately eighty-foot-high bank of the San Antonio.

We left the plantation the next morning and marched down on the left bank of the river toward the little fort of Goliad, which with La Bahia, a little town, is about 105 miles from San Antonio. We decided to await reinforcements and then to undertake a major movement against Matamoras.

Colonel Johnson and Major Morris were in command, but in reality it was Grant, the beloved Scot, who led us, in spite of the fact that he constantly refused to be regularly elected.

The sixth day showed us again the waters of the same stream that pushes its way through between the Alamo and San Antonio. On the right side and about a mile from the ford lay La Bahia and a little higher up, the little fort, Goliad, which a few Texans under Dimmit had recently captured from the Mexicans.

For a few days we lay on the left side of the stream where we drove up several herds of horses and selected the best ones for our use. Here we unsuccessfully followed a small division of Indians that had attacked several ranches.

Finally, on the ninth of January, we marched through the deserted streets of the town, and only occasionally one could see the wrinkled face of an old Mexican looking out of the little loopholes that served the block huts as windows. The larger buildings were deserted; at the beginning of the war, their inhabitants had taken refuge on their ranches along the wooded banks of the San Antonio, where they decided to await the results of the war. Others had openly taken unfriendly issue with us and had hurried off to the Rio Grande to enter the field against us united with Santa Anna's first invading forces.

Our numerous assurances that we had taken up arms only to protect the nation and the Mexican confederation and that no Mexican would be compelled to bear arms in the war for freedom availed nothing. Even Colonel Grant, who had lived a long time in the northern provinces of Mexico and who had at least the appearance of being highly respected by the inhabitants of that region, urged them in a friendly manner to unite with us and to shoulder the muskets for the general welfare and to defend their herds and homes united with us against the oppressions of Santa Anna, but everything was in vain. They either moved away or lurked around only to report faithfully our plans and movements to the usurper.

We here met a Doctor Bunsen from Frankfurt on the Main River, who had recently arrived with a company from Louisville, Kentucky, to participate in the storming of Matamoras. Also a certain Patton of the same place was in his company.

The total number of our troops now stood at six hundred men, and we were waiting only for powder, lead and provisions to be ready to march. But these articles were to appear from day to day, and as one period after another passed by and we were meanwhile obliged to lie idle, a general feeling of ill-will broke out among us against Governor Henry Smith, who let the army lie idle here under all kinds of hardships. Instead, if he had supplied us with lead and powder, we might now have had Matamoras, which the enemy, since he knew our purpose, fortified more strongly from day to day.

Many, dissatisfied with the irresolute government, had already directed their steps northeastward to their homes. But we had not considered that it might be as difficult for the provincial government to get moneys together as it was for us; not one citizen had paid in any money for the purchase of war supplies, and those supplies which the generous-spirited citizens of the States had bought and gathered were still on the sea. The only mistake of the government was that no proclamation called upon the people to support the army.

The collection of supplies would, no doubt, have been sympathetically supported everywhere, as everywhere the volunteers passed through the country the colonists gave us the best of everything that they had in the house and placed their herds at our disposition. Nowhere could we ever induce the owner to take pay for them.

The army had now melted down to approximately 450 men. If the army were not to break up altogether, something had to be done to employ the energetic fiery spirits.

In a general meeting it was decided to march to Refugio, thirty miles nearer our aim, and to wait there at the outside eight more days. From the dispatches of the Governor we could hope that certainly within this time a considerable detachment of volunteers from Georgia and Alabama under Fannin, who now was colonel, and a large consignment of supplies for the expedition would arrive.

I cannot fail to mention here one of the most peculiar cannon of Goliad. It was a two-pounder that the Mexicans fastened on the back of a mule and used in pursuing the Indians. The mission of Refugio, to which the army directed its march and where it arrived two days after its departure from Goliad, was formerly, like the mission buildings of San Antonio, inhabited by Spanish monks whose object it was to Christianize the Indians. Now only the high, decayed walls and the weatherworn roof gave evidence of the Christianizing zeal of the Spaniards. The priests desired not only to rule in the spiritual realm, but also wanted the physical power to be in their hands. Trickery and force of arms were alternately brought into service against the wild and numerous inhabitants of the prairie. The Comanches tell even now of a frightful scene where around eight thousand of their tribe were destroyed. Scattered about the church were the little houses of Powers's Irish colonists, who had only recently settled here. The place was located on an elevated prairie; and as health and contentment of the inhabitants beamed from their features, I believed that the climate here was well adapted to the Europeans. The splendid, fresh, green meadows on which numerous herds of cattle were grazing, each colonist owning at least from two hundred to five hundred head, made this little village one of the most pleasant in the former province of Texas. Towards the southwest the Rio Blanco[8] ripples down between high rocky bluffs. It begins to be navigable for small craft within a half mile of here from where it winds down to Copano Bay through dense forests. The tide of the bay drives the fresh waters of the river far back into the level country at regular intervals. Thousands of water birds swim about on the rising and falling waters, while there are countless numbers of fish in the water that come up into the country with the flood of the tide and mostly hurry back out into the bay again with the ebb. The dense forests are alive with beautifully feathered southern songsters, and the pecking and knocking of the flocks of woodpeckers united with the constant gobbling of the turkeys reveals to the hunter a hunting ground which cannot be surpassed anywhere in the world. When one passes out of the dense forests that seldom permit a friendly ray of sunlight to pass through, up into the countless little savannahs, he discovers a country that is covered from November to May with countless flocks of wild geese that walk about perfectly unconcerned among great herds of wild horses, cattle and deer and appear not to be any more afraid of the coyote or the large wolf than of any other of the wildlife. One is charmed with the luxuriance and the grandeur of the southern climate, and few would care to wish themselves a more beautiful paradise than this one. The dwindling tribe of Caranchuas seldom make inroads into this rich region in which their fathers, once a mighty nation, chased the fallow deer and peacefully enjoyed the wild honey

---

[8] Ehrenberg errs: it was the Mission River.

mixed with the roasted game. But those times have disappeared and that region abounding with game is void of people; their bones are bleaching on the prairies with those of the Comanches, their eternal enemies. The Caranchua tribe, which now consists of approximately thirty to forty men, now roams over only the lagoons and the low, narrow islands of the Gulf along the Texas coast, where they take the redfish and the buffalo for their daily needs out of the waters of the roaring sea.

It was in this region, called by the Mexicans the Eldorado of the West, that the army pitched its camp a little below Refugio during the latter half of the month of January 1836. Here we waited again for a few days on the arrival of fresh reinforcements and dispatches from the governor, but nothing appeared. We had already decided to leave without further delay on the morrow for the town of Matamoras, one hundred and sixty miles distant, when General Sam Houston, the commander-in-chief of the army, suddenly appeared in the midst of the camp. The various companies immediately assembled and surrounded the field marshal, already renowned from Niagara Falls to the Rio Grande. His patriotism, his democratic views and his liberal actions had won for him the general love and confidence of all the Texans. Difficult were the problems that he had to solve. He was to quiet down the restless heads, concentrate their forces and to prepare them for the work that had to be done with the approach of spring. The whole plan, to create a completely independent state, now stood clear and in the brightest colors before the mind of every citizen of Texas. The Mexicans, instead of supporting us in our efforts to throw off the yoke of tyranny, rather joined the tyrant, and enormous preparations to destroy the settlers in Texas were being made by Santa Anna, eagerly supported by the priests.

There was no other way open to us; either separate from Mexico and found a new republic, or else leave all our property in Texas and flee over the Sabine into the States.

"Comrades!" began the general, "it is with pleasure that I find myself in your midst again after long separation, and I notice with astonishment that the keenest anticipations that I had of the patriotic spirit of the army have been far surpassed in reality. Comrades, we must seek to maintain such a patriotic fire and not consume it where it will be of no benefit. Soon, friends, I believe, soon will the enemy under Santa Anna raid our peaceful savannahs, soon will their bugles urge the soldiers to our destruction, but that mighty word—freedom—will inspire us, the thought of right and religion, of wife and child, will make us heroes. And disregarding the superior number of the enemy I hope that our army will defeat his purpose on the foaming Guadalupe and before the next summer has faded away the flag of Texas, the true symbol of freedom, will wave in all the ports of the land. But to be victorious, citizens, it is necessary that we stand united and that we extend each other our hands in firm union. United we stand, divided we fall.

"You aim to take Matamoras. I praise your courage, but I must candidly tell my friends that this plan does not please me. I see no advantage that can emanate from it. I see only an unnecessary sacrifice of the blood of Texans for a town that can have no value for us and that lies beyond the border of our territory. If it is meant to injure the enemy, let us await him and let his forces, fatigued by long marches and privations, feel the work of our guns. Let us prove to him what a nation united, though weak in numbers, can do when it rises up en masse and boldly speaks out: 'We want to be free!' Let us show him that where the nations rise up for the cause of justice the

Almighty will carry the banner. But I see, comrades, by the expression of your features, the disapproval of my opinion, but it is just my opinion. I thought to act only for the interest of the new fatherland, but my voice is only one, that of yours is to Matamoras. Well, then, to Matamoras be it. But at least wait a short time until the troops from Georgia and Alabama land and, united with them, what power of the enemy can withstand us?"

The Artillery Captain Pearson stepped forth and addressed himself to the army: "Comrades! as much as I respect General Houston, I cannot approve his suggestion. We have already lain here idle too long and the consequence is that the larger part of the army has left us. Too long we have waited in vain for munitions; in vain we looked for reinforcements from day to day that the government had promised. It would be for nothing that we would stay here longer, hesitating, idle, enduring the hardships of a campaign. If we shall endure, let us be acting, and I herewith call on all who are in favor of an immediate departure for Matamoras. Colonels Johnson and Grant and Major Morris are in favor of the expedition and will participate in it. Once more, let us not hesitate longer, and, all who endorse my position, be ready at noon to leave for Matamoras!"

These two speeches, coming one after the other, called forth various feelings, and as the army had voted decidedly for the storming of Matamoras, it was only Houston's eloquence and popularity that induced the larger part of the army to wait and to begin the march in conjunction with Fannin's reinforcements.

Another time the old General stepped forth to give us a sample of his eloquence, and I will try to write down a brief outline of his speech: "Comrades, Citizens of Texas! Another time I am appearing before you, and it is with the most fervent desire that this time, at least, my words will find general approval.

"Our proclamations to the other states of the Mexican Confederation, asking them to support us in our struggle for the restoration of our former rights and for the protection of the Constitution of 1824, have, as you all know, been without results. Even many of the Mexicans who live between the Sabine and the Rio Grande have disdainfully forsaken the cause of freedom, and have not only denied us their support but united themselves with the troops of Santa Anna and as enemies waged war against the land. Others have gone beyond the Rio Grande in order to smother us in conjunction with the next invasion. Still others have gone to their plantations on the banks of the forested rivers, apparently to idly observe the war. These, comrades, are for us the most dangerous because he who is not with us is against us. Also, from the otherwise liberal inhabitants of Zacatecas we have observed no movement in our favor. No other help remains for us now than our own strength and the consciousness that we have seized our arms for a just cause. Since it is impossible to call forth any sympathy from our fellow Mexican citizens and no support is to be expected from this side and as they let us, the smallest of all the provinces, struggle without any aid, let us then, comrades, sever that link that binds us to that rusty chain of the Mexican Confederation. Let us break off the live pad from the dying cactus that it may not dry up with the remainder. Let us plant it anew that it may spring luxuriantly out of the fruitful savannah.[9] Never will the vigor of the descendants of the

---

[9] Houston is alluding to the Mexican coat of arms, which was a prickly pear cactus with one pad for each Mexican state in the union.

sturdy north ever mix with the phlegm of the indolent Mexicans, no matter how long we may live among them. Two different tribes on the same hunting ground will never get along together. The tomahawk will ever fly and the scalping knife will never rest until the last of either one tribe or the other is either destroyed or is a slave. And I ask, comrades, will we ever bend our necks as slaves, ever quietly watch the destruction of our property and the annihilation of our guaranteed rights? No! Never! Too well I know my people. The last drop of our blood would flow before we would bow under the yoke of these half-Indians. On my journey through the province I have had opportunities enough to learn the wishes of our countrymen. All of Texas is for separation. Even some prominent Mexicans, who are living among us, are preaching loudly that we should sever the bond that binds us to Mexico. 'Texas must be a free and independent state,' is the general word.

"A general convention of the representatives of the people will be held at Washington on the first of March of this year. It is the duty of the army to send several representatives, and I hope that my comrades will elect only men who will vote for our independence, who will fearlessly proclaim our separation from Mexico. And what they decide upon, comrades, we will defend with force of arms.

"For a few moments more of your attention I must beg, my friends. There is general complaint about the negligence of the government in supplying the troops with war materials. But to eliminate the causes for this complaint lies beyond the power of the governor. Shiploads are on the sea, and only unfavorable northwest winds have prevented their running into our harbors. Possibly even now they lie safe in the Matagorda Bay, and the citizens will hasten to deliver the cargoes to the army."

Loud applause greeted the commander-in-chief as he left his position, and all his friends and old comrades heartily shook hands with him.

However, a small detachment of seventy men, including the whole artillery company, insisted on immediately advancing at least to San Patricio, forty miles nearer Matamoras, a decision that they executed that very day. They left us under Johnson, Grant and Morris, taking two pieces of artillery to immediately fortify San Patricio, while Colonel Grant with a small detachment intended to scout the western border and purchase horses on the Rio Grande for the whole army. Bunsen and Langenheim were with this expedition. On their departure we wished them good results on their undertaking and hoped soon to see the domes of Matamoras, united with them.

After general Houston's departure, our two companies, the Greys, crossed the river and camped two miles from Refugio not far from the plantation of a Mexican named Lopez,[10] who showed astonishing interest in the war for independence. That he was a spy we were soon to discover. From here we made excursions into the surrounding forests and prairies and waited with ardent desire the arrival of Fannin, who was to land with his troops at Copano, fifteen miles away. The remainder of the army was quartered with the citizens of Refugio and came over to us only when they wanted to catch fish and turtles. The rest of the time they consumed in catching and breaking the wild mustangs that ran about on the prairies between here and the bay.

As it was necessary for a small guard to go down to the coast to await the arrival of Fannin and to immediately inform

---

[10] "*Lopus*" in the original German.

the army of his appearance, four other Greys and I offered ourselves to attend to this post for a week, which was approved. We immediately equipped ourselves. A young hog that we had killed constituted our main store of supply. Besides, however, we had a small quantity of dried beef, a small amount of cornmeal and a little coffee and sugar. Thus equipped we proceeded on our journey, our baggage and provisions being packed on one horse.

    Although the ground was very dry, high sage-like grass covered the level country down to the bay. Groups of mesquite bushes and small trees concealed the coyotes, which were found here in large packs. They were not shy in the least. Surprised to see a caravan of this kind moving through their quiet domains, they left their retreats and trotted in rows a short distance away alongside of us with their interesting heads constantly turned toward us. A hurricane was roaring from the Gulf over the prairie toward us; and if we had so desired, we might have loaded our horse down with wild geese that, on account of the storm, would not venture out of the tall grass and often came within reach of our pistols.

    When we were still eight miles away from Copano, we could hear the roaring of the surf as plainly as if we had been in front of the foaming waves. We hurried forward anxiously to get the first glimpse of the majestic mirror of the bay, which we expected at every turn of the road around a point of mesquite forest. But we constantly deluded ourselves. None of us had ever been in this region before. As we were walking down a little hill that was unusually luxuriantly overgrown, we amused ourselves by setting the grass on fire. Barely had the flames taken hold when they rushed forward with amazing rapidity. Within a few minutes they had disappeared beyond the hill down which we had just come. The black stripe before us and the just as dark cloud of smoke that accompanied the fire indicated to us that the mighty fire column would soon hurry past our comrades at the mission. The cries of the frightened-up winged flocks had died down again. The thundering of the waves sounded ever clearer over to us. We had just stepped out of a group of trees into that immense prairie that lies all along the coast of Texas.

The open, winter-bleached plain on which we now stepped was encircled on the north by forests, while in the far distant east and west it rose to meet the moving sea of clouds. But to the south roared raging waves, whipped by the hurricane against the sandy bank of the bay. A lonely one-story wooden building, which had formerly served as warehouse for the goods of the people moving to San Antonio, stood on this immensely beautiful shore.

Years ago the inhabitants of this heavenly landscape had left their lonely habitation. The only human beings that still frequented this place from time to time were the fishing Caranchuas or possibly Castro with his Lipans, who occasionally roamed this far but whose domains really extended only to the right bank of the Nueces.

It was in this old warehouse that we established our quarters, and in spite of the hurricane, which was expending its fury on this stable-but-trembling building, we had soon started a merry fire on the wind-protected north side of the house and dinner was being prepared.

The first evening approached, and with the disappearing sun the howling of the storm died away. As it was very sultry and as we would anyway rather sleep in the open than in houses, we lay down on the gallery. After we had stacked all of our belongings at our heads and placed our guns as usual under our blankets, we slept splendidly in spite of the roaring surf that rolled over Copano's strand.

Towards four o'clock in the morning we were awakened by a strange noise, but we could see nothing that might have disturbed us. We were on the point of lying down to sleep again when we saw a number of dark figures at some distance on the prairie slowly approaching us. It required only an instant and our guns were in order to do their part. Not a sound escaped our lips; no movement betrayed our wakefulness.

If we were quiet, our unknown enemies were dead. Not the slightest noise revealed their movements through the dry grass, and still the group was approaching us. Suddenly the deadening lead took flight from our guns, and in a few seconds everything had noiselessly disappeared. We jumped up and approached the place to which we had fired. Although we were sure that we had hit, we found nothing.

The night was so exceedingly beautiful and we were so thoroughly awake that we sat down on our spread-out blankets near a small group of aloe plants and gazed out on the still restless waves that occasionally threw a fine spray over us.

The morning set us clear on the adventure of the night before. Not very far from us lay two dead wolves, the victims of our guns. But imagine our consternation when we returned to prepare our breakfast and found that all of our provisions with the exception of the meal had disappeared. Even the coffee lay emptied out about twenty steps away. Imagine our rage. Certainly each one resolved henceforth to shoot every wolf that crossed his path and not to be as considerate for them as we had been on the previous day.

Departure for Matamoras

But in order to get breakfast we had to use some other means besides to rage, especially as we had no inclination to cut beef steaks from the hind quarters of the wolves. Consequently, two men were sent out to hunt game, while I and another one went down the bay for half of a mile to secure a load of oysters that had settled there in mighty colonies. When we returned, the hunters had already brought in a turkey and two ducks and in a short time the fifth man, in spite of the wolves, had prepared a brilliant breakfast that could not have been served better by Jacob Astor's in New York.

For eight days the light forest, the coasts of the bay and the waters supplied us with fish, oysters and game birds of many kinds.

Fannin's Landing

ON THE SEVENTH DAY, after we had given up all hope of seeing the so anxiously awaited flotilla run into the harbor during our watch period, we sat on the shore and looked at the undulating bay that lay in enormous waves before us, the billows not breaking, however, before reaching the beach. Thus one generally sees the sea just before or immediately after a storm. Then one sees with amazement the water in terrible battle with itself while the greatest quietness prevails in the atmosphere.

But we were not to have watched in vain. On the southeast horizon, apparently, two grey cloudlets just then rose up out of the water. An inexperienced eye would not have taken them for the work of human hands. But with every moment that they approached us, the mist disappeared; and the cloudlets unfolded themselves into two slender figures, two speedy frigates, that were dancing toward the shore under a light southwest wind and full sail on the rolling waves. From the loopholes the cannon thundered a friendly greeting from Fannin's Free Corps towards us, and their threefold hurrah greeted the new home. One of our comrades rode at full speed through the prairie toward Refugio to announce Fannin's successful arrival. He arrived just in time to set bounds to the dissension and discontent which, occasioned by the inactivity, would have brought about a complete dissolution of the army in a short time.

After a few hours the larger part of the troops were busy at the shore or on the waves landing the supplies that they had brought along.

Among a few companies I can here mention only that excellent Georgia battalion under Major Ward, all herculean and muscular statues. But the best ones were the Red Rovers, well-made native sons of Alabama. All were dressed in brown hunting shirts and trousers and were armed with pistols and guns. Dr. Shakleford, their captain, was respected by everyone as their father, as he was the only aged man among them. His son and his nephew had shouldered their guns with him for the sake of our cause.

It was ten o'clock at night and the bustle was not yet over. The whole shoreline was lit up with many watch fires, and instead of the howling of the wolves that in the previous night roamed the savannahs, one could now hear the step of the relieving sentinels and occasionally loud, hearty laughter of a group sitting around a campfire. But suddenly four riders on foaming horses from Refugio rode through the outposts. They brought dispatches from the government according to which all Texas should elect representatives today for the first national congress to meet on March 1, 1836.

As only two hours remained for holding the election, the work proceeded rapidly, and by twelve o'clock candidates for independence were elected by an overwhelming majority.

The next three days were consumed in unloading the supplies and transporting them up to the mission. Shortly thereafter the two frigates turned their prows seaward. While the little cannon of Fannin's people fired them a farewell, the star-spangled blue field, the flag of Uncle Sam, waved wishes of good luck from the slender masthead down to the single star that beamed from the light blue flag that led the Georgia battalion to the mission.

A few days after Fannin's arrival in Refugio we saw all of ourselves deluded in our hopes; the prospect of marching to Matamoras had disappeared, and many left the army again. Fannin would have been glad to take part in the expedition, but he feared—and he had reasons to—that he would not lead the command while the universally very popular Colonel Grant was present. He, therefore, advanced other reasons and remained steadfast in his decision to await the enemy on this side of the Rio Grande. Consequently, he marched to Goliad in order to fortify the place and make preparations for the spring campaigns.

The part of the army that lay at Refugio before Fannin's arrival had dwindled down considerably and remained as before in its old quarters. Captain King's company alone, which would play a heroic role next spring, had melted down to thirty-one men.

The Greys marched to San Patricio to inform that little advanced detachment of the army of the present state of affairs and to induce the men not to expose themselves longer to the danger of being cut off from us. And should they yet be unwilling to follow us, to induce them to at least put the cannon under stronger protection, either to turn them over to Fannin or to await the disposition of the government.

Our march led us over a high prairie that was strongly overgrown with mesquite bushes and on which many varieties of cactus covered large stretches of now very dry ground. Frequently we saw the wild herds of the former Irish inhabitants who, practically all good Catholics, had moved over the

Rio Grande in order to avoid coming in contact with a host of heretics like us.

Here also, as everywhere else, exceptions were to be found. An especially noble-spirited example of patriotism was given by a high-hearted individual of this nation. Mr. Fagan placed his whole, and not very small, crop and several hundred herd of cattle at Fannin's disposition without any prospect of ever receiving any pay for them, as it was possible only for a Texan to hope that we would be victorious.

As a warning for the lonely wanderer, several crosses stood on the side of the road. Beside the crosses rested the bodies of several Mexicans that had fallen under the scalping knife of the Comanches or the Lipans.

Late on the second day after leaving Refugio we arrived at the little, though neat and regularly laid-out and built, San Patricio where, as already mentioned, only Irish lived.

Johnson and Grant with the rest of them had taken possession of a few vacant buildings. Although many other houses were unoccupied, we preferred to throw up our quarters on the edge of the forest that bordered the Nueces. As we were much fatigued, our old companions soon had a row of lively fires burning and, not satisfied with providing us with provisions, they would not in the main surrender the work of preparing them, which was in general the custom with the San Antonio army.

The next morning awoke us for the chase, as the whole densely wooded Nueces valley seemed alive with turkeys. Their cries sounded from every direction. By nine o'clock approximately forty of them were in our camp, besides several rabbits. These were the first real rabbits that I had seen in America; they are fully as large as those in Europe, but have a much lighter hair color, also lighter than the smaller kind that one finds in the States.

The landscape was beautiful. While the left bank of the Nueces borders a perfectly level plain covered with a growth of mesquite bushes, the opposite one revealed, after we had passed through the dark forest of the valley, a laughing, rolling region. The prairie was in places decorated with groups of live oaks and other varieties of trees. At the foot of a chain of hills lay a bright narrow sea that billowed with fish. This region had been turned over to a German by the Mexican government that he might here found a colony of his countrymen. The disturbances in Mexico and then in Texas itself prevented the execution of this plan.

Colonel Grant had already bought up a large number of horses and was willing to leave for the Rio Grande in a few days to supply the whole army with fresh horses, as they were unusually cheap on that river.

On the third day after our arrival at San Patricio we received news from Matamoras. The citizens of that city were wishing that we would appear. Then they would seize their arms and drive out General Cos, who was now commander there. Since so many contrary reports from there had come to us, we did not trust them. Although Colonel Grant tried to induce us with our approximately one hundred and fifty men to attack the city by night, we considered it as such a foolhardy undertaking that we could not give his proposition consideration for a moment. We would not rely so easily on the persuasiveness of the inhabitants on the other side of the Rio Grande as Colonel Grant did. This credulousness was Grant's only weak point.

In vain we tried to induce him and his little division to retreat. Since we were aware of their bitterness toward Fannin, we proposed returning to our old San Antonio; but no one was willing to follow our advice. After a few days we were obliged to leave with only the cannon. At the same time Grant and Johnson with their divisions rode off in different directions through the mighty Tamaulipas prairie to their destination, the Rio Grande. With the promise that they would follow us within six weeks with enough horses for the whole army, they left us.

Nothing of importance transpired on our march back to Goliad, where we arrived in the beginning of February.

From here we purposed to march to San Antonio to reunite with our companions who had remained behind, as Fannin's method of commanding the army did not please the free principles of the Greys so well as to tie them to the walls of Goliad.

But we were obliged to stop there for a while at least, as Fannin would not give us provisions except while we remained in his camp. He assured us, however, that he was shortly expecting the arrival of two ships in Lavaca Bay that were being loaded in New Orleans with all kinds of supplies. So we remained and began busily with Fannin's troops to secure the fort, which, with the cooperation of our Polish officers, soon took on the appearance of a fortress; but for treachery, the Mexicans would barely have succeeded in taking this fortress from a Texan garrison, even though small. It lay more advantageously than the Alamo and was not spread out so much.

Our task was now to demolish the low buildings around the fort under whose protection the enemy could approach the walls unhindered and to destroy the four- to five-foot-high and three-foot-thick hedges, in which task we utilized wind and fire. After just a few days the artillery had a free view all around.

The Campaign of 1836 Begins

IT WAS TOWARD THE LATTER PART OF FEBRUARY that dispatches from the government and newspapers from New Orleans arrived telling us of the defeat of the Blues who had sailed to Tampico.

General Mexia, who had fought against the destroyer of the constitution of 1824 during the war with the several states in 1833, and who was compelled by Santa Anna's superior power to clear the field and, after the last battle, to flee from Mexico, was now living quietly in New Orleans, hoping that Mexico's lucky star would rise again someday. He determined, in that event, to draw anew the sword for his unfortunate fatherland. For such an opportunity he was not long to wait.

Santa Anna himself, who judged him according to his own character, gave Mexia the opportunity, sending him thirty thousand dollars with which to purchase arms and other war supplies in the States for the campaign in Texas, to return home with them, a pardoned man. 'Tis true, Mexia bought arms, but not to deliver them to Santa Anna and to become a traitor to his country; but, on the contrary, to equip several new companies that were assembling in New Orleans with them. With these he sailed with two schooners to Tampico in order, once more, to unfurl the tri-colored flag for the restoration of the Constitution of 1824 and from there to act in conjunction with the Texans. He was influenced in coming to this decision by several Mexican army officers who were in secret correspondence with him and who promised him on their word of honor to go over to him with the troops under their command immediately on his arrival.

After the Blues had drawn in the sails outside of the well-known dangerous Tampico Bank, they waited for a small steamboat that was just coming down the stream from the town to tow the unknown schooners, which it took for freighters, over the foaming banks. Soon they were masters of the boat and directed the pilot to take the ships up the stream and to cast anchor immediately in front of the city.

But they had barely gone halfway when the schooners suddenly stuck fast as the pilot either unknowingly or intentionally had driven out of the channel and onto the sand bank.

Just opposite lay a little fort that commanded the river, from which a boat was now coming to examine the schooners. The officers and men on the boat were immediately taken prisoners, and since everything was now revealed, the Blues immediately stormed the fort, which capitulated in barely a quarter of an hour.

All of Tampico was alarmed over the inroad of the, as it was believed, Texans, and as Mexia and his troops, completely fatigued, arrived at the city during the night, everything had been prepared for their reception.

The battle continued until the dawn of day. The garrison had concentrated in a single position, and if Mexia's allurers had kept their word, Tampico would have fallen. Being either base or cowardly, they forgot their promises and instead of going over to the attackers they opened fire on them. After sunrise they were on their way back to the little fort to return to Texas or New Orleans from there. But many were missing, and under another article in the *New Orleans Bulletin* we found where twenty-nine men of the Blues were shot on Santa Anna's order during the early part of February. They had lost their way and fell into the hands of the enemy. Two Kentuckians, when they saw that they were going to be shot, sprang forward against the soldiers and fought a despairing fight. But it was in vain. And although they wounded several, they were finally overpowered and, though heavily wounded, shot.

This was the prelude to the tragedy that was enacted in the western prairie during the next spring, where the Mexicans unfolded their character in the clearest colors.

By these reports we saw what fate awaited us if the enemy through negligence or dissension on our part should surprise us. The most advantageous time to march was now arriving, as the fresh grass was coming out abundantly, although our well-known northwest storm, the aftermath of the winter, still blew across the prairies.

More bad news came a few days later. Johnson himself with the four remaining men of his detachment arrived from San Patricio. Five days before they returned from the Rio Grande with several hundred pretty horses and as formerly took up their quarters in the now completely vacated town. As the trip had somewhat strained the horses, they were turned out on the green meadow during the night and guarded.

Towards midnight as the guards sat carelessly on their horses, they were suddenly surrounded by several hundred mounted Mexicans and shot down without mercy after they had defended themselves like mad, as several of the enemy subsequently admitted.

At the same time the fatigued troops in the town were awakened out of their deep sleep by the enemy bugles sounding the signal for the attack. Many hundreds of them sprang through the town under incessant shooting and with the cry, *"Viva Mexico!* Down with the Americans! Death to all Texans!" They located the scattered houses in which our people were quartered. The largest band of the enemy now surrounded the blockhouse in which twenty-two of our men were located. Their position was revealed by the still-flickering fire in front of the door. The other five men and Johnson rushed out of their little house that was surrounded by at least twenty times as many of the enemy and broke their way through the line. Only one fell, and while the circle opened in a cowardly manner, the remainder rushed through and out on the open prairie, from where they set out toward Refugio.

For several days they lived on spherical-shaped cactus of various varieties with which this prairie especially is covered, as they had either forgotten or lost their ammunition in their haste.

The remainder defended themselves desperately. Already many were wounded, but nevertheless they continued to fire vigorously on the encircling enemy, whose musket balls, in conjunction with balls from the artillery, punctured the walls of the block house by the hundreds. Suddenly there was a lull on the enemy's side and those that were ordained to die could breathe freely again. A short stillness set in, interrupted only by the yelling of the distant Mexicans who were driving together the frightened horses. Then a Mexican officer stepped forward and offered the surrounded ones mercy if they would surrender without further contest. Since they had nothing to risk, several stepped forth, but Pearson and the oth-

The Campaign of 1836 Begins

ers declared that they would rather die fighting than to surrender themselves to the mercy of such enemies. Barely did the unfortunate ones stand before the house before a volley from the enemy wounded several and killed one. The others fled back into the house that they had just left, and all were now determined to sell their lives as dearly as possible.

The firing continued through the whole night, and only when the sun rose did the guns quiet down. And only occasionally did a single bullet from a crack in the block house knock down a Mexican from his horse as he raced by.

Toward eight o'clock, the blowing of the bugles indicated the arrival of a high officer, and shortly several of the enemy appeared with a white flag before the block house that protected the few still living heroes and requested an interview.

Hope never seems to completely leave the human heart. Practically all the wounded Texans again trusted the sham promises of the enemy and soon stood among their ranks. But only for a short time; before noon their bodies, full of holes, watered the soil of the prairie with their blood.

Only two of them, Langenheim, the tall Brunswicker, and a young creole from Missouri who spoke Spanish, were saved for other sufferings.

Independence

ON THE FIFTH OF MARCH we received inspiring news from the General Convention at Washington. On the second of March our first congress had solemnly proclaimed the independence of the former province of Texas from the Mexican Confederation, and declared that the district lying between the Rio Grande, the Sabine and the Red River from this day would take its place among the nations of the earth under the name of the Republic of Texas.

Today was as stormy as the rejoicing that swept through the colonies, and the new star that waved over Goliad for the first time today trembled and battled on the blue flag with the roaring hurricane. But barely had it waved from the walls in its splendor for an hour when suddenly a new attack of the storm hurled flag, star and staff in a terrible whirl down into the fort. This was in fact an evil omen, but what state, just springing into life, will not have to battle against reverses for the sake of independence. But after only a short time the blue banner again waved in the enraged elements. The storm soon abated, and the unassuming sun cast a golden hue over the purple vault that was showing us the last traces of the departing storm on the western horizon.

The beginning of the new month brought us many important events. A new government with Burnet as president and Lorenzo de Zavala, a Mexican, as vice president was installed. General Houston issued orders to destroy Fort Goliad and the Alamo and for the troops immediately to withdraw behind the Guadalupe, as Santa Anna was said to be on the march to Texas with twelve thousand men.

Houston's orders probably reached Goliad in time, but not the Alamo, as a messenger from there advised us that the garrison there, composed of 150 men, was already surrounded by several thousand Mexicans and had been summoned to surrender by Santa Anna, which, however, they indignantly rejected. Meanwhile the blood-red flag waved from the enemy's quarters. They urgently solicited aid from Fannin and Houston. Houston lay at Gonzales higher up on the Guadalupe with five hundred militia.

Another order from General Houston gave us the alternative of either retreating behind the Guadalupe or, if it were the wish of the army, to march on to San Antonio. In the latter case his troops and ours were to unite forty miles on this side of the Alamo at Seguin's ranch. At the same time, he observed that it was the wish of the militia to rush, united with Fannin's division, to the relief of the garrison at the Alamo.

But Fannin was inclined neither for the retreat nor for the march to San Antonio. On the contrary, he would rather face the enemy in the fort of Goliad as reinforced by him. In Goliad he undisputedly held the leadership, which rank, however, he would have had to resign if he combined with the main army. Our efforts to induce him to march to San Antonio were in vain. In vain we pictured to him the fate of our brothers. Nothing could change his ambitious determination! He remained at Goliad. Often one could plainly see ambitious and better feelings battling within him, and during one of those moments he gave orders to march to the Alamo.

We camped on the other side of the stream and expected to break camp for San Antonio the next morning. Suddenly we heard the words: "Back to Goliad! The majority of the troops prefer to defend the fort."

From where Fannin derived his conclusion that the volunteers were not inclined to rescue the lives of their brothers in the Alamo was not explained to us, and without taking the vote of the army, everything went back to Goliad.

The Greys moaned and complained about the fate of the besieged ones to whose reinforcement they had been on the march, only to be detained by Fannin. Soon it was too late, as Santa Anna in person closed in around the Alamo with seven thousand men, and with every day the enemy works moved closer and closer around the decaying walls of the Alamo. The garrison had already gallantly repulsed several attacks. Even if they could hold out for a short time, it was self-evident that they must finally succumb. At the beginning, to be sure, it would have been easy to fight their way out during the night, but they did not wish to leave the walls that we had so honorably taken away from the enemy during the previous campaign.

At the risk of their lives, one or two came daily through the enemy lines and brought us the pleadings of the garrison and especially the private letters of Travis, the commander, and letters from Bowie and Crockett. These two renowned backwoodsmen of North America begged the volunteers at Goliad to help in saving the Alamo.

As said before, Fannin could not be moved to evacuate Goliad, and he still believed that the besieged forces, if they so desired, could surely withdraw. This is the only thing that I can say in his justification. I cannot believe that he feared to face the miserable and partly conscripted hordes of Santa Anna in conjunction with General Houston.

Another message of horror came to us from the southwest. The last three men of Grant's little detachment sprang into the fort and brought us the details of the destruction of that gallant Scotsman and his men.

As they were returning home with approximately four hundred pretty horses, their detachment of thirty men was suddenly attacked. On each side of the road were heavy thickets that converged toward each other a little ahead of them, where an opening of about one hundred feet remained. They were in the act of driving through there when several hundred enemy lancers streamed forth from the thickets and, without paying any attention to the drivers, gave immediate chase to the horses. But Grant, who did not want to lose the horses and who had seen unbelievable examples of cowardice in these half-Indians, drew his sword and attacked the enemy at least ten times as strong as he. Their guns immediately sent a number of the enemy to the ground. After the pistols also were fired off, there was nothing left for them to do but to draw out of the confusion and reload and attack anew. The commands of Grant were drowned in the general din and only a few could execute them.

It was a terrible confusion; the wild horses that had been made frantic by the firing stampeded across the dry prairie enveloped in a cloud of dust. The Texans, who—except for Grant—had no other arms than their guns, pistols and Bowie knives, were now busy warding off the lances of the enemy. Woe unto them that fell slightly wounded from their horses, or otherwise did not sit fast in the saddle and were torn down! Woe unto them, as the whole herd of wild, panting, half-mustangs galloped over them and battered them to pieces.

The little troop of Texans melted together more and more. One after another, pierced by the lances, disappeared under the all-destroying hoofs. Only Grant and the three men who brought us the news appeared on the outside edge of this terrible whirlpool and would have been unhindered in taking to flight if Grant, who saw several of his men still battling against enormous odds, had not rushed back into that whirling mass of confusion, frantically meting out stroke after stroke to the cowardly hirelings—he wanted to save his companions or die with them. Everything gave way before this gallant one as his Scottish arm and his Scottish sword whirled around dealing death among the enemy.

After the other three had loaded, they rushed after their leader to support him, but they had not reached the battling mass, when suddenly—Oh, pity!—the lasso flew through the air and falling, looped the body of the noble Scotchman, who strove in vain to throw off the claws of death. He struggled fruitlessly, and with a hurrah from the hellish breed he sank, torn from his steed, and disappeared like his comrades under the hoofs of the foaming horses that were thundering away enveloped in a cloud of dust.

Consternation pierced the hearts of the three that were approaching; for a moment they stood still and gazed after the disappearing mass. Then all three, without saying a word, turned their horses toward the northeast and rode in a full gallop along the road toward San Patricio. Here they found the enemy already in possession of the town. Since it was dark, they rode right through between the outposts and did not discover their error until their bullets whistled about their heads. They barely had time to take another road when the bugles of the enemy sounded the alarm. But the good, faithful horses again strained their already exhausted strength and carried their riders safely and quickly far out on the open prairie from where they again galloped away after a short rest. And after three days they rode slowly into the gates of Goliad.

The day after they came in, a considerable consignment of cornmeal arrived in Lavaca Bay, and on this and the following days about eight hundred beeves were slaughtered, from which meat was cut in long strips and dried. Great quantities of supplies were to be accumulated to avoid any suffering in case of a long siege.

A detachment of one hundred and twenty men went thirty miles down the San Antonio river to fetch up a large quantity of corn that the planters there wanted to turn over to the army and to protect them from the restless Indians that had been stirred up by the Mexicans in Texas and that were making occasional raids. Our sleep on the plantation where we remained for the night was interrupted by Fannin's cannon, the pre-arranged sign that he was to give us if he deemed it necessary. We marched during the whole night, and by nine o'clock the next morning we had covered the thirty miles. Nothing of particular importance, however, had happened. Only a few scattered enemies had appeared in the vicinity of the fort.

A few days before, Captain King's company, which was, as previously stated, composed of thirty-one men, had been ordered down to Refugio to protect several families that had requested Fannin's aid against the Indians on their way to Goliad and the colonies. But these soon sent news that they were enclosed in the church by at least one hundred and fifty Indians and Mexicans and requested immediate help from Fannin.

The Georgia Battalion were therefore dispatched; but just as this arrived at Refugio, King was marching over the little Rio Blanco to follow the enemy that had slyly fled. Ward also, who had heard of a little fort that was said to have been erected by the Mexicans and Caranchuas five miles from Refugio, departed the next morning to the designated region to destroy the same. But as he found nothing of importance, he returned to the mission. Barely had he re-entered the old church when toward six hundred cavalry of the enemy and a long twelve-pounder appeared on the opposite bank of the river and immediately began to bombard the church.

Toward four o'clock in the afternoon the enemy received several hundred infantry reinforcements, which, like the cavalry, had come from San Patricio. The church was now completely surrounded, and several efforts were made to take it, which, however, were bravely repulsed. But the Mexicans remained in possession of the low houses of the settlers that stood in moderate distance and did some damage from there, which caused the besieged ones to make several sorties, and soon the buildings that were so dangerous for the Texans were enveloped in destructive flames.

During the whole night the Mexicans kept up a vigorous fire. But barely had the midnight hour passed when the Georgia Battalion marched unnoticed through the encircling enemy line. It did not march off toward Goliad, but, on the contrary, toward the sea coast, where it soon lost itself in the broad prairies.

The morning revealed to the Mexicans that they had shot their powder away during the night for nothing. They were on the point of leaving for Goliad to storm this fort in conjunction with Santa Anna and the remainder of Urrea's troops from San Patricio when the unfortunate King and his company appeared on the opposite bank of the river. As he noticed the enemy and was at the same time noticed by the enemy, he took a favorable position in a little dense forest and defended himself with incomparable gallantry against the Mexicans and Indians that pressed in on him from all sides. Even to this day one hears them speak of King and his people with horror.

In vain, General Urrea offered them honorable capitulation, but at the time surrender was out of the question, and the departing day left the gallant defenders unvanquished. As darkness set in the little troop slipped through the tall grass and past the enemy posts. They already believed themselves to be safe, when suddenly a hellish war whoop of a Caranchua broke the stillness of the night. In a few moments hundreds of Mexicans surrounded them, and further fighting would have ended with the destruction of all, although King was ready to fight to the last drop. But the repeated assurances from the officers present that they would be treated respectfully finally caused them to surrender.

On the next morning, however, their bloody corpses lay about on the high banks of the Rio Blanco. Mexican bullets had murdered them, and the butt-ends of the muskets of the soldiers horribly smashed the skulls of any quivering bodies so that the brains spattered about.

Only two Germans of King's unfortunate company were saved, by a German, a Prussian, who was an officer in the enemy artillery. His name is Holzinger,[11] and he will be mentioned again later.

At this time the Mexicans living in Texas were sneaking from one camp to another. Where anything was to be gained,

---

[11] Juan Jose (Johann Josef) Holzinger.

they served as spies. Nothing was sacred to them. This time, they were the first to bring us the news of King's destruction. But we hesitated to accept as true any information emanating from such sources.

The Fall of the Alamo

FANNIN'S LITTLE ARRAY MELTED AWAY more and more. We heard nothing further from the little detachments that had left us. Enemy cavalry often appeared in sight and Colonel Horton and his thirty horsemen already had several skirmishes with them.

No courier appeared from San Antonio; the Alamo was too closely surrounded, and it was now a matter of impossibility to pass unnoticed through the numerous posts of the enemy.

Soon after King's battles and murder we received news from General Houston at Gonzales that did not leave us in any doubt about the unhappy fate of our comrades in the Alamo.

"The signals," ran the dispatch, "that some of my men were in the custom of receiving every morning at sunrise from the unfortunate Travis and his comrades have died away. It is possible that all our heroes are buried under the debris of the Alamo, whose walls were too dear than to turn the trophy of the previous campaign back to the enemy. The next point of the enemy attack is the walls of Goliad, and may the army there consider what power will surround its walls. I, therefore, beseech you another time to make a speedy retreat and to unite with the militia behind the Guadalupe. Only if we are

united will we be in position to achieve anything. Furthermore, it will be impossible for me, in case the detachment at Goliad is besieged, to stake the fate of the Republic on a single battle in such an unfavorable position for our troops as are the open prairies. Therefore, another time, Colonel Fannin,
"behind the Guadalupe!

"Sam Houston"

A little detachment of thirty militiamen fought their way in broad daylight through the enemy lines that surrounded the Alamo, and a few days thereafter the main attack began. After Santa Anna, the Napoleon of the West, as this miserable braggart called himself, had been repulsed several times with severe losses, he took refuge in infamous trickery which consisted of his requiring several Mexican women to secretly sell poisoned food to the besieged ones. Traffic in food, although in secret, had taken place up to this time between the people of San Antonio and the besieged men. Consequently, the latter did not at this time suspect the hellish plan. But soon some felt the effect of the poison and presently death rolled through the veins of those that had partaken of the food. Fortunately, only a few had to suffer, as only a small amount had been consumed 'til then. But the gallant Bowie lay dying on his bed when the bugles from without sounded the signal for the attack.

Among the seven thousand to eight thousand men in Santa Anna's army there were twenty-five hundred men composed of criminals of the blackest kind that were being kept under the watch of the remainder of the army, which, however, was not composed of much better elements.

This host of gallants was placed in front, and behind them were the cannon and the bayonets of the other soldiers.

They were now unchained, as they were still in fetters, and the blood-red flag was placed in the hands of these that had escaped execution. Santa Anna now stepped out in front of this herd that, clothed in rags as they were, and with the Napoleon of the West in the lead, looked more like a bandit corps than an army.

"Mexicans!" he cried as he passed along the lines. "Mexicans! Today is the day when you shall show the rebels the spirit that you have already proven to us in the fatherland. Today is the day that shall make you free and guiltless again when you scale yonder walls of the Alamo and plant the flag that leads you on the holy walls of the church; but today is also the day when your eyes will behold the blue heavens above you for the last time if the blood of the dogs behind the walls of the Alamo does not flow, and if your flag does not wave from the church instead of the star. As sure as your work is bloody, if you do not complete it you shall surely fall with the cannon placed behind you and the bullets of your comrades. Look around you and behold the thousands of bayonets, and consider the few in front of you.

"A bold attack and you are free.

"I know that you are gallant, and for that reason I am letting you do your own leading. But I will follow for your protection. Consider once more, your freedom is at stake. Forward! *Viva Mexico!*"

The cannon chimed in with the call, and the bugles accompanied the weak applause of the prisoners, on whose features could be read a deathly fear. In despair they rushed forward against the cannon of the Alamo that immediately spit forth volcanic flames, their grapeshot raising havoc in the ranks of the attackers. Two times they turned to flee, and two times the artillery of their brothers thundered them to the ground by the herds. In despair they stormed forward once more to scale the walls, but only a few succeeded.

Around the walls the dead human bodies were stacked up in layers, and over these Santa Anna now led the charge with the fresh reserve. But these also gave way before the small group of defenders. Urged on anew, the troops rushed forward again. On the opposite walls just then appeared another detachment of the enemy. The wall was completely unguarded and their passing over could not be prevented by the Texans because of the shortage of men. Attacked from all sides one little group after another fell and died the death of the hero.

Only David Crockett and six other men were still fighting when the core of Santa Anna's army scaled the walls. As the hunter had from six to eight loaded muskets lying beside him, he piled a circle of dead bodies about him. But he fell also, shot down by the bullets of the rejoicing enemies.

Everything had quieted down and the dead men were lying about in the fort when suddenly a man gesticulating wildly appeared on the ruins of the flat buildings and all alone defied the enemy. Wildly he cried: "A few minutes, only a few minutes, you bloodhounds, shall you rejoice in the fruits of your victory and then shall you fall victim to our vengeance!" With these words he fired at the moving mass and then looked rigidly down on the other side, where a single Texan, Major Evans, bleeding at many wounds, was rushing wildly toward the powder magazine with a burning torch in his left hand. The latter had not been noticed by the enemy, and in triumph the man on the wall followed all of Evans' movements toward the magazine. The Mexicans stared at the madman without shooting at him. Fleetly he ran along on the old decaying walls, and the old masonry under his feet fell into the depths some forty feet below.

Then did they first notice the madman with the wildly flickering torch, without being aware of the danger that threatened them. A moment later and the ruins of the Alamo would cover the Mexicans and their victory. But before Evans could rush into the deadly magazine he himself fell, pierced with a bullet, to the ground. A loud cry sounded down from the building and, as if he would ignite the powder himself, the last fighter flew with mighty leaps among the bloodthirsty enemy.

Colonel Bowie, who was lying on his deathbed, was shot by orders from General Cos. Twenty-two hundred slain Mexicans covered the battlefield; scattered among them lay the 180 men of the garrison.

Finally, but unfortunately too late, did Fannin decide to follow Houston's instructions. The affairs of the Republic stood in a critical condition. San Antonio was lost; the volunteer army was practically destroyed; an enemy army eight thousand to ten thousand men strong was in the land; there was no prospect for aid in case of a long siege; nor were there enough provisions. These were the important causes that finally moved Fannin to evacuate and destroy Goliad. But so tenaciously did he cling to the walls of Goliad that he, in doubt, several times recalled the already issued orders.

The Battle of Coleto

UNDER THE LEADERSHIP OF COLONEL FANNIN, on the 18th of April, 1836, we began our retreat from the demolished and partly still-burning Goliad, on whose fortification we had all worked with great zeal. A stack of dried meat from near onto seven hundred steers and the remainder of our meal and corn were set on fire, the columns of smoke from which ascended to the beclouded heavens.

All the artillery, with the exception of two long four-pounders, a regular mortar and a small mortar, were spiked and left behind as we left the ruins at eight o'clock. Nowhere was there a trace of the enemy, whose spies for several days had revealed themselves westward toward San Antonio. The number and size of the provision and ammunition wagons that we took with us were too large and the power to move them was too small, so that before we had gone half a mile, the way was strewn with objects of all kinds and here and there a wagon that was left standing or knocked to pieces. The rest of the baggage remained standing a mile from Goliad on the romantic banks of the San Antonio, or was dropped in haste into the clear water of the river.

Chests filled with musket provisions or the belongings of soldiers disappeared in the waves. All the horses and oxen were used to transport the artillery, two wagons and the powder magazine. In this way we went slowly forward without even getting to see an enemy.

Our route led us through one of those charming landscapes where little prairies alternate with thin forests of oak without any undergrowth. We frequently saw herds of cattle grazing on the luxuriant grass, and immense herds of deer looked with amazement at the little army winding its way through the stillness of the west. The noble Andalusian horses, which had their beginning here with the horrible conquest of Mexico by Cortez, stampeded away in close formation over the undulating prairie and, long after they had disappeared, one could still hear the rumble of their fleeing hooves.

Eight miles from Goliad begins a considerable treeless prairie, known as the nine-mile prairie. It was in this prairie that the army had wearily advanced from four to five miles by three o'clock in the afternoon. A few of my friends and I were bringing up the rear guard about two miles behind with instructions to keep a watchful eye on the forest, which was several miles away to the left of us. Since not the least trace of an enemy had shown itself so far, we rode carelessly along until we accidentally turned around and noticed at a distance of about four miles a figure in the part of the forest through which we had just come that looked like a rider on horseback. Since, however, it did not move, we came to the conclusion that it was a tree or some other lifeless object. Without taking further notice of it, we rode on. A quarter of an hour might have passed, and as our army at a distance of one to one and one-half miles was moving at snail's pace ahead of us, and since we did not wish to catch up with it, we decided to halt a little while to graze and rest our horses. Now, as we let our gaze wander over the immense prairie to enjoy the beauty of the scene, we saw behind us, near the edge of the forest, a long black streak on the plain. It was impossible for us to tell what it was. A few thought that they might be large herds of cattle that the settlers were driving eastward out of reach of the Mexicans. But this seemed improbable, as all of those that stood on the side of the Texans had cleared the region west of the Guadalupe, since they would rather lose everything than to further bear the yoke of Santa Anna. As we looked more intently and observed the disturbing object more closely, we noticed a moving and twisting in the dark mass that grew larger and larger and in proportion to the distance ever plainer. We could no longer doubt that it was the Mexican cavalry that was following us in full gallop. Hastily we mounted our horses and dashed off at full speed to our comrades to prepare them for the reception of the enemy. The news was received with a hurrah. Everything was at once prepared for battle. A hollow square was formed, and in this way, of course very slowly, we continued our march. Fannin, our commander, was a gallant and spirited warrior, but for the commanding officer—where he should act with independence, understanding and decision—he was totally unfit. Instead of trying to reach the forest one mile away for the sake of our safety, where the Americans and the Texans are invincible, he decided to offer battle on an unfavorable open terrain.

The Mexicans sped up and at a distance of from five hundred to six hundred yards gave us a volley from their carbines, to which, however, we paid no attention, as the balls flew in respectable distance over our heads. Only occasionally one would whiz up entirely exhausted as if it were breathing its last breath and strike the ground in front of us without even knocking up any dust. Only one, an innocent thing—the sender probably never suspected that he was that near taking a human life—whistled through between me and the next man to me and tore off a part of the cap of my friend Thomas Camp, who, after me, was the youngest man in the army.

We remained completely passive and let the enemy approach. They fired volley after volley at us as they came nearer. Our artillery officers—mainly Poles and fine, tall men—patiently waited for the time when they could reply to the unholy greetings to advantage. The moment arrived, our ranks opened, and the artillery hurled death and destruction among the enemy. Their horses, to which the confusion of battle was a terror, reared up wildly.

The effect of our fire was frightful. Herds of horses were running about without rider, while others were wallowing in blood and kicking about furiously. The resulting confusion to some extent retarded the attack of the enemy, and consequently we began to move forward again. But we could do this undisturbed only for a short time, as we were soon threatened with a new attack. Fannin ordered a halt in spite of the fact that his attention was called to an enemy corps that was pushing through the forest to our left and which probably intended to cut us off from the woods ahead, while the detachment in the rear of us only aimed to detain us. Either Fannin did not grasp the danger of the situation or his ambitious nature held him back, because someone else had discovered the maneuver of the enemy before he did.

Finally, after we had repeatedly protested to him in vain that it was imperatively necessary for us to gain the woods, the Greys saw themselves obliged to indicate to him that they would march off alone. But it was now too late. The enemy had already appeared on the elevation ahead of us, and there was nothing for us to do except either to fight our way through or to offer battle in the unfavorable position in which we then were. Fannin was for the latter; and before the captains, who had assembled for consultation, could reach a definite conclusion, the countless bugles of the Mexicans from all directions sounded for the attack. The cavalry itself rapidly advanced from all sides at once, not in closed ranks, but in broken formation with yelling and constant firing.

Their wild cries, with which they sought to intimidate us, because they could not do it with their guns, stood in clear contrast with the composure of our people, who waited for only the best opportunities to use their guns. The thunder of our artillery soon rolled peal upon peal and the balls flew devastatingly among the enemy. The attack of the cavalry had so far been fruitless, but the infantry had just arrived. All of his forces were now put into motion by the enemy, and we were attacked from all sides at once. Besides this, there were three hundred Caranchuas and Lipans cooperating with the Mexicans, lying in the tall grass on the left of us toward the San Antonia River.

We did not become aware of this contemptable, although due to his position dangerous, enemy until a number of our people had been wounded by their bullets. Whereupon we sent a few loads of grapeshot into the tall grass that freed us from them in a moment as they hastily fled in every direction.

Meanwhile the enemy infantry, which had combined with the cavalry, advanced step by step with constant but irregular firing. We made use of our guns and sent well aimed shots into the advancing hosts. We were soon enveloped in such dense smoke that we were occasionally obliged to cease firing and to advance slightly on the enemy in order to see our sights. The whole prairie as far as one could see was covered with powder smoke and thousands of lightning flashes quivered through the dark masses accompanied by incessant thunder of the artillery and the clear crack of our rifles. Among them sounded the scattered bugle calls of the Mexicans, encouraging the men to battle. From time to time our grapeshot hailed death into the ranks of the enemy under the majestic roll of thunder. I do not believe that a coward was to be seen on the battlefield at this moment. Who has time and disposition then to think of himself and his life in such tumult? Who is not inspired by the lusty blowing of the bugles and the thunder of the cannon? One pays no attention to death that holds his reward. All his senses are dulled. One sees nothing, one hears nothing except his enemy and only partially does one hear the commands of the officers. That is the way it was with us. As the dense smoke only occasionally permitted us to see the advancing enemy, we stepped forward to meet them. Foolhardily, several of us stood in his midst and fired.

I myself had gotten so far ahead in the general tumult and fired so incessantly that I did not notice how I stood right among the Mexicans. Everything was confusion and it seemed as if we were shooting each other down for pleasure. When I discovered my error, I hastily went back to my position as my ignition tube was stopped up besides. On my return to my comrades I stopped at each fallen enemy and fired the often-loaded musket at the living ones.

But how did it look in our camp? Many of our people were either severely wounded or killed. All of our artillerymen with the exception of one Pole had fallen and built a wall around the now-silent cannon, whose power had now passed as the range was now too close to do effective service. The whole battleground was covered with dead men, horses, guns and all kinds of objects. I did not spend much time in looking at the battlefield, but ran about to try out the guns of the fallen ones as quite a while would probably have been necessary to put mine in order again. I searched a long time before I found a usable one, as the damp, almost wet air had made practically all unfit for use. Fannin himself was wounded three times. The third bullet had penetrated through a waterproof coat, a summer coat, the trousers, a pocket in the overcoat in which he had a silk handkerchief and into the flesh. But strangely enough it did not tear through the handkerchief, and as he pulled it out the bullet fell on the ground. Now first he felt the pain of the wound.

It was now between five and six o'clock; the enemy cavalry had tried in vain to drive its horses against us, but the terrible effect of our artillery and gunfire brought all its effects to naught and it was obliged to withdraw. The infantry was also compelled to follow without waiting for the signal to withdraw, and our cannon, now operated by the Greys, sent its parting greetings after them.

Seven hundred and twenty-odd enemy soldiers lay on the prairie; we had lost about the fifth part of our men. With the exception of the massacre at the Alamo, this was more than had ever before fallen in any one battle.

Meanwhile the enemy remained in possession of the elevation and seemed disposed to renew the attack on the following day. The so anxiously anticipated night broke in soon after the close of the battle, but it was to be no period of recovery for us. A fine rain was falling and spoiled the remaining good guns that we still possessed. Every moment we expected to be attacked by the enemy, who had posted himself in three detachments around us. The first was placed toward Goliad; the second, on our way to Victoria; and the third to our left and equally far from the other two, so that they formed a triangle. Their signals indicated to us their exact positions. Under these circumstances it was impossible for us to retreat without being noticed. No other way lay open to us than to spike the cannon, abandon the wounded and all the baggage, set our guns in order, provide ourselves with sufficient ammunition and fight our way through the enemy, that is, through that detachment that blocked our way to Victoria. If we could only reach the forests, we would be safe and no power that Mexico might be able to send over could battle successfully with the Texans. The Greys would rather sacrifice a part of the force for the young Republic than have the memory of having turned the whole force over to the gruesomeness of an enemy upon whose honor and humanity no one could rely. Fannin, however, was of another opinion. Was it possibly the three not very dangerous wounds that had exhausted his spirit, his well-known gallantry, or was it the groans and wails of the dying—as practically all of the wounded would have to die, because the enemy here also used mainly copper bullets—or was it the hope that our advance guard, which had reached the woods before we noticed the Mexicans, would return with help? Only from the reports of our artillery could they infer that we had been attacked, and then, only as the echo hummed through the forest. It was too late for them to re-unite with us, since, as stated before, the Mexicans had surrounded us. They were thus also cut off from us. Consequently, they could not do anything except to ride hastily to Victoria, which was ten-miles away, and to lead the militia there—which was erroneously reported to run up to six hundred men—to our rescue.

    Fannin constructed his plan on this hope, and in vain we beseeched him to use the darkness of the night to cover his retreat. He decided to remain and wait until eight o'clock in

The Battle of Coleto

the morning. If no help should appear by that time, we could beat our way through the ranks of our contemptable enemies by day; and if we could not be victorious we could at least die fighting.

"Until then," he said, "Comrades, grant my words consideration; listen to the cries of pain of our brothers whom the skilled hand of a surgeon can save from the hands of death! Are we willing, are the Greys of New Orleans, the first company to enter the field for freedom, willing to leave their wounded brothers to horrible death that the barbarous enemy has sworn to them? Friends, another time I beseech you by the patriotic and humanitarian feelings that live in your hearts, do not forsake the helpless ones here.

"At least give them protection until the break of day. If no help is here by that time, fellow citizens, do your duty; I will follow you!"

We felt the seriousness of the moment and the heavy responsibility of our plan and hesitatingly remained. Sadly and without consolation we stared into the night. What an awful choice: to leave our friends and brothers to certain death or to sacrifice ourselves for them! Only weak was our hope for reinforcements from Victoria, as we were not convinced of the correctness of the report that militia were there.

But we resigned ourselves to our fate to wait for the next day. Meanwhile our few vehicles, dead horses and any other solid materials were laid up around our camp as breastwork in case of another attack.

The groans of the dying friends and enemies far and near was heartbreaking. With shudders we heard their moaning and the hollow noises of the construction of the breastworks as they sounded through the black night across the dark prairie. At regular intervals the signals of the enemy sounded over to us. Otherwise everything was quiet, not even a breath of air moved. Only the cold, misty rain helped to stiffen the half-dead bodies of our comrades, while others, who were burning with fever caused by poisoned copper bullets, were pleading in despair for water . . . only a swallow . . . only a drop.

But there was not a drop with which to quench them. We had nothing to give except our heart's blood. God alone could help. He heard, He saw everything and helped. A fresh rain cooled the bodies from without and with the gradual disappearance of the outward heat, the terrible inward fever subsided also.

To combat the stiffening of my own joints, I walked up and down in the camp while I cast useless glances into the impenetrable darkness.

No rescuing sound could be heard from the east, no star was to be seen on the horizon, no hope flickered in the heart. Broken German speech startled me out of my musings. "Friend," it said, "lay this carpet bag under my head for me."

I did so and asked in the same language after the name of the unfortunate comrade.

"I am . . . a German," was the answer. "Oh," he continued, "I would gladly . . . gladly . . . have fought . . . ten more . . . battles for Texas . . . but it's over . . . with my . . . labors . . . I'm done, my countryman . . . I am dying . . . my name . . . Eigenauer from . . . Lauterbach . . . friend, if you ever get home again . . . think . . . of me . . . my old mother still lives . . . write . . . I died . . . for Texas . . . write I died . . . for Texas, write her . . . my land . . . all . . . all . . . ."

He could not speak any more. He was at the point of death. Three bullets had passed through him after he lay bleeding in the ground. I heard his last groans, and I went out, toward the enemy.

Black figures not very far away passed by me from time to time. They were the Indians, who were carrying off the fallen enemies to conceal from us their real loss with the coming of day. Moodily I wandered about, and only at the break of day did I return to the camp.

Everybody was already awake in our little fort. Quietly and expectantly our looks wandered over the forest wall from where our rescuers were to burst forth. But with the advance of day our hopes, on whose fulfillment Fannin had yesterday believed so faithfully, began to disappear. Doubt after doubt rose up like thunder clouds whether the whole report that a large number of militia were at Victoria was false, since it was difficult to get quick and accurate news in thinly settled country.

The artillery of the enemy that had not arrived on the battlefield yesterday was planted in position this morning with the detachment that blocked our way to the timber. Our labors during the night were now in vain. The enemy commanded the elevation and our breastworks were useless as his artillery could now reach every nook and corner of our camp, a circumstance that was not noticed yesterday in the heat of battle.

We could not remember ever having seen Fannin, usually so gallant and at times almost rash, so undecided as he was during the last eight days. Especially since yesterday it seemed that one plan after another passed through his head. The large number seemed to confuse him and to hinder him in his usually prompt manner of reaching a decision on a given matter and putting it into speedy execution.

The groans of our wounded had now ceased. They had died either from their wounds or from the cold and wetness of the night, or the rain had somewhat alleviated their pains. Scattered far and near about our camp lay the dead Mexicans that the Indians either had not found or could not carry away. A few of our men went over to view the dead bodies of the enemies, and not very far away from us they found the banner of the Mexican army under a pile of dead riders and horses and brought it into the camp. But no rejoicing hurrah came over our lips. All knew that the deciding moment that was to decide over life and death was soon to strike. The flag was thrown without consideration on the debris of the camp.

It was approximately seven o'clock when we had given up all hope for reinforcements and had assembled to decide on which manner to attack the enemy and on how we could beat our way through, when suddenly the Mexican artillery bellowed out a good morning to us and grapeshot whistled through and over the assembly, which at once caused us to decide to attack the detachment on our road with our guns and Bowie knives in order to gain the timber. Everything was in readiness; even some of the severely wounded would rather die fighting than be helplessly murdered.

See! Unexpectedly the white flag, the sign of peace, rose before us and halted us in our progress. Being suspicious, we even then wanted to put our decision into execution, but Fannin's command fettered our movements.

New hopes had arisen within him to save the men who had been placed in his care and who were in this desperate situation because of him, even if it be through honorable capitulation.

Three delegates of the enemy approached our camp, two Mexican cavalry officers and a German who had worked himself up to colonel in the artillery and had won the favor of Santa Anna. He was, if I err not, from Mainz and originally a carpenter. He probably possessed mathematical and architectural talent and offered his services to the German-Mexican Mining Company, which, however, was not accepted. Later he went to the English company and was employed by it and was sent to Mexico. Here Santa Anna noticed his talents and had him to build the beautiful castle Mango de Clavo for him. Through the construction of this castle, which completely filled the expectations of the owner, Santa Anna gained a very high opinion of the knowledge of the builder, which in reality was very meager, and he employed him as an engineer in the army from where he was later advanced to Colonel of Artillery.

This German, Holzinger, was the only officer of the three who could speak English. As it was, however, only in a broken manner, it was often necessary first to translate our transactions into German and from there carry them over to the Spanish.

After long negotiations Fannin finally agreed that we should surrender all of our arms, that our private property should be respected, that we ourselves should be shipped through Copano or Matamoras to New Orleans and set free, and that as long as we were prisoners of war we should receive the same rations as the Mexican army received. Our obligation was to be our word of honor not to fight hereafter against the present Mexican government.

With misgivings we stood around our Colonel after the Mexicans had ridden back to Urrea, the commander of the Mexican army, to have the ratification of the agreements completed.

The united volunteer Greys from New Orleans and Mobile protested loudly: "Forward? Is this the way that Fannin fulfills his promises? Is this his gallantry? Has he forgotten Tampico, San Patricio and the murder of our brothers in the Alamo? Has his long sojourn in Texas not acquainted him with the character of the Mexicans? Never will the Greys agree to a capitulation that will remove them from their precious new fatherland. If the Mexicans should keep their word this time, it will be the Greys who will not feel themselves bound by the terms of this capitulation. Citizens, comrades, we now appeal to you. You do not yet know the false character of the Mexicans. You have not yet had enough intercourse with these barbarians to be able to judge them accurately. Believe the Greys: surrender, capitulation in Mexican is to die. If it shall be to die, let us die fighting for Texas, a sacrifice for freedom. With us hundreds of the Mexicans will fall, and possibly we will succeed in breaking through their ranks, although they are probably ten times as strong as we. Think of the few of us who succeeded in taking San Antonio away from them. Two hundred and ten men. against two thousand! Why should we not at least now risk the battle?"

Thus we spoke, but our speech had missed its purpose. The prospect of soon being back in the States again and of reentering upon their former conditions of life moved the other troops to give preference to the capitulation. Certainly the life of a soldier in the wilderness is irksome, and the privations that he must endure are not few. But they did not know the charm of the life that the prairies, teeming with game, offered those who, like the red Comanches, hunt through them during all seasons of the year. No worry about house, nourishment, and dress weighs on the fantastically dressed ranger. Everywhere he finds nourishment in abundance, and the few remaining necessities that he is obliged to draw from the regions of civilization are earned with the gun. Happy because he freely roams through the splendid west and he seldom sees the settlements. But when the day of election approached, when the highest officer of the land is to be elected, then the ranger stands with his countrymen to cast his vote for the best interests of his country.

It was, therefore, useless to talk against such inclinations. They decided too credulously to sign the capitulation and the Greys and a part of the Red Rovers, who still held to their former position, were obliged to yield to the majority and like the others hand over their guns.

Inwardly deeply humiliated, which showed itself on our faces, we walked up and down in our camp, casting angry looks at Fannin and the others that had voted for the capitulation. Some sat lost in thought with eyes fixed stark on the ground and envied those who had died during the battle. Despair stood on the features of many of the men, who only too well foresaw our fate. Especially one American named Johnson made himself conspicuous because of his anger. Gnashing his teeth, he stamped on the ground. Thick clouds of smoke from his glowing Havana twirled about his head. Like the smoke from a steamboat, cloud after cloud streamed from his mouth, and quicker and quicker they issued forth. Denser and denser did the cloud mass become until it seldom revealed the head, in which now, as it seemed, a terrible plan was being worked up.

Curiosity had brought many Mexicans into our camp, and in company with the Greys they wandered over the field covered with debris and corpses. Nervously, they glanced at the stern grey cannon, which had always been frightful to them, as if they were still afraid of this now-unarmed enemy that had driven their dried-up soldiers from house to house in San Antonio.

Now of course they looked down with contempt on the spectacle, to have prisoners of the Texan army. Never before in their lives had they experienced a thing of this kind.

Group after group of the Mexicans crowded over into our camp to see the pretty guns that we had surrendered. Everybody was in fervent emotion in that the ones were possessed with malicious joy of victory and the others with shameful despondency, and I have said what the Greys felt. Suddenly a light flashed through the misty morning, a dull report followed, and a terrible jarring of the air combined with it. And then deathly stillness fell over the prairie, which was again covered with wounded men.

Impenetrable suffocating smoke, held down by the damp air, rolled heavily over the dark green prairie. Wildly the horses of several of the senior officers reared up and, frantic with fear, rushed out with their stupefied riders in uninterrupted speed with ruffled-up manes and flying tails into the safe distance. All had either done so themselves or were thrown to the ground by the concussion and after a while, still half-stunned, we went toward the place where the explosion seemed to have broken loose.

The powder magazine had disappeared; only a part of the lower framework remained. Around the place lay several men wounded, although not severely, and about fifteen yards away from the wagon lay a black body that barely looked like one of a human being. It was still alive but not able to speak. It was burnt coal-black like the color of a negro, and it was impossible to tell who the unfortunate one was. Our glances wandered searching around; the roll was called and the missing man was Johnson.

No one had noticed him before. Was it an accident or was it really his plan to kill himself and as many Mexicans as possible at the same time? At what he considered the favorable moment, he must have ignited the magazine. But as the lid was not locked, the main force went upward, and in this way the terrible plan missed its purpose.

The confusion was not yet over, the rage of the Mexicans had not yet subsided, when suddenly the clear signal of alarm sounded over to us and the enemy hastily assembled his troops. Soon this movement explained itself. Our true advance guard appeared in the forest together with all the militia that Colonel Horton could get together in the short time. The report on which we had built our hope was certainly untrue, that is, that there were from six hundred to eight hundred militia at Victoria. Instead there were from thirty to forty men who were waiting for Fannin's arrival and who now appeared under Horton's leadership, forty-odd men altogether, with the positive determination to help us.

"But what fright," said the brave Horton later on, "took possession of us as we concluded the results of the fateful morning from the position of the Mexican troops! We stood in astonishment and were undecided what to do when suddenly the war-like bugle notes of the Mexicans sounded. No time was to be lost; quickly we had to counsel and just as quickly we were ready. If Fannin had so far forgotten his duty as to surrender, we were obliged to save ourselves for the Republic. Now was the time when Texas needed our arms and our guns. All of our volunteers were now either taken prisoners or were murdered. Consequently, we turned our horses and speedily galloped back to Victoria to unite with Houston's troops at Gonzales."

As Horton and his men fled, the Mexicans hastily pursued, however without results. Safely the former reached the dark densely forested banks of the Guadalupe and disappeared in the forests that were well-known to them, which offered safety in their closely interwoven plant world and their cane breaks of ten to fifteen feet high, and the enemy dared not follow them.

If our troops had arrived a half hour earlier, we would have frustrated the bloody catastrophe that soon followed, but it was written otherwise in the book of fate. The volunteers were to die that Texas might step forth from her entirely precarious position with greater splendor. A sacrificial offering had to be made for freedom in order to fire up anew that spirit that was for a while slumbering so carefree, especially in the hearts of the settlers. It was necessary to execute a bloody act to demonstrate the difference between the blessings of a free system of government and the injustice and presumption of a tyrannical absolute government such as Santa Anna had introduced by the overthrow of the liberal Constitution of 1824 and its conversion into a centralized governmental system.

The Imprisonment

AT TWO O'CLOCK WE RECEIVED ORDERS to return to Goliad to await Santa Anna's designation of the port through which we were to be shipped to New Orleans.

We, therefore, left the battlefield where we had the day before victoriously defended the rights of freedom, and in the evening by the clear light of the moon we entered the old church of the still-smoking fort, our prison quarters.

Fort Goliad and the town of La Bahia lie on the right bank of the San Antonio River, here high and bare, about thirty miles from its mouth in Espiritu Santo Bay and from fifty to sixty miles from the main waters of the Gulf of Mexico. The whole region on which the town stands is composed of white broken sandstone, though the water has washed deep furrows. Toward the stream barely a twig or tree is to be seen to soften the dead view of this desolate place. A number of stone houses that are always one story high and resemble chests turned upside-down and painted white more than they do human habitations, project like high walls out of the surrounding huts, which are built of unhewn tree limbs set up vertically and finished with lime. As viewed from the opposite bank of the river, this scene has something of unusual interest. After one has traveled for months through the green and fruitful forests and prairies of the West and has searched in vain for sights of antiquity, with the exception of San Antonio and its missions, at La Bahia a town lies spread out in an unfruitful location before the visitor, but its style of architecture makes a very favorable impression at a distance.

The houses that rise in terrace formation one over the other on the slopes of the high banks are a counterpart of the ruins in the Arabian desert, especially when the scorching sun of the south sends its pale rays down upon them and the eye is not able to long endure the blinding glare. Higher up than the town and toward the east, Fort Goliad lies on a little plain.

It consists of a rectangle about twelve hundred feet long and one thousand feet wide enclosed by a wall, in part seven feet high and provided, largely by Fannin's command, with bastions at each corner. On the south side is a large built-over gate, which formerly contained on the one side the sentinel room and on the other the prison. On the north and opposite side of the fort stand the ruins of an old church with a flat roof on which had been placed several small cannon. Westward from the church there is a row of one-story flat-roofed buildings of equal height. From the left bank, as I have stated before, the town and the fort have such a desolate and yet such a highly interesting position that we were agreeably surprised as we for the first time turned around the point of the forest and saw the place lying before us in all its beauty. On the opposite and left side of the San Antonio lay the ruins of the old Spanish mission of Espiritu Santo in a densely wooded region. At our feet lay the clear San Antonio. Toward the right and left were dark forests. Before us lay Goliad and La Bahia in their blinding sand. And behind these toward the southeast, south and southwest lay an immense prolifically green prairie on which the great herds of cattle and horses of the inhabitants of the town had quietly grazed before the outbreak of the Revolution. It is worthy of note that only the small spot on which the town stands has sandy soil, while all around the soil is rich and overgrown with a luxuriant growth of grass.

Nobody had yet entered the fort when we returned from the battlefield after an absence of thirty-six hours. The Mexicans evidently feared a concealed mine or some other plan through which they might suffer injury. Consequently, we were the first ones to enter the desolate ruins again, but as prisoners, and we were stuffed into the old church for the night. Literally stuffed, as we stood so close man to man that it was possible at the highest for only one-fourth to even sit down. It was well that the inner room of the church had a height of thirty-five to forty feet. If it had been lower, we would have suffocated. As it was, the air remained fairly fresh.

Thus the first terrible night passed away. A burning thirst had taken possession of us. Parching with thirst we called loudly for water, and finally toward eight o'clock six of our men were instructed to go to the river. The first load disappeared like a single drop on a red-hot stove. Only after the vessels had been filled and emptied three times was our thirst slaked, and we awaited the moment when we would be released from this dungeon and be given nourishment. But our hopes were in vain. We received nothing but water toward evening and the second frightful night broke in upon us. The heat was much greater and more suffocating than the night before. Many slept while standing as the bodies pressed so close against one another made it impossible to fall over. Some of the smaller ones, who were fortunate enough to cower on the floor, could rest at least for a short time. The awfulness of the damp atmosphere that prevailed here was suffocating and it was possible to tolerate it on the floor for only a short period.

The next morning finally appeared, but with it still no liberation from this deathly dungeon. Our breakfast, as before, consisted of water. Strong guards stood in front of the side doors and before the main entrance several cannon, but neither the sharply loaded muskets nor the cannon could suppress our rage. Fannin's men loudly demanded the fulfillment of the terms of the capitulation. They clamored for food and demanded to see the commanding officer, or they would not consider their lives too dear to sacrifice them for their rights.

  The colonel of the Battalion de tres Villas appeared immediately after these utterances in company with Holzinger and assured us that he would do his utmost to drive up some steers and butcher them for us as they themselves were not supplied with the least of any other kind of provisions and had not issued any rations to their own army in two days. Although we knew that this was untrue, we promised to remain quiet until evening. Since the cannon at the door were heavily loaded and the men were standing by with burning torches to suppress the slightest movement among us, I am convinced that it was intended to exhaust our patience, to provoke us to the limit, and then, when we should venture to obtain justice with force, to fire on us with grapeshot and then to kill the rest of us with the bayonets. In this way Santa Anna and his henchmen could later have announced that they were compelled to shoot us down in order to save their own lives. In fact, they were the first to violate the terms of the capitulation, and a disturbance among us would have been perfectly excusable.

  If it really was Santa Anna's plan to murder us in this way, the commander at Goliad did not have the courage to execute it. That evening at about six o'clock we received beef—at the most six ounces to the man and promises for more as soon as more cattle could be driven up.

Now we had meat but it was raw, and we had neither fire nor room to cook it. With a few small pieces of wood that lay about in the church and a little paneling that we tore from the walls, our resourceful comrades soon had two fires going—very small ones, as the heat and thirst were already almost unbearable.

On account of the smallness of the fires only a few at a time could roast their meat. Before they all could have gotten through, the whole night would have passed away. Consequently, those farthest away from the fires renounced their claims and ate their meat raw, an example that was generally imitated as the fire only added new miseries to the other privations of the body.

After we had spent another night in distress like the preceding two, the command to vacate the church was finally given, not to march away but to exchange the roof of the church for the open heaven and to take a position within the walls under heavy guard.

Opposite us were a few companies of infantry that were ready every moment to shoot us down in case one of the many sentinels that stood around us should give the alarm.

At the large built-over entrance stood four pieces of artillery, although they were not directed at us. It was raining lightly as we were leaving the church. In spite of that, our condition was considerably improved because, although we were still close together, we could at least get fresh air. Today also we did not get anything to eat, and we began to give away our things and also our little money for something to eat. For this the soldiers charged enormous prices, so that a man, not a very hungry one, could eat about ten dollars' worth of tortillas, a delicacy made of corn, salt and water and in the form of a little pancake of the thickness of the back of a knife, baked on a hot tin or even on the open coals under constant turning over and over, after the corn had first been soaked in suitable lye, then pounded to pieces by the artful grip of the Señoras aided by two stones and finally freed from its mealy mass. According to my opinion this is a discovery of the Mexicans, and the aforesaid tortillas would probably let themselves be assembled into a very good grade of leather if passed through a better pounding-machine than the women of Mexico. But what does not taste good when one is hungry? Trousers, shirts and other articles of the wardrobe quickly disappeared among the greedy and half-civilized Mexican soldiers, whose only good trait of character is that they divide with the poor what they steal from the rich. To steal is natural with them, and they do it even when they are not in need. Consequently, travelers who travel through the northern states of the Mexican confederation must be very watchful not to lose one or more of their horses every few weeks. First a hired man that one usually takes along for a servant or a guide will disappear with one, or possibly a ranchero, who probably has thousands himself, may entertain himself by stealing one and driving it into his own herd.

It was about four o'clock when all the wounded from the battlefield were brought into the church and a few small buildings. The number ran to approximately two hundred men among whom were about thirty of our comrades.

The enemy army was without physicians. Consequently, Doctor Shackelford and another of our men had to serve as surgeons, an Englishman and George Voss of Hamburg as assistants and Joseph Spohn, a young attractive creole from Louisiana, as interpreter. These alone had permission to

The Imprisonment

go about freely, and also to see Fannin and Chutwick,[12] a young cadet of West Point from the States, who had a room to themselves.

On the fourth morning we each received three-fourths of a pound of beef that we roasted on little fires. Just as we were busy with our meat, one hundred and twenty new companions in misfortune appeared to our surprise under heavy guard. They were the troops of Major Ward, who, after wandering about in the completely unknown prairie for eight days, surrendered on the same terms after hearing of our capitulation.

Twenty-six men of them, all carpenters, were left at Victoria on Holzinger's direction, who indicated that he needed them in getting the artillery over the river, as the Mexicans were of no value at heavy work. Although we barely knew each other, we sorrowfully shook hands as friends. Ward, who now saw how wrong it was not to have obeyed Fannin's order to return to Goliad at once, did not wish to leave his companions in this sad condition into which his ambitiousness had brought them, and shared the privations of the imprisonment with us instead of living in the room with Fannin to which he was at first directed.

When I think of that time, my hands involuntarily clench together, and gnashing with fury I would like to strike out the time that has passed since that day and lead my comrades against the planted cannon and the bayonets of the Mexican devils that I might not die unavenged.

On the next morning, the fifth of our imprisonment, all Germans were called out by Holzinger, the Prussian; I, however, did not step forth but remained with my high-minded

---

[12] Joseph M. Chadwick

friends, the Americans, as I was determined to share everything with my companions in sorrow. And according to my mind matters of racial differences were out of the question, as like feelings and like misfortunes had united us. No difference existed. We were neither Englishmen nor Germans nor Americans, we were one nation from the time that we entered Texas together. We were Texans.

This was not my opinion alone, but also that of all of my friends and my fellow countrymen, who, like I also would have done, in proud feeling of independence contemptuously rejected Holzinger's offer to take service with the Mexicans as artillerymen against our dear second fatherland, Texas. What a disdainful offer! It could emanate only from a creature like Holzinger. We should offer our hand to destroy a young nation that was fighting for its rights, for the rights of humanity!

"No," answered Mattern, "if you would leave me the choice between a brilliant position in Mexico or a life in the mines among the criminals, I would choose the latter rather than that this arm should do service in the suppression of freedom! No, Mr. Colonel, I thank you for your courtesy, but our views are different! Our spirit advances with the times, yours and that of the priesthood battles in the opposite direction. It is in vain, your time is past. The people know that they are the ones that have the right to make the laws."

The last words were not heard by Holzinger as he turned around to walk away. Neither could he deny his displeasure nor force himself not to admire the spirit of our Mattern.

On the sixth we received the third and last ration of one pound of beef in the fort. All of our things had passed over into the hands of the Mexicans, and we possessed possibly only a few precious objects, which, however, did not escape

The Imprisonment

the greedy glances of the enemy soldiers, who tried by every means and trick to entice these away from us also, to steal or to simply take away, as we were not permitted to follow them through the guards. Naturally, compensation was out of the question, as well as the consideration of our complaints.

From me they stole one of those large, pretty, woolen covers which are made only in the mountain lands of Mexico and are completely waterproof. But they also had an enormous price. Mine, that I had bought twelve to fourteen days ago for ten dollars from a Mexican spy that we had captured, was probably worth from forty to fifty dollars. In the center of these blankets are openings for the head to pass through, the sides of which are usually surrounded with either stitched or worked-in garlands. The four outer corners are ornamented in the same way. If the ends of these covers, especially the finer ones that are usually white, are gracefully folded back so that the right side falls over the left shoulder, this ornament makes a very good impression on many a fantastically dressed ranchero or officer. Besides that, they are light and warm. In vain I asked Holzinger to have mine sent back to me. In answer he told me that that would not do, as I as a prisoner would have to put up with many things. During the afternoon I had the pleasure of seeing the cover wrapped over the body of the same villain whom I had paid ten dollars for it when he was our prisoner.

In order to attain their greedy purposes more easily, our customers came and acquainted us with the highly gratifying news that we would all be shot. Very humanitarian of them, giving us an opportunity to sell the few things that we still possessed in order to sweeten our last days.

"What good will it do you?" they said, "In a few days you will be shot anyway."

But we could see through their plans and it helped them very little, as we could but believe that the enemy officers, even if they should be conscienceless enough to do such a deed, would be restrained for the sake of their honor, since they would be called word-breakers and murderers before the world. We knew that they were Christians only in name, but they held just that much stricter to the forms of Catholicism.

We were momentarily expecting a courier from Santa Anna, who was just then making preparations to follow Houston.

General Urrea had crossed the Guadalupe immediately after our capitulation. He accomplished this because the militia had evacuated Victoria without firing a shot.

Probably from six hundred to eight hundred men were now at Goliad. Among them was the previously mentioned Battalion de tres Villas. The name of its colonel, who was also the commander of the fort, has slipped my mind.

On the seventh morning at about nine o'clock the Mexicans brought in another one hundred prisoners, volunteers from New York under Colonel Miller, who were captured immediately after their landing at Copano. Since they had not heard anything of the arrival of the Mexicans in Texas, they believed themselves perfectly safe and went unarmed in boats, on account of the shallow water, to a landing one-half mile away. Barely had they arrived at the shore before they scattered, glad to set their feet on solid earth again after a journey of several weeks. Suddenly hordes of the Mexican cavalry rushed out of the mesquite timber, through which the road to Refugio winds, and upon them, and before they could recover from their astonishment, they were prisoners. They received other quarters outside of the fort and they were also permitted to move about freely. In order that they could be recognized by the soldiers, they wore broad white bands around their arms. From Colonel Miller and especially from Joseph Spohn and George Voss we have the report of what transpired at Goliad after our departure.

Today also went to a close without any food passing over our lips except the refreshing drinks from the San Antonio. Terrible thirst must have been raging within the unfortunate ones, who, disregarding the same, were in good humor and so full of hopes that they were planning what they were going to do after their arrival at New Orleans. Others were picking bits of meat here and there from the bones that we had thrown on a pile to burn several days before our retreat. They were the bones of the eight hundred steers from which we had cut the meat that we had then dried and later burnt.

The Murder of the Prisoners

THE CLOUDY MORNING OF THE EIGHTH DAY DAWNED. If the enemy had not changed our situation, we would have forcibly freed ourselves or ended the imprisonment in death. But it was to come otherwise.

Grey clouds encircled the horizon, while not the slightest motion occurred on the surface of the earth. A damp sultriness lay on the prairie, capable of inciting feelings of misgivings among those who had nothing to fear, whose own horizon was clear. How much more must not our imagination have depicted the impenetrable future with dark pictures that were too soon to become reality! A courier with the disposition of our fate from Santa Anna probably arrived during the night.

Anxiously we looked forward to the news and keenly hoped, in conformity with orders, immediately to break camp for Matamoras and to greet the free, blue gulf from there, to pierce its waving billows and, finally, to sail up the mighty Mississippi, the father of the rivers of North America, to the city that we had seven months before left in merry enthusiasm. Bright and dreary glimpses into the future alternated in rapid succession.

Henceforth we were to view the battling nations from out of the distance, without ever more being participants in the contests between freedom and despotism. This was a sad picture, but several of us, including myself, saw a drearier one ahead of us. We already saw ourselves in the mines of Mexico, heard the clatter of chains about us and saw ourselves compelled, like the criminals, to bring the ores to the light of day. Viewed from another standpoint, even from here a hopeful side showed itself as we still had the hope and the right to take up arms again for Texas and to fight another time under the banner of the young republic. If we should ever get back by flight or other aid, we would be bound by no oath, no word and no capitulation.

The cannon that had formerly guarded the entrance were turned around during the night and directed at our quarters. Apparently they were heavily loaded. On the other side of them stood the artillerymen with burning torches ready to fire at the first wink.

In front of us stood several companies in dress uniforms, which, however, were very shabby and made of the coarsest material. They did not have the least camp equipment with them, which, however, we did not notice, as they as a rule had little or nothing to take with them. I believe that I can frankly assert that not one of the Texans noticed it.

At last an officer stepped among us with Santa Anna's orders in his hands, of which he did not let us know any more than that we were to march off at once. It was eight o'clock in the morning.

Where to? To Copano or to Matamoras? The answer was not revealed to us and we were left to surmise.

Short time was necessary for us to make our preparations to leave this place of misery, and in a few minutes we stood in position two men deep, with the exception of Colonel Miller's detachment, which, as previously stated, lay outside of the fort. Furthermore, Fannin, the physicians and assistants, the interpreter and the wounded were missing, who were later to be brought to New Orleans by a nearer way.

After the roll had been called for the last time and after the last echo of the oft-repeated "Here" that accompanied the calling of the different names had died away, the order to march was given and the Greys marched ahead under the command of First Lieutenant McMannemy of the Greys of Mobile through the dark gate. Singularly enough both the captains had left for Houston's headquarters on company business a few days before the retreat began.

Outside of the gate we were received on each side by a troop of Mexicans. Like us, they had been placed man behind man to form two rows. Thus enclosed we marched forward.

We were close to four hundred men and the enemy at least seven hundred, not counting the cavalry that was swarming about on the prairie in little detachments.

From now on it is possible for me to give an account of my own experiences and to tell that of the others according to other, already named, sources that are no less reliable than mine, I can assure you, as three and sometimes more eyewitnesses told identically the same account. And the Mexicans did not deny the things maintained by them.

Quietly the column marched forward on the road toward Victoria, contrary to our expectations. Where they were going to take us in this direction was an object of general consideration for us. Most of us seemed to think that they were taking us to an eastern harbor in order to ship us to New Orleans from there, which finally would be the same, and it would even be nearer and better for us this way.

The intolerable silence of the usually talkative Mexicans and the sultry heat increased the nervous expectations that were now lying on the breasts of all of us. This death march, as one can with justice call it, often recalls to my memory the bloody scenes that I was to witness at that time. Anxiously I looked back to the rear part of the column to see if Miller's' people were marched off at the same time with us. But imagine my astonishment when neither Fannin's men nor the last captured Georgia Battalion was to be seen! They had separated us without our noticing it, and only the Greys and a few of the colonists were marching in the detachment with which I was. I glanced over at the escort and now first I noticed their festal uniforms and the absence of camping equipment. Bloody pictures rose up in my mind, among others those of Tampico, San Patricio and of the Alamo. Then I thought of the character of our enemies, their duplicity, their banditry and their exultation in bloody deeds. All of these together prepared me for the worst, and there were moments when I was on the point of acquainting my companions with my apprehensions. But the never-dying hope detained me. It showed me the future even now in brilliant colors and, absorbed in thought, I continued to step forward. The pictures of our probable fate became ever livelier in my imagination, and soon the happy ones of the future exchanged places for the painful ones of reality. The next moment my few remaining articles rolled through the lines of the Mexicans out on the fresh green prairie so that I would not be hindered in my movements in case of need.

      Probably a quarter of an hour had elapsed since we had left the fort, and not a word had passed over our lips nor over those of the enemy. Everyone seemed to have dropped into deep reflection. Suddenly the command of the Mexican sounded to march off to the left from the main road; and as we

The Murder of the Prisoners

did not understand, the officer led the way himself. My companions in misfortune still carelessly followed the leader. To our left a little five-to-six-foot-high mesquite hedge extended straight about a thousand yards to the roaring San Antonio river, whose clear waves, at a right angle with the hedge, pushed their way through bluffs between thirty to forty feet high, which rise practically perpendicularly from the water level on this side. Our feet were directed down the hedge and towards the river. Suddenly the thought seized everyone: "Why are we going in this direction?" This and several mounted lancers to our right, to whom we had previously given no attention, confused us. And now we noticed that the line of the enemy between us and the hedge had remained behind and was now lining up on the other side so that they formed a double file here. Unable to comprehend this movement, we were still in a maze when a "Halt!" was commanded in Spanish, which ran through us like a death sentence. At that moment we heard the muffled rolling of a musket volley in the distance. Involuntarily we thought of our companions, who had been separated from us and evidently led off in that direction.

Astonished and confounded, we looked at each other, and cast questioning glances first at ourselves and then at the Mexicans. Then another command rang out—"Kneel down!" from the lips of the Mexican officers. Only a few of us understood Spanish and could not or would not obey the order.

Meanwhile the Mexican soldiers, who were barely three steps away, had leveled their muskets at our chests and we found ourselves in terrible surprise.

We still considered it impossible to believe that they were going to shoot us. Otherwise, what would we not have done in despair in order to sell our lives dearly! If we had been compelled with unarmed hands, we would, like Winkelried,[13] have grasped into the bayonets of the enemy; and many a one of our murderers would have let his life bleed away on the green carpet of the savanna. Even the constantly fleeing coward will become gallant when he sees certain death before him and all hope of saving himself has disappeared. Then the raging fury drives him forward to throw himself on his enemy and in the attack of despair to draw both down together in destruction.

Only one among us spoke Spanish fluently; the words seemed incomprehensible to him. In doubt he stared at the commanding officer as if he wanted to read a contradiction on his features of what he had heard. The remainder of us fixed our eyes on him to thrust ourselves on the threatening enemy at the first sound from his lips. But he seemed, as we were, possessed of the unfortunate hope that this order was naked threat to force us into Mexican service. With threatening gestures and drawn sword, the chief of the murderers for the second time commanded in a brusque tone: "Kneel down!"

A second volley thundered over to us from another direction, and a confused cry, probably from those who were not immediately killed, accompanied it. This startled our comrades out of their stark astonishment which had lasted from five or six seconds. New life animated them, their eyes flashed and they cried out:

"Comrades! Listen to that crying—it means our brothers, hear their cries! It is their last one! Here is no more hope—the last hour of the Greys has come! Therefore, Comrades—"

A terrible cracking interrupted him and then everything was quiet, A thick smoke slowly rolled toward the San

---

[13] Arnold von Winkelried, a legendary Swiss hero.

The Murder of the Prisoners

Antonio. The blood of my lieutenant was on my clothing and around me quivered my friends. Beside me, Mattern and Curtman were fighting with death. I did not see more. I jumped up quickly, concealed by the black smoke of the powder, and rushed down the hedge to the river.

I heard nothing more and saw nothing. Only the rushing of the water was my guide. Then suddenly a powerful sabre smashed me over the head. Before me the figure of a little Mexican lieutenant appeared out of the dense smoke, and a second blow from him fell on my left arm, with which I parried it.

I had nothing to risk, but only to win. Either life or death. Behind were the bayonets of the murderers, and before me was the sword of a coward that crossed my way to the saving stream. Determinedly I rushed upon him. Forward I must go, and the coward took to flight in characteristic Mexican gallantry. Now the path was open, near was the point of my escape. Another few moments passed. The smoke rolled like a black thundercloud over to the other side, and I stood with rapidly beating heart on the rocks on the edge of the water. At my feet rolled the water and back of me the hangmen were pursuing.

Like a corps from hell they set in after me, but with a "The Republic of Texas forever!" I threw myself into the rescuing floods.

Swimming slowly toward the opposite bank and prodded from time to time with the poorly aimed bullets that the enemy sent after me, I swam through the current of my savior. But another victim was to fall through the Mexican barbarity, namely, our faithful dog that had accompanied the company from the beginning to the end and that now sprang into the waters after me to share my pleasures and sufferings with me in my flight through the unknown prairie. He had already reached the center of the stream when the Mexicans made a target of him, and although they seldom hit, the faithful friend, wounded, disappeared under the waves.

Arriving at the other bank of the river, I looked around once more to where my comrades were dying, while the bullets of the still-firing enemies whistled about me. The hellish exultations of the enemy mixed with the cries of pain of my dying brothers sounded over to me. What feelings took possession of me here!

I was saved. I saw my enemies, threatening, standing on the opposite bank. The scene of the butchery seemed like a dreary dream to me, and yet I saw the terrible reality before me. As through a miracle I was saved, had escaped certain death, and now first, after all danger was over, I began to tremble.

I had read of crimes of the most terrible kind, but I could never have attributed to a people who called themselves Christians an infamous deed of this type, to shoot down prisoners with devilish delight who had surrendered themselves in confidence of oath and word of honor.

The houndish, cowardly, bloodthirsty race, these desecrators of religion, who parade their only saving religion, and pretend to worship Christ who commands to love the enemy and do good unto him! But such is the weakness of Catholicism. Instead of giving its followers moral strength and an invigorating, rational faith, it blinds them with outward display of splendor and gives coarseness and immodesty full freedom, and absolves every crime from punishment for money and feigned atonement.

I cast another look and a farewell greeting to my dead companions and turned to flee. I had to hasten if I did not wish to fall into the hands of the lancers who were now on this side of the river, less than half a mile below me.

I threw away everything that I could spare, as the water had made my clothing considerably heavier, and, unfortunately, in the haste my diary also, that I had kept to this time. Provided with only the most necessary clothing, even without coat and cap, having lost the latter in the stream, I set out across the heavenly forests and prairies of the west.

Fannin's Death

THE DEED WAS DONE; the horribly mutilated and naked bodies of the warriors of the Coleto lay about on the green slaughter places in the vicinity of the walls of Goliad, as the Mexicans had completely plundered the dead bodies of the men.

But the last act of the drama was played within the walls of the fort.

The wounded lay groaning in the old church, and all of those who were not seized with a raging fever, as is usually the case with those that are struck by copper bullets, heard the volleys that struck down their comrades. In a rage they tried to free themselves from their bandages in the hope, by loss of blood, to anticipate the devilish enemy and to rob him of the triumph of digging into the hearts of the dead.

After the last shot had been fired outside of the walls, the curtain rose for the second-to-last time and the orders of the commanding officer of the enemy reached the ears of the wounded.

"All Texans come out!" he said, "and the lightly wounded bring the heavily wounded into the center of the fort."

Those that were able to do so immediately arose in resignation to step before the judgment seat of Almighty God on the same day with their brothers to ask for justice. But nothing could induce them to bring their dying or raging comrades to the place of murder, and only the attendant, Voss, who had hopes of not being shot, with the brown murderers, carried the dying ones out, of whom several died before they reached the fateful spot. Barely had they been pitched on one pile when the order in Spanish was given and another bloody heroic deed of the Battalion de tres Villas was finished.

Not a word was said to indicate to them that they were going to die. Not a minute's time was granted them to ask the mercy of God. Without any previous preparation they also were murdered by the disciples of the Jesuits.

Fannin himself now stepped forth from his prison and Joseph Spohn was at his side. With indescribable sadness he looked at the still-bleeding bodies of the wounded. Deeply he regretted that he had not hastened to the aid of the fallen garrison of the Alamo, or that he had not sooner followed Houston's orders to retreat behind the Guadalupe. Tears of deepest sorrow ran down his cheeks during the slaughter of his true and faithful comrades. They were not the tears of cowardice, not the fear of approaching death! No, no, it was the unhappy fate of his brothers. Fannin was too gallant to fear death and to cry about it like a child. No, they were the bitter tears of repentance and of sympathy that moistened his cheeks.

He had composed himself when he left his prison, and in spite of his strongly inflamed wounds, he advanced with a firm step to his executioners.

Having arrived at the place of execution, he drew out his costly gold watch and handed it to the leader of the Mexicans who had the orders to shoot him.

"Sir!" he said, "divide the worth of this watch among your people. Tell them to aim well—here." He covered with both hands the region where his heart was to beat only a short

Fannin's Death

time longer, "Here, sir, tell them. I wish that their bullets may drill through me."

Hereupon Joseph Spohn laid a white sheet over his eyes, and a few moments later, as the smoke had cleared away, the Colonel lay on the ground with shattered head.

The drama had ended.

Joseph Spohn, who was saved afterward, sat on the carriage of a cannon and gazed starkly at the corpses of his comrades. He barely noticed the blood-greedy glances that the triumphant enemies cast toward him.

I must mention one more scene. As was already said, Dr. Shackelford was taken from our midst to serve as a surgeon. It was now impossible for them to get along without him, and in order to save him, he and another American were forcibly concealed under buffalo hides in the tent of an officer.

Imagine the feelings of a father whose only son and beloved nephew came to such a horrible and traitorous end. At every volley, at every shot the unhappy father groaned; "My son, my son, my brave Red Rovers, all, all are murdered—Oh it is horrible! Shackelford has robbed the citizens of Alabama of their sons—Alabama is bereft of its sons! No, not orphaned, there are still enough men in the state—I will thither," he continued at short intervals, "I will go there—

"I will speak, they shall shudder, the stones shall soften. The Union must shoulder the guns—old Shackelford will call through the states: Citizens! Americans! To arms! To arms! The blood of our brothers cries for vengeance from the prairie beyond the Mississippi—to arms! is the call, like the old weak Shackelford—to arms!" Several shots fell, and he continued in indescribable pain: "Oh my son, my only one, my nephew" he wept. "My sons! Yes, all! All you Red Rovers, you were my children, I was your father, you loved me as a dear father, and now?" A long pause, but then again, throwing the buffalo skins from him in despair: "Ha, Red Rovers! Children! countrymen! What shall I tell the people of Alabama? Where shall I hide my face, when they will point at me with their fingers? 'That is Shackelford,' they will say, 'the Red Rovers are dead, but Shackelford lives!'" Out of himself with pain, he fought with the strong carpenter to get on the outside.

"Let me loose, let the old father die with his sons, let me—but I have the right. I will live—live—to call the States to war. My call shall sound from the gulf to the Niagara Falls and from the Mississippi to the seas. We will, yes, we will revenge, bloody revenge will we have."

Long he raved away after this manner, and cost his companion in misfortune no little effort to keep him in the tent.

But soon the usual solemn quietness lay over the prairie again, which was only occasionally interrupted by the creaking of the ox carts of the enemy dragging the pale, naked, bleeding bodies onto a funeral pile where they were only partly burned. On the next night packs of wolves assembled on the place of execution, where they could be seen gnawing on the partly burnt bodies. On the following day the black vultures encircled the corpses and the wolves and the walls of Goliad. Cawing, they prophetically announced the overthrow of the Mexicans.

My Flight through the Wilderness

MY COURSE WAS DIRECTED TOWARD SAN ANTONIO to the northwest, but only to deceive the enemy, as my real direction lay toward east-northeast on the Brazos. But after I had wandered through the wilderness for about two hours, I struck a little brooklet that meandered off to the San Antonio. I walked into it, and as it occurred to me that it would obliterate my trail, I walked up in it for a while.

It was strange that not the slightest fear had taken possession of me, and I walked forward as courageously as if I were walking through the charming surroundings of the mighty New York. Serious thoughts floated about in the sea of my feverish imagination, and as the American coast for the first time arose before the fleet of Columbus, so the future rose up before my soul. The Greys had fallen but I was alive, the only one as I thought, saved by the Almighty to inform the world of this infernal deed. In my imagination I already saw how the troops and the old general himself listened with shuddering and rage to the account of this infamous act. I already heard the solemn vows that brother made brother, that father made son, and that the son made the loving father. I saw the bandit army annihilated, fleeing across the Rio Grande. And behind it all, I saw the single star in its splendor once more rise victoriously over the prairies. Splendid dreams! It was the prophetic spirit that rent the veil of the future; it had granted a deep look into the book of fate.

Exhausted from the rapid walking, I lay down in the tall grass on the bank of the little stream, and after I had noted the direction in which I was to go, I closed my eyes. A deep dullness filled my mind. No terrible dreams, no feverish fantasies, no pain from my light wounds, no fear, nothing hindered the refreshing repose that had possessed me for the strengthening of my mind and body.

A stormy sea of clouds, the remnants of a hurricane, rolled for the first time in a long time over the skies, and a fine rain was falling on my face when I awoke. Dark night lay on the prairie; the tall grass before on the hill waved in the wind. The undulating outlines of the elevation appeared to me as if a band of Mexicans or a troop of roving redskins were sneaking over the hill. I listened, but as I could not hear a human sound, I concluded that I was in error, which in reality I was.

I stood still to recall the map of the Republic and to take my course accordingly; it took only a few moments and I was ready. Northeast seemed to me to be the best direction. But what object was I to take as a guide in this dark, starless night? The only one was the wild current of the clouds, but it is not a good one. Consequently, I gave the rain that struck me on the right side of the face the preference.

My arm pained very much and was at first so stiff that I could not move it. But the penetrating rain soon softened the swelling and cooled the heat and alleviated the pain that was raging in my head. Toward four o'clock in the morning I found an inviting hole in the treeless bluff of a bayou that I had to cross. Being exhausted, I lay down in it and soon fell into a deep sleep from which I did not awake until about nine o'clock in the morning. It had ceased raining, but the several-feet-high mesquite grass wetted all my clothing. Toward the right a line of forest extended to the Guadalupe, the first stream on my wanderings that I had to strike and cross. Therefore, I turned my steps toward the oak-overgrown section where I had the advantage of not having the grass as high as it was on the prairie.

The whole evening after I had left the woods I wandered through one of those regions where the traveler sees nothing but hills overgrown with waving grass. Not a tree, not a bush, not even a cactus, that is found nearly everywhere in the west, broke the endless oneness. From my feet all around to the cloud layers chasing along the encircling horizon I saw myself as the only living being. No herds of deer grazed here, no gobbling turkeys passed through the prairies and no song of a bird interrupted the solemn quietness of the solitude. During the winter this region must be covered with geese, but they had a month ago undertaken their great journey to the northern prairies and waters of the Missouri and the Mississippi.

Disregarding the loneliness and filled with dauntless hope, I went forward with long steps, constantly and almost unconsciously whistling our favorite march.

Toward five o'clock I heard, as it seemed, subterranean thunder, but soon I saw a herd of wild horses on the horizon speeding over a hill. They came in close formation directly toward me, but stopped about one hundred and fifty paces away and gazed at me in consternation. At the loud signal of a fleet-footed mule, the whole herd of about three hundred dashed away with flowing manes in the same direction from which they had come. And soon they had disappeared behind the hills to which I was directing my steps. Finally, as I reached the highest of these, I saw before me the deep forests of the roaring Guadalupe. Soon I reached the light forest and, true to my course, stepped confidently forward under the post oak trees. Momentarily I expected to see the stream itself where I expected to spend the night. The night approached ever closer, and I crossed several roads, which however, I dared not follow, as Urrea's army was ahead.

Only in the dense forest was I safe from the Mexicans even if not so completely from the scalping knife of the roaming Caranchuas or the Lipans, although I had little fear of these, as they will attack only when there is something to be plundered.

The second night after my flight had already set in when I prepared my bed from Spanish moss that, hanging in long festoons from the trees, indicated the nearness of the stream. But I still could not hear the roaring of the water.

Toward midnight a majestic thunderstorm, such as an inhabitant of the north has no idea of, awakened me. A powerful, foaming current rushed down the ravine in which I was lying, and half of my body lay in the water. This was a warning not to sleep in the ravine in the future. I sprang up and sought shelter under a powerful pecan tree, where I was to some extent protected from the rain. After half an hour, the moon and the stars looked down so clear from the blue skies through the tops of the old oaks and hickories as if the whole night had been quiet and pretty.

Fresh moss was town down from the gigantic limbs and a new bed was prepared. Although I was soaked to the skin and did not have a very good bed, I soon went to sleep as soundly with the calling of the whippoorwill as if I had lain between cover and mattress since sundown under the roof among the colonies. But when I awoke with the sun, I could barely move my left foot. Practically my whole left side was stiff, and as I moved forward I experienced a cutting pain in my hip. After walking for a quarter of an hour, the pain disappeared and, strong and vigorous again, I swam across the charming Guadalupe, where I had just arrived, much to my satisfaction.

During the first half of the day my wanderings led me through the rich, prolific, densely wooded green of the stream where it was difficult for me to follow my course. But, in spite of all obstacles, everything went well. I was guided partly by the bark of the trees and partly by the sun shining down from the clear sky, which, however, is not a very good pilot during the midday hours. During the afternoon I entered the prairie that spreads out between the Guadalupe and the Lavaca rivers and the night overtook me in it.

As I again found myself on a treeless, recently burnt-off plateau, I placed my pilgrim's staff in the ground in such a manner that its upper point indicated the direction in which I intended to go the next morning. If it should be cloudy weather the next morning, I would at least know my direction.

But the whole of the next day was pretty, and I roamed through a heavenly region. Countless numbers of little prairies, tree courses, and islands grouped endlessly alternated one with the other. Barely would I pass around one far projecting point before other, new points, new forest lines and new projections, interspersed with green island mottes, would appear, while in the distance dark blue forest lines would disappear at the horizon. Now, too, the region began to have more signs of life. Small herds of horses and cattle that here often wander far away from the colonies grazed in company with countless herds of deer on the spring green of the savannas.

With the exception of the first day of my flight, I had not experienced the slightest hunger, in spite of the fact that I had eaten absolutely nothing so far. Neither did I experience any appreciable decrease in my strength, and while I momentarily hoped to see the black forests of the Lavaca, I stepped forward with the time of our favorite march.

Although my stomach showed no craving for anything except clear water, which I found in abundance so far, I believed it best to give it something to do, and in view of this decision, I picked some green leaves in walking along and tried to make a frugal meal out of them. But it was "no go" as the Texans say when a thing will not work. The early spring in this region does not offer the white man the least thing with which to satisfy his hunger if he is not provided with a gun, while the region west of the Guadalupe is sown with cactus, which, in case of necessity, can keep one from starving.

On the fifth day the sun rose again clear and bright on the deep blue sky, and very early it sent its almost-burning rays down on the enlivened but ever-changing landscape,

A trip through the Republic may be compared to a trip through the galleries of the new museum at Berlin. As one hurries through the rooms from one creation to another, so one wanders almost carelessly in the paradise of America from one park to another, and then first is the eye—dulled by the ever fresh beauties of nature—pleasantly surprised when it beholds the sandy beach, the raging surf and the waves of the Gulf of Mexico.

Meadows and islands of black forests lay about me. Numerous herds of horses, cattle and deer stared at me as I walked past them. Many a flock of turkeys marched around in procession and observed me with misgiving, while the sand grouse trumpeted its monotonous morning march. Anxiously my eyes hung on the dark forest line ahead of me in which I hoped to find the clear Lavaca. I carelessly continued my journey on a broad road that meandered off in my direction between the island mottes. Since yesterday not a drop of water had passed over my lips and, panting for water, I looked around for a sign of a spring or stream. My eyes scanned the endless expanse to the right and to the left, but they could discover nothing of promise. On a projecting forest my hopes were fixed, and the road that I was following led toward it.

I had to throw away a small turtle that I found on the road because I had no means of opening it. Not a single stone had I found on my flight, and I constantly wandered on a red brownish soil which was dark, almost approaching black, in the valley of the Guadalupe.

I almost despaired of ever reaching the dark forest and I could distinctly feel how my strength was leaving me, and my spirit with it. Slowly I dragged myself forward, and my active fantasy was apparently the only driving force of my very heavy feet.

It was about noon when I rounded the forest projection, and before my eyes, which seemed to be veiled with crape, another immense expanse danced and glimmered. Islands, horses, deer and cattle floated and tumbled about before my gaze, and miles away it seemed to me that a forest was again stretching its black arm out to the west.

I stared out into the glowing prairie. Confusedly the landscape rolled before my eyes, and I collapsed.

About twenty steps from me stood a majestic live oak tree under whose dark noble branches a whole battalion could find protection from the hot rays of the sun. I saw it as I fell, but I was not able to drag myself to it. Neither did I care to; since it seemed that I was to die, I wished, parching with thirst under the perpendicular rays of fire that fell from above, to breathe out my confused spirit as soon as possible. My eyes rolled like balls of fire in their sockets, and there was a beating in the forehead as if it were being clubbed to pieces.

As I assumed, it was evening when I awoke, since the sun stood deep and bloody on the horizon. I was somewhat refreshed and dragged myself to the shady oak. Another time I closed my eyes to spend the night here and to push forward anew with the early morning. After an hour, as the unbearable thirst would not allow me any rest, I opened my eyes again and believed that the night was still hanging over the prairie. But, oh horrors! High and clear hung the sun, a sea of flame in the unending field of indigo. Not the refreshing night but the glowing day was before me, and I must have slept near to eighteen hours in the wild fever.

But if I were to save myself from an unavoidable death, I must get away from here to search for water, and my only hope was the black arm reaching toward the west ahead of me. I staggered forward. There was no shady tree, no bush, no twig on my way. Nothing but an endless waving flower bed lay around me. At last I reached the border of the forest. But there was no trace of water; everything was dried up. I would probably have been eaten up by the wolves here if I had not discovered at a considerable distance out on the mighty treeless plateau that lay spread out before me, a clear blue sea, whose opposite bank seemed to be enclosed with dense forestry and along which several plantation houses lined themselves.

Seized with new courage, I stepped forward in spite of the unexplained question of how a person was to strike a sea here when none such was charted down on any map of the region. I staggered forward, and only the hope of reaching the water gave my nerves new strength. Again the sun burned down on my feverish and moss-enveloped head. The waves on the depression twittered and blinded my eyes. The buildings on the edge of the forest stepped forth more and more out of their misty veil, and with every approaching step the outline of the inviting mirror changed.

The region now began to take an unusual aspect, similar to that which borders the sea. Thick, strong grass, reed-like growths, palmettos and other things covered the dry earth which now took on a wave-like appearance. I had just walked over one of these waves and was standing on the crest of another and directed my eyes anxiously toward the sea. But what hellish delusion! What awful deception! Where was the sea with its quivering waves? Where the settlements that I had seen so plainly? Everything, everything had disappeared. Terrible! All hopes were momentarily destroyed.

I could not and would not believe it. I peered to the left and stared to the right, but discovered nothing. I turned my gaze from whence I came, fearing that I had gone around in a circle in a fit of fever. But there I saw the islands that I had recently passed. Another time I looked to the region where the blue water had appeared, but nothing was to be seen. The grasses trembled and vibrated, and even the rays of the sun that fell on the prairie quivered. The houses of the settlers had disappeared. But dreary forests spread themselves out before me, and several powerful moss-covered live oak trees stood in front of the mighty forest like the outposts of a great military camp.

I threw myself like an insane person on the prairie, buried my face on the earth and broke the hot rays of the sun by covering my head with a handful of grass. But I could not stand it long this way. Raging fever rolled in my blood and pounded in my head. In despair I would have put an end to this earthly suffering, but the necessary means to do this act were lacking. Feverishly I sprang up, and Oh what joy!

Dark clouds like the many chains of the San Saba mountains were stacking themselves one over another in the east. A fresh gulf breeze blew out of the same direction, and with new spirit and new hope I walked on toward the dark forests again.

A fine rain soon fell and refreshed the surrounding creation. Fresh and green the grasses and plants lifted their heads that had been hanging sadly downward before, and out of the timbers great numbers of horses and cattle that had gone under the shady trees during the hot noonday sun drifted out on the prairie. Their great numbers and their various brands indicated to me that I had reached American colonies. But where and which was impossible for me to say. I believe that I had covered from eighty to one hundred miles in a straight line, but I could not depend on this assumption since I had never been in the coast lands east of the Guadalupe.

The rain had almost completely relieved my thirst and the fever, and fortunate it was, for the terrible heat in my veins would have killed me in another night. Here I wandered until nine o'clock through the light forests, and I was rather sure to find a stream in its depths. Being exhausted, it was necessary for me to look up quarters for the night at this time. I soon found a dry creek on whose banks, as usual in the forest, I carried some moss together for a bed. Since I found that the sandy bed of the creek was still damp, I dug a hole about eighteen inches deep in its bottom in order to get a good drink in the morning from the water that would collect there during the night. I then threw myself on the moss and slept until the crowing of several cocks awoke me the next morning.

The Colonies

A POWERFUL DRAFT OF THE PRECIOUS WATER that had gathered in my spring during the night was my morning's refreshment, and then I looked around and discovered that I was within a hundred yards of a large plantation. The order of the fields, the fences and the buildings and the large quantity of poultry was to me a sure sign that the enemy had not defiled this section with his presence. My heart beat with joy on seeing a human habitation again. Happy beyond description on being near civilization, I walked with new strength to a clear stream to my left, whose crystal ripples murmured over a gravel bed. Another time I quaffed from the most precious of all drinks and then went across the stream without entering the plantation, as I was convinced that the buildings were vacant and that the inhabitants had destroyed their food and fled toward the east. Besides that, I expected to find some more plantations on the other side of the stream.

And so it was. When I stepped out on the prairie from the strip of woods about one thousand yards wide, I discovered eight or ten habitations on the rolling rim and numerous herds of cattle roaming about. The places were alive with poultry, but not a sign of a human being was to be seen. Everybody was gone, far away, to escape the murdering bands of Mexico.

Every convenience that a person could wish was at hand, but, with the exception of corn, there was not the slightest trace of any food. Everything had been concealed or destroyed.

Hunger I had not, I can assert that on my honor, or I would have given chase to the poultry. But a number of eggs looked so inviting to me that I ate about a dozen raw since I could not start a fire. After this meal I fell into a sound sleep on a pile of cotton. Being refreshed, I felt for the first time after my flight a gnawing hunger. As I searched through the buildings another time for food, I found two names written with charcoal on one of the doors, one of which was the name of my friend, Thomas Camp.

Up to this time I had the positive conviction that I was the only one to have luckily escaped the massacre. But here the names indicated to me that there were others who had escaped and were already ahead of me to inform the world of the infamous murder at Goliad.

Enraptured, I sank down to thank the great spirit.

In the rejoicing of my heart I could have kissed the black lines and embraced all of humanity with the exception of Santa Anna and his henchmen.

I searched in vain for food. All that I could find were the remnants of dried beef that were left on the rods when the rest was hastily cut down, together with a few little sacks of seed hanging on the wall of one of the outhouses. I took one of these and all the remnants of the beef that I could find, hung them around my neck, and thus equipped I proceeded on my journey. I had also improved my wardrobe. A large, grey, so-called Kentucky felt hat that cast a shadow about three steps in diameter now sat on my head instead of the moss cap. I, therefore, marched in the shade. At my side hung a canteen well-filled with water that I had borrowed along with the grey helmet from my friend the absent planter, for which my name as debtor was written alongside of the other two.

It was as hot as yesterday, but under the grey felt I marched like under the evergreen live oaks. Ahead of me lay, as I presumed, the forests of the Navidad from five to six miles away, which formed with those of the Lavaca that I had just left, a great, green, oval meadow on whose borders all around one could barely make out the numerous homes of the colonists, while the great plain itself was occasionally broken by groups of live oak trees. But that much greater was the bustle of the animal world that now left the timber to eat off the freshly springing grasses in spite of the very hot sun.

The angry, blood-red face of the sun god had just disappeared behind some layers of clouds on the horizon when I stood on the crest of a prairie elevation within a thousand yards of the timbers of the Navidad, on whose border I noticed two horsemen. I was in doubt about their nationality, but the sudden sound of military music and the appearance of a troop of dragoons around a forest projection indicated to me that Urrea's whole division was advancing.

It was only a moment and I lay safely in the tall grass. I crept to a small, dense island motte and concealed myself at the foot of a magnolia tree in some vines and Spanish moss. Here I determined to await the night.

Barely was I through before the enemy put out his sentries, and my whole island domain was within his lines—by the way, not a pleasant observation from my nest, but I was consoled by the fact that that there was nothing to do to change it, and I anxiously looked forward to the coming of the night.

Darkness had finally enveloped the green savanna in its dark mantle in whose tall grass I now crept out between the sentries that stood from fifty to sixty yards apart. The watchful blue frocks, who suspected no heretic in their vicinity, stepped together, the three in a group, and were lustily jabbering, probably about the large amount of plunder that they expected to draw back to Mexico. I had a strong inclination to take along with me the musket of one of the gentlemen that stood guard, instead of its master. But I was liberal-hearted, and besides, the musket was such a contemptible weapon in the eyes of the volunteers that even the man who carried it fell heir to its contempt. In our opinion as well as that of the inhabitants of the Free States of North America, it was fit only for hirelings. I, therefore, followed my course and was soon out in the open again where I could walk on after the manner of a human being.

But I now had to hold a council with myself about a number of things that crossed through my mind in the same manner that I crossed through the prairie.

The first question was: Where am I? Then: Had I gone forward in the contemplated direction? Was this timber the Navidad? Where would Sam Houston probably be? What should I now do and what course should I take to reach the Texan army? After much debating back and forth I decided to direct my steps toward Washington, where I had some prospect of striking the army of liberation. It was my definite opinion that this would be the best course that Houston could take in his retreat from the Colorado to the Brazos, as the deep, almost impenetrable primeval forests that covered the rich valley of the red Brazos would be the best terrain for the backwoodsmen to give the firm of Santa Anna and Company a little demonstration of their marksmanship. The next question was: Where was Washington? And could I depend on my skill to work my way through the wilderness and also the redskins at the same time? Vividly that awful day still stood before my mind when I, with a thousand ill wishes and filled with fire from within and fire from without, fell unconscious to the ground. But I remembered that the eastern part of Texas was more densely settled and that larger forests covered the soil than the western. Musingly I went forward when I suddenly came upon a plain road, which I followed without thinking.

After going a few miles, I came to several plantations that stood from two to three hundred yards from the road, but I lost not a moment and hurried on with new life along the road. After I had wandered for about six miles, I found myself between two large cotton fields that spread out on the sides and before me as far as I could see in the pale light of the moon. Black timber surrounded the field, and on the opposite side lay a number of dark mounds that I took for the outlines of the residence and other buildings. Cautiously I left the road and went slowly through the dry, rattling cotton stalks. Several times I stopped and listened, but not a sound of a living being could be heard in the houses. Only the owl carried on a wild confusion with his companions in the nearby forest. On my approaching nearer, I could recognize among the different buildings especially the negro quarters, the mighty cotton gin and the blacksmith shop. It was evident that this was the property of a rich settler.

Something dark moved in the shadow of the gin and the cotton press. I listened but could not hear a sound. I advanced a few steps nearer, when suddenly the whole creation seemed to wake up. A terrible flapping of wings and a wild confusion of cries sounded all around me. Countless shrill cries filled the air and an endless cloud of wild geese rose up into the sky, darkening the moon and the scenery that lay about me.

Honking constantly, they swung around several times to the border of the forest, and it roared like a storm when they were over my head. Finally, however, they settled down at the other edge of the field.

The drunken army of the Dictator could not have given me a greater fright than this wild flight of these knights of the feather, especially as I was of the opinion that these annually welcome guests had already set out on their northward flight.

The presence of these creatures here substantiated my former conclusion that neither friend nor enemy resided in the houses. Without further hesitation I now stepped among them, between which stood a number of inspiring china trees. Hundreds of chickens and turkeys were roosting on their branches. In the pretty garden surrounded by fig and peach trees lay large herds of snoring hogs, and through the yard walked a bunch of cattle that looked at me as if they had not seen a human soul for years.

As I entered the dark door of the main building, something stumbled towards me from within over the carpeted floor. I sprang to the side and behind the door and a perfectly white mule walked majestically by me. He looked out of the door like an Imperial excise officer during bad weather, raised his head to the moon and so commandingly brayed "Peace," that the whole plantation trembled. I took a breath and landed him a powerful blow with the door, and now the scare was on him. He stampeded out as if possessed through the frightened cattle, and his fading form finally disappeared in the dark timber.

I walked through several rooms, and everywhere the greatest disorder prevailed. Tables, chairs and beds lay scattered about. Everything indicated that the inhabitants, like all the colonists living west of the Colorado, had taken flight in the greatest haste. The set table stood in the spacious, elegantly—for Texas, almost aristocratically—furnished dining room. The dishes contained untouched victuals that needed nothing but warming. But a soldier who has had no cooked food for fifteen or sixteen days is not very particular, as the Texans say. And anything that satisfied hunger is first-class for a patriot. Excellent beefsteak it was in fact. Since I had now suddenly become a rich plantation owner, I seated myself comfortably at the table and set the dishes in order. One pan or plate after another was emptied, and in a short time the ghostly moon looked sadly with me on the clean, empty, shining table.

Everything would have been good if I could have brought fire from heaven like Prometheus, or if I had had such a confidential acquaintance with the redskins as I had a few years later, or if my somewhat too patriotic fellow Texans had suspected that a poor devil from Fannin's butchery would have arrived here, practically starved to death. They would certainly have rioted, destroyed all the food and would possibly have left a gun and a little powder and lead. They had destroyed everything in their rage. Only the barns were filled to the roof with corn, but the mills were gone. Consequently, the enemy could not make much use of it. But neither could I.

If I remained here, I would in reality be no better off than I would be out in the prairie. I would either have to eat corn with my donkey, who still looked suspiciously at me from the side, or make a daily club-chase on the poultry and eat the captured game raw like the Indianized Hungarians did a few years ago in Vienna, when they appeared as American man-eaters who a thousand miles west of Philadelphia ate each other and tore living chickens to pieces and ate them before the very eyes of the good-natured people of Vienna.

After considerable calculating back and forth, it occurred to me to slip around the camp of my neighbors six miles away and possibly get a firebrand from them. If I should succeed in doing that, I would not exchange my abode for the Arcade or the Bishop in New Orleans or for the Astor house in New York because, in my mind, there was nothing to be more desired than freedom.

With a box half-filled with ashes I stole down the Navidad—it was this little river that bordered one side of the plantations—under the protection of the forest along the watercourse. I pressed over the cultivated fields of several squatters, and just as I was about to step out of some bushes, I found myself directly in front of a Mexican outpost. I hastily withdrew and tried my luck at several other places. But wherever I approached, I found a closely picketed chain of sentries. I consequently returned without results to my plantation.

On the next day I made another attempt, hoping that the enemy had broken camp and moved on. But I deceived myself. The same thing transpired the following two days, on the last of which I was almost captured.

Disappointed hopes and the many fruitless marches to the camp of the enemy had made me bold, and I impatiently threw my ash box away. I believed now that the Mexicans intended to settle down here in one of our richest colonies, which made it look very gloomy for us and especially for our independence. While I was thus fruitlessly calculating on what to do and on how far the Colorado probably was away, a heavily loaded donkey, a companion mule and two iron-faced Mexicans armed with carbines and pistols came panting around a forest corner about four hundred to five hundred yards away. The donkey brayed. The Mexicans looked surprised at each other and then around. And the one with a mustache looking like horns in the distance saw something dark, my insignificance, sink into the tall grass. With a frightful "*este carajo Americano,*" he and his hesitant companion hurried in a large semi-circle past the spot where the dark object had disappeared. They did not trust the situation and, from a considerable distance, took a shot at me, if, as the hesitating one said, if it really was someone.

But I stole slowly toward the timber, carefully laying the blades of grass that stood in the way to the side. I was particularly careful not to show my head. I was already forty to fifty yards away while the one with the twirling mustache was still firing at the spot where I had disappeared. Suddenly, however, I heard some confused calling. I looked up a little to run hastily to the timber if more of the bluecoats should appear. Instead of that I saw the donkey going off in a full trot with his noble companion, paying no attention to the load on his back and braying lustily. My Mexicans *carajoed* after them. And their long drawn-out "Mu-u-ula mu-u-ula hoi mu-u-ula" sounded most charming on this occasion. I did not contemplate long, but hurried away with steps that Hopping Johnson would barely have been able to surpass. I myself marveled at the fleetness of my feet when I again entered my natural domain, the primeval forest. "Texas forever!" I cried again after I had escaped the bluecoats for the second time.

Urrea's Camp

"LUCKILY ESCAPED, LUCKILY GAVE THEM THE SLIP," I observed out of the cotton seed, like the fox when the trap snaps shut in front of his nose. "Happily at home again!"

But here I now sat among immense piles of cotton seed that were stacked up in the gin, like a cricket in his sheltered hollow. I might expect the enemy at any moment to come for more provisions, as the loads of corn on the donkeys were from my plantation.

Thousands of plans crossed through my mind, but they exploded as quickly as many a steamboat on the Mississippi. I wanted to go to Washington, but I did not know where it lay. Neither did I know where I was nor where Houston was. Neither could I play the settler until the republicans came back, because I had no fire and because it was not safe here. I worried and studied a long time. At last a bold thought passed through my mind, namely, to go directly into the Mexican camp, to present myself to the general as a traveler, to solicit his protection in this unpopulated Texas and to sail to my countrymen with the first favorable wind.

A queer notion this, in fact. But the same evening I was on my way. It was already dark when I walked through the Mexican outposts, who were very energetically calling their "*Alerta*" to each other, yes, in fact, so energetically that not a soul noticed how one of the accursed rebel array wandered through their watchful chain.

Close to two thousand men lay before me; the prairie, covered with watch fires, spread like a dark star-spangled heaven. I walked through the rows of the heroes of Santa Anna sitting around the fire. They were a picture of comfort as they sat with crossed limbs cracking pecans, cooking *caldo*, smoking *cigarritos*, or playing cards for their wages that the Napoleon of the West had owed them no telling how long. Some were cursing us heretics and others were innocently enjoying a mental plunder of the city of New Orleans. They were determined to punish this city exemplarily because of its participation in sending the Jews[14] to the aid of the Texans, and the Queen of the Mississippi was to congratulate itself if it escaped without being burned to the ground. In passing, I wished them good luck on their journey. "Go to it, my boys," I said and walked on through the irregular fires to a few tents on a slight elevation near the forest where I expected to find the headquarters.

A group of jolly women that sat in front of a tent attracted my attention. They were busy shelling corn for a noisy herd of mules. Several keen-looking men on horseback surrounded the herd of mules, which were fighting for something to eat. With incessant cursing and other long, drawn-out words, the men endeavored to establish quiet among the restless mules. If quiet for a moment should set in, a hail of the aforesaid articles would start the revolution anew. A prime enjoyment among the Mexicans!

---

[14] In a footnote, Ehrenberg makes the dubious assertion that all non-Catholics are called Jews in Mexico.

I stepped closer to the women and the fire must have strangely illuminated me, as the ears of corn fell from the hands of the Señoras from fright. I do not know whether it was I who looked so frightful or whether it was only my prodigious Kentucky felt hat. At first they looked at me in surprise, but when they heard *"muy buenas noches"* they cried as in one chorus *"un carajo Americano,"* our usual title. I bowed very respectfully to the Señoras and thanked them, with a few courteous Spanish words that I had learned, for their very flattering welcome and then asked for the location of the tent of the general.

"*Capitan*," they called to a little son of Mexico sitting on a horse. "*Capitan*, come here quickly, *un Americano!*" The captain came up and looked at me with his one weak black eye. The other one had been shot out by one of Dimmit's men at the capture of Goliad. He demanded to know what I wanted from him and how in hell I got in here.

The man looked so barbaric, his face was so overgrown with whiskers, and he spoke such frightful English that a braver heart than mine would have lost courage. But I had over time become so remarkably careless that I looked him independently in the eye as if an old acquaintance of mine stood before me.

"My gallant captain," I answered, "You see here a perfectly peaceful traveler, who has something of importance to tell the general."

"Something of importance? Importance, Señor?" he asked, staring at me in excited curiosity. "But," he continued, "have you appetite, Señor—probably are hungry—drink a cup of cacao? Come, let us talk—come—but Señor," measuring me from head to foot, "You do not look as if you had anything of importance, I mean, but if you know anything, I would be glad to learn something of importance."

"Sir," I said, "I have things of importance for a general but not for a mule-captain; but in spite of that, I will drink this cup on your welfare."

The mule-captain felt himself flattered that I at once titled him captain in the presence of the women, as he really was only a lieutenant of the herd that had just been fed.

"Señor," he continued more considerately, while I enjoyed another piece of cornbread, "do you know we soon go to Washington to whip the damn Yankees? You no be one of them? I see the kinky hair. Are you not, Señor, of black and white blood?"

"I cannot say, Señor, that I have the honor of being related to the black gentry. But I presume you are—hmm?"

"Right, Señor, right—but you look so brown—your hair so woolly, Señor." He shook his head.

"Do you mean Washington in Texas?" I interrupted him, "I presume that Mexico will not wish to tie up with Uncle Sam?"

"Uncle Sam we want to whip, Señor. We want to drive them out of America and the blacks shall become free men, Señor,"

"Very humanitarian, sir, wish you good luck on your journey. But if I may ask, my brave captain, who so disfigured your noble features, and who had the inexcusable impudence of knocking out your eye?"

"Señor," he answered solemnly, "a *carajo* Americano, sir, when we were at Goliad. Señor, we were behaving like good Christians as we often do. A plot—the bandits—the *Americanos* saw us over the wall, Señor. Saw us peaceful. That made them mad, Señor. They shoot, my companion falls—me,

Señor," he added gnashing his teeth, "They shoot out my eye, and I want to get my *fusil*, Señor. The bandits—the Jews—come over the wall on one side, and the *Mexicanos* go away over the other now, Señor. I not be strong enough to fight all. I leave my *fusil* and walk away over the wall, and run to Matamoras, Señor, with one eye," He took a deep breath and continued: "My wife, Señor, will not have man half blind—takes another one—I nothing can do. Padre say, she has right, forgives my sins for three years for nothing—very kind. But it was very good I no *fusil* had . . . would have shot myself . . . Señor."

"Psah, captain, you shouldn't be a fool. You are still as fine a fellow as ever trotted in his own boots. What, commit suicide? Shame! A man like you speaks of committing suicide, and because of a petticoat who flutters with the wind and changes color like the lizard for the stakes! Psah, captain, I thought the sons of Mexico were too gallant to speak like this."

"Señor, I courage enough have. I no shoot myself. Been went to General Cos, tell him, been was a patriot, tell him, have fought at Goliad, tell him I was last one run away, tell him lots more, Señor. Cos sent me General Urrea, was commander at Tamaulipas, but in Texas, Señor . . . became *capitan de las mulas,* have a very good salary, Señor, but have not yet received anything. The padres have said that we will get much, and Santa Anna has said that we will get very much, and Cos and General Urrea have promised us great piles of doubloons and pesos in New Orleans and Philadelphia, Señor, we going there. You do better going with us, get rich, awfully rich."

Martiny,[15] a neat little adjutant of Urrea, just passed by in company with another officer. I remembered him from Goliad and knew that he had been reared in the States and that he spoke English very well. I sprang up hastily and followed him.

"Señor, Señor," cried the commander of the mules, "you me not want to tell the important news, the important news, Señor." But I did not hear him and asked the adjutant where the general was to be seen.

Surprised to see one of the rebels here, he looked at me and asked from whence I came, if I were one of Fannin's men, or if perhaps one of the rebel army, and if I had possibly deserted?

At first I had an inclination to play the role of a deserter, but I could not persuade myself to carry such a disrespectable name for even a few weeks. In order to forestall any further questions, I told him that I would report only to Urrea in person and that all further questioning would be useless. This had a powerful effect.

He, however, was very friendly and observed that the general could not now be seen for half an hour as he was eating his supper and that I might meanwhile go with him to his tent to take a cup of warm drink.

I still had an appetite and could easily manage an adjutant's portion, as the Mexicans eat very little. And as our people are accustomed to say, they eat like canaries, quarrel like sparrows, consist of skin and bones like a crane and run like a horse when they perceive powder behind them.

Beefsteak and frijoles is an excellent meal for a person who had tasted nothing warm for fifteen to sixteen days with

---

[15] Martinez?

the exception of a cup of cacao. But what surprised me the most was the excellent beefsteak, without which the American and the Texan could not live very long.

I ate my portion in good Yankee style in about five minutes, while the two officers, with constant questioning, required over half an hour, after which we broke up to see the general.

A mustached triumvirate sat on gigantic trunks around a table that was still set with a simple meal. The first one to draw my attention was a black-brown individual with a singularly small face, which compared to his broad-brimmed hat like the head of a peacock to its tail, and what was not concealed by the shadow of the broad brim of the hat was obscured by a heavy mustache over the lips and a dark beard under. While the sparkling little eyes cast piercing glances at the entering Texan, I at once recognized him as the death messenger who brought orders for our execution from Santa Anna to the commander of Goliad—at least we believed that he had brought the orders from San Antonio. At his side sat another notorious individual, a Mexican Rhine-Prussian, in reality a noble fellow, and already known to us from Fannin's capitulation. I mean the p.p. Holzinger.[16] With him, as with all the Mexican defenders of the fatherland, the most important and dignified thing was the aristocratic, barbaric looking mustache that was nicely twisted to a point. I marveled that a carpenter had risen so high after I had seen his twisted beard, and that he was able to produce such a noble decoration, as these usually only grow on noble soil. Bold drawings on the paper that

---

[16] The abbreviation "p.p." is an odd choice. Commonly used in German, it stands for the Latin "*per procurationem*," referring to someone who acts as an agent, as when a person signs a document for another. It amounts to referring to "the agent Holzinger."

lay before them came from the hands of the latter—too bold, it seemed to me, for the hand that executed them. His constantly moving mouth entertained the officers who were sitting by. But in spite of his explanations they looked at the plan as if everything was Greek to them.

The third, finally, was a five-foot-ten-inch, rather pale-looking man. Only a small amount of beard was discernible on his face, and his eyes, which did not sparkle as fiery in this proud, descendant of Spain as did those of the little half-Indian death messenger, left the drawing on the table after a time and rested on the adjutant and me.

General Urrea, for it was he himself, addressed me in a very friendly manner, asking who I was and from where I came. As I could speak very little Spanish, he asked me what other languages I could speak, upon which I answered: English and German. He paused for a moment and then spoke with the other two, but it was so rapid that I could not understand a word that he said. Whereupon Holzinger addressed me in a very angry manner and directed me to answer his questions to the minutest detail. "First," he began, "from where do you come? Who are you? What in the devil are you doing here? And what do you want?" He then was silent, however, first warning me not to say anything but the strictest truth.

"On question number one, Colonel, I must answer you that I am a citizen of the North American Union, and that I am under the protection of the twenty-four stars, which, as I believe, stand in unshakable bonds of friendship with their southern sisters and, as I hope, are worthy of the confidence of Mexico." Here I took out my pocket knife and began to whittle like a Yankee when something of importance is up, so that my inner consciousness would not play on my features.

Holzinger mumbled, "Very well, very well spoken," smiled and translated this part of my examination.

"On the second," I continued, "I can only answer that I hope to be called X. X. and that I was born in a land called Prussia."

"Prussia? Prussia? I thought you were a Prussian. Prussia stands in good relationship with our republic. I am, therefore, not surprised that you are a Prussian."

I behaved as if I had not noticed his insinuation and proceeded to answer the third question. "Quite a while ago a kinsman of mine disappeared from his home. We have never been able to find the trace of him. And it was only in the year 1834 that I was informed by a German newspaper editor in Cincinnati by the name of Hartmann that my lost uncle, or at least a gentleman by that name, was in Mexico and was employed by the English Mining Company at Real del Monte. Since I for the longest time cherished a desire to wander through the plains of Tlaxcala and to visit the battlefield and place where Cortez gave the world a bloody example of gallantry when he destroyed Montezuma, I set out last summer when I was in New Orleans and went with a schooner to Matagorda Bay, where I bought a mustang to ride from there on. I began my journey in July but became ill in this vicinity with the chills and fever. I did not get well until the fall. That season, as you know yourself, Colonel, is not adapted for traveling on account of shortage of grass for the horses. During the winter I remained with Mr. Williams—that was the name of the owner of the plantation where I had been staying—who lives about six miles from here. Last March I took another fever, the so-called bilious fever, and I cannot say how long I was laid up. Neither can I remember anything except that the planter came to my bed one day and told me that he and his family would have to leave the plantation at once, but since he had no light wagon in which to take me along, he would be obliged to let me stay here for a while. I should, however, be without fear, as my good old black servant, Jack, would come within three days and get me. I saw him enter, I heard him speak, the kindly Williams, I saw him set food near my bed, I felt the warm grip of his hand, saw him leave—but I did not understand anything. I again fell into feverish dreams and must have lain there a long, a very long time, until a few days ago when I recognized my sad situation.

"After I had eaten a little of the practically dried-up food, I felt somewhat refreshed and decided to wander over to the houses of the neighbors. But all the houses to the right and to the left were deserted, and I did not see a human being until I stood in the center of your army."

"A very touching account, Mr. Prussian," said Holzinger, and translated the last part thereof with doubtful smiles to the General.

"The fourth and last question, Colonel, is easily answered. I come to you as a man in need, who would ask nothing but the sympathy of his fellow man. I am through, Colonel. Kindly ask General Urrea's permission for me to accompany his army to the next settled region."

A long debate followed in the triumvirate. The mustaches were thoughtfully rolled. Martiny was questioned, and I had to endure the penetrating looks of first one and then the other and, at times, of all three.

"Now, Mr. Prussian," Holzinger finally began, stroking his beard, "this is a very nice little story, and I must admit on my honor that it has touched all of us. But we do not believe a word of it. If we did, every Yankee could come with his false pretenses. Consequently, another time, the unadulterated truth, you know that we do not trifle. Also, where is the army of the rebels now, and are you not a spy?"

"Spy, sir!" I responded angrily, but composing myself again, I answered, "I am not thinking of playing such a role," but I asked, "what did you say of a rebel army?"

"Do not dissemble yourself," he continued, "the Texans I mean, where are they?"

"I do not know a word of them, much less why they are called rebels."

The colonel was surprised, the general was much surprised, and the death messenger more surprised. They looked at each other, debated, shook their heads and shrugged their shoulders.

"Have you never heard the name of Fannin?" asked the Colonel. "Only the direct truth," said he with threatening, drawn-together eyes.

"Fannin, Fannin," said I, rubbing my forehead slowly, "Fannin? No, no, I think never."

Again the triumvirate counciled awhile. Then they were silent and so steeped in thought that not a joint moved. The polished beards were gripped in the hands as if these important parts of the Mexican officers were in danger. The Texan incognito sat quiet and, while whittling figures, speculated on what the mustachios would bring forth next.

Suddenly, it seemed, a great thought struck Holzinger. Unceremoniously, he released his mustache that he had been holding with both hands. In doing this, however, he brought it into such disorder that he was obliged to pause to put it into sightly appearance again. Hereupon he first spoke in a loud tone in Spanish to General Urrea and then in German to me, while the other two rubbed their hands between their knees.

"Now, my dear Prussian," he said, giving his mustache another artistic turn, "I presume you know the name of your uncle in Mexico."

"On this point I can fully inform the Colonel," said I. "My uncle is Señor Antonio X. X. in Real del Monte, twenty-two leagues from Mexico," and I continued to whittle slowly and carelessly. Without hearing another word, the inquisitor turned to the General and informed him of the correctness of my answer. Holzinger knew the whole mining personnel, or at least the officers, as he was formerly counted among the latter himself.

After another little conference in which, as I believed, they mutually expressed their doubt about my statements, the inquisitor addressed himself another time to me, and after assembling all the dignity that his black mustache would permit, he said in a fear-inspiring tone, "Listen, professed Prussian, do you not know that we shoot everyone that we find in Texas?"

"Uncle Sam, sir, would probably attend to that," said I, giving my figure the last cut with the greatest composure. "Uncle Sam doesn't trifle, especially when some of his component parts are concerned, and every citizen is a part of the republican colossus."

The Colonel translated this into reckless Spanish, indignant that I should have dared to threaten the Catholic priestly authority. Urrea heard the blustering translation and smiled a little, but the death messenger set his mustache in order, doubled his brown fists and struck on the table so that the dishes rattled, and this blusterbuss slung curse after curse over to me in such rapid succession that the sum total sounded like one long, drawn-out word.

Urrea, for whom things seemed to get too warm, and who had remained passive up to this time, arose, looked around, and his majestic figure alone commanded silence. A single look and a carelessly spoken word with a well-sounding voice at once destroyed the anger and the raging of the other two. A number of slowly spoken words, among which he directed Holzinger to take care of me for the night, fell on my ears. The manner of the half-breed had appreciably changed in typical Mexican fashion even before Urrea ceased speaking. His barometer had fallen and corresponded with that of the General.

As I was leaving the tent, the General called to me in Spanish but very distinctly, asking if I wasn't hungry, and before I could answer, the young adjutant and I had to sit down at the table. The young man was Urrea's favorite, and although he was very young, he deserved the favor above all of the other officers. During his stay in the Union he had absorbed the tireless spirit of "the brother Jonathan" and had acquired such knowledge as probably no other of his comrades could demonstrate. Withal he possessed such a lovely character and had such a fine, tender appearance that he was irresistible.

Honestly said, it was time that the hearing came to an end, as I barely would have been able to carry the mask much longer. My only means of salvation was my whittling, which concealed my feelings and gave such a composed, careless manner that it surprised the three.

As Holzinger assured me, my hearing was to be continued the next morning. But the good countryman must not have been able to bring it that far. When I came to Urrea, I found that there was nothing to it and that the General was very friendly. He ordered Martiny to give me one of his uniforms. And even the Rhine-Prussian, to avoid seeing the frightful Kentucky felt hat, gave me an officer's hat nicely decorated with gold cords. Toward ten o'clock the next morning, I was, without previous notice, confronted with several Texan prisoners, all of whom with one exception did not know me.

This one was Jack Rees, who like me had succeeded in escaping from the massacre but was later likewise compelled to surrender on account of the shortage of food. A wink from me cautioned him and we stared at each other's faces like two figures in a wax museum. But the inward pleasure at seeing another comrade saved threatened to break our assumed masks.

I stood this last examination also, walked free through the Mexican lines and lived in the tent with the General, who seemed to have a special pleasure in the little Prussian, as he now called me.

As I went through the camp the next day, I saw Holzinger's cook, a Hamburger by the name of Gansen, whom Holzinger had rescued at Refugio. He belonged to King's company, and as the men were to be shot, Holzinger threw an artillery mantle over him and drew him out of the confusion. The heroes fell and a scoundrel was saved who, at the Fannin massacre, as Martiny told me, offered his unrequested services to operate one of the cannon against his comrades, but Urrea, indignant at the meanness of this person, which is saying much, ordered him to leave the cannon at once and to attend to his kitchen duties. To this fellow, whom I didn't know any further than that he had once been one of our men, I confided my condition, as I was glad to see that another of our unfortunate companions had been saved. He also was very happy, pressed my hand and gave me the advice to act as if we had never seen each other, which I promised, although it did not make much difference to me as I was of the positive conviction that I was out of all danger. As I entered General Urrea's tent that afternoon, he smiled at me, threatened with his finger and told me that he had discovered who I was.

"Well, General, your assumption, or rather your knowledge, is correct, and I cannot and will not further deny it. But I would be grateful to know from what source you have your information."

"Your countryman did not act as befitted him," he answered, "but the little Prussian need not be concerned. He to whom Urrea gives his word may rest easy."

I was inclined to ask him who gave Fannin his word on the Coleto, but wisely held my peace.

"If the little one asks it," he continued, "he shall at once have a horse and a pass to Matamoras, and from there he can go wherever it pleases him. But it would be pleasant to me if he would remain in Texas until the close of the campaign, which can now be considered as practically ended, and then go with me to Durango; if it should not please him there, he will be at liberty to choose another place."

"Thank you very much, General, for your kind consideration. I would rather remain in Texas, but allow me to observe that it does not appear to me as if the campaign is nearly ended. In the first place, the Mexican troops are not nearly at the Sabine, and in the second place, I do not believe that the militia of the land will forsake all of their property without trying a battle. The backwoodsmen, General, are no cowards, and I will venture the opinion that you will yet have many a round with these cold-blooded, constantly calculating squatters. Up till now the Mexican armies have fought only with volunteer soldiers from the States, who must ascribe their fall to their own internal disunion. No one was willing to take orders from anyone else, and each one fought on his own account. Even in such circumstances the little groups have shown you what the determination of the will can do. 'Be free!' was their motto, but 'Texas or Death!' is that of the militia."

This conversation was conducted in English and had to be partly translated by the adjutant. The General smiled as I ended, tapped me on the shoulder and said in questioning tone, "Still rebellious?"

"General," I responded, "as long as I live this should happen only for freedom. If new flowers should appear on the old stem beyond the Rio Grande, General Urrea can depend on it that his prisoner, who went into the field for the broken off and singly planted leaf, will just as willingly fight for the buds on the old plant."[17]

"This is very good, a praiseworthy zeal," said Urrea, "However, we have dispatches from the commander-in-chief that leave us to infer that we will soon depart for Durango." He turned to Martiny and directed him to translate the main sentence of a dispatch from Santa Anna, which he did as follows:

"Much to our indignation the old Tennesseean[18] everywhere runs out of our way, so that not even our dragoons can catch him. Soon he will be beyond the Sabine and all of his rabble with him. Then the brave officers may enjoy a period of rest or follow me across the Sabine. Our national honor demands of me that I at least most severely punish that town of

---

[17] This is a repeat of the metaphor of Mexico as a prickly pear cactus with many pads. The Texas pad has been torn off and planted alone for freedom; Ehrenberg would fight to bring freedom to the old pads as well.
[18] Sam Houston.

shopkeepers that dared to recruit troops against Mexico. Another time I remind you that the Congress of the Nation has ordered to shoot everyone. Remember this . . . ."

He stopped.

I laughed over this boasting, and considered it to the advantage of my country to encourage the enemy in it. The question was also on my tongue to ask what kind of a congress this was that had passed that order. Was it composed of representatives elected by the people? If this was the case, was the law passed through the house of representatives with the bayonets of Santa Anna or with the pesos of the Catholic priests? But I chose the wisest path. I held my peace and left the tent to get fresh air.

Old Sam

THE GUADALUPE ROARED DOWN between its banks past the little town of Gonzales, where the Texas militia under Sam Houston had thrown up its quarters. A singular stillness prevailed in the camp. With dark and moody expressions, the tanned planters stared into the fires, and barely a word passed their lips except an occasional taunt at Fannin. Even the whittling had ended. Instead of that, the men played with their powerful Bowie knives. They threw them alternately into the ground and drew them forth again. One could easily see that a bloody, frightful catastrophe was playing before their imagination in consequence of which they would from time to time make fierce gesticulations. It was the fall of the Alamo and the death of the heroes that had so gallantly died there that put the whole camp in this mood. Since the sixth of March the signal cannon that Travis fired regularly every morning had not been heard, and the worst was feared. And today the worst had been substantiated as the exact news of the battle and the death of the unfortunate ones became known. Imagine the mood of the little army of slightly less than six hundred men.

    Several were sitting around a large fire and were reading the letters that Travis had written to the National Assembly shortly before. In a soft voice the reader, an old brave planter dressed from head to foot in Indian attire—he was our old acquaintance from San Augustine—continued:

"I am besieged by a thousand men or more under Santa Anna. I have sustained an incessant bombardment for the last twenty-four hours without the loss of a man. The enemy has demanded my surrender at discretion, or to expect no mercy if the fort be taken. My answer was a cannon shot."

"Hear it, boys, did you hear it? It was a cannon thunder, boys! That was the proper way to answer those bloodhounds," the old man interrupted himself, and then continued: "Our flag still floats on the walls, I will never surrender or retreat; Victory or Death!"

"Victory or Death! Yes, you brave Travis, Bowie, Crockett, Evans, Paw and all you heroes are no more.[19] But boys, boys, I swear to you these old bones shall never find rest if a terrible vengeance be not taken for our comrades. Boys, you hear it, you may accuse me in high heaven if old Jack doesn't do it."

A long pause followed, No one spoke until it seemed that the spirits had somewhat quieted down.

"But father," hesitatingly said a slender boy, "let us read the last letter from Travis. I have not yet heard it—just came back today from mama after whom you have not even inquired."

"Ha, you saucy brat, who would speak of mama in times like this? Go, you pin-feather hero—help the old woman cook her tea! Who think of wife and child when such giants like Crockett and Jim Bowie fall? Who would think of kitchen affairs when the hell-hounds, the Mexicans, aim to bring the

---

[19] "Evans" is likely Maj. Robert Evans, the master of ordinance. "Paw" may refer to Capt. John J. Baugh, the adjutant of the Alamo garrison.

red cock into our midst? But we'll give it to them. Damn it, they shall have it. Jim Bowie, my old boy . . . have fallen in honor . . . are great forever. All of you, old comrades, are gone, are happy. But the old Jack from San Augustine is still here, and is weeping bloody tears. Yes, you old comrades, Jack is weeping blood, and Jack is thirsting for blood. Blood is his rallying-cry; either the blood of your murderers or mine must flow."

Great tears ran down the cheeks of the old hunter as he sat poking into the fire. None of his sons nor any of his listeners dared to try to stem the relieving stream.

Finally, after a while the old man began to read the second letter, which Travis had written on the third day of March.

"The enemy has continued his incessant cannonading to the present time and surrounded us on all sides with fortified positions. However, thirty-two men from Gonzales have stolen into us and my couriers have passed out and in.

"I have this place fortified so that the walls are ball proof and am strengthening them with earth walls. We have been lucky enough not to lose a man, but have killed many of the enemy. We have now fought for ten days against a force estimated from fifteen hundred to two thousand effective men. A reinforcement of approximately two thousand men is now moving into the town. And judging by the general cheering, Santa Anna himself must have arrived.

"Colonel Fannin is said to be on the way with reinforcements for us. Unfortunately, I fear that this is not true, as my several appeals to him for aid have remained unanswered. From the colonies alone I am expecting help, and without its speedy arrival, I will have to fight the enemy regardless of the consequences. I trust that my countrymen will not lose courage in this hour of death. If they themselves should fall a victim to the vengeance of a barbaric enemy, this one shall cost the enemy more than a defeat. God and Texas! Victory or Death!

"The Convention must declare our independence. Then we will know for what we are fighting, and the world will understand us. If our independence is not declared soon, my men and I will lay down our arms. But under the flag of independence we are willing to risk our lives daily and to resist the monster, who is fighting us under the red flag and is threatening to murder all prisoners and to convert Texas into a desert. I will have to fight the enemy at his bidding and am ready to do so. If my fellow countrymen do not come to my support, my bleaching bones shall be an eternal reproach to them. With five hundred reinforcements I would drive the enemy back over the Rio Grande and reverse the vengeance against the enemies of Texas regardless of whether they are inhabitants of it or not. All, who are not for us, are against us. The government should declare them enemies of the land, or it will act as murderer against itself."

"Women!" constantly mumbled a voice of a man about six feet high and stout, who walked through the rows of fires with a grey, broad-brimmed, kinked-up felt hat pressed down on his face.

Yellow leather trousers and high-water boots dressed the lower part of the gigantic figure while a Cherokee hunting shirt with fringes hung over his shoulders. And a rather long vest, reaching well down to the hips and buttoned halfway up, added a quiet dignity to the figure that not even his enemies could deny. The collar and bosom ruffle of his fine linen shirt hung crumpled up out of his vest, and the white throat and chest formed a sharp contrast with his brown, although friendly, facial features. But now his brow was laid in powerful folds and with a morose expression and arms crossed on his back Old Sam—it was he—walked through the camp. Working out plans, he walked up and down and did not hear the report that the Mexican cavalry had arrived on the other side of the river.

As he returned, the old planter was just reading the last lines of the letter, and a "How, man?" he growled forth. "How can you now read so quietly? Have you no feeling, man? Every line, every word tears and rakes like a dagger in my heart, man, and you read as if it afforded you pleasure. Speak it with such emphasis as if it were fiction, man! Ha, must Sam Houston have such men in his army. Hadn't expected it. All our healthy young men dead! Their blood cries from heaven for vengeance, and here you sit and don't give a damn!"

In a rage the old planter from San Augustine sprang up before Sam Houston and, gnashing his teeth, broke the silence with the words: "Halt, Halt! Not another word! Not another word! Outrageous liar! Outrageous liar! Who dares to say even now that Jack has no feelings? Who dares?"

"I! I! Sam Houston said it!"

"It is a damn lie! I say," answered the planter, out of himself.

"And who dares to call Sam Houston a liar to his face, who dares it? Who?"

The old general, who had not looked at his opponent in his rage, now fixed his stark, protruding eyes on those of old Jack. Piercing glances shot back and forth. And with arms directed backward and clinched fists, the two gigantic figures stood opposed to each other. Neither breathed. Nobody, not even the militia itself that had gathered in a circle about the two, dared to interrupt the pause with even a syllable. But the clinched fists dropped, the stark eyes began to sparkle anew, the rage changed into sorrow and "Jack!" said the one.

"General!" the other.

The hands fell into each other, and they shook heartily. Again the tears ran over the cheeks of the old planter. But the old general, as morose as before, walked his usual way through the surprised militia with his hands crossed on his back. After a while the General had disappeared in his tent, but his gigantic mind worked as usual with astonishing cold-bloodedness.

Order after order flew into the colonies, to Fannin, to the National Assembly, to the States and to his own men.

In a short time, the light artillery of the Texans drove the Mexican cavalry far out of reach. It enlivened the discouraged militia.

"Remember the Alamo!" was heard from every direction. The folding of the tents and the packing up of articles of the soldiers of the little army proceeded rapidly in order to break camp speedily for the Colorado, there to assemble the whole military force of the Republic and then to destroy the enemy.

"Sam Houston is himself again!" cried the troops as they marched away. With the cannon in the lead, they marched off to the Colorado forests, where they arrived late in the evening of March 11.

Here Houston pitched his camp in the hope that after the latest news the hitherto tardy citizens would hasten to his standard. Heretofore people had regarded the Mexicans as too contemptible to be accorded any attention; but after such a deed was committed, everybody could see that only the speediest general cooperation would save the Republic.

The Texans threw off their apathy, but in spite of their general uprising, the army did not increase in the least. In fact, it dwindled down to an insignificant mass as the citizens who composed the army at Gonzales were obliged to leave the colors to take their families over the Brazos to safety. Then who could with certainty foretell the results of the first battle?

The General had deluded himself, and his only hope was to obstruct the passage of the enemy over the Colorado until the returning citizens and Colonel Fannin, who had received repeated orders for an immediate retreat, had united with him, and then to make a sudden attack on the main division of the army of the enemy that was rushing forward, which was divided into three divisions, and cut off the other two divisions from Mexico.

On the Colorado

BY THE TWENTY-FIFTH OF MARCH the army had increased to thirteen hundred men, but one dispatch after another with terrible news had called forth a murderous spirit among them. The murder of Grant and his men, of Johnson's detachment, of Captain King's, the inexplicable disappearance of Ward, who was wandering around somewhere in the wild prairie,

Horton's final report of the capture, for which Fannin himself was to blame, together with the fall of the Alamo, called forth such a rage among the backwoodsmen that only a Sam Houston was able to lead them.

The old general sat on a stack of saddles with several letters and a map of the former province of Texas before him, and the captains sat or stood propped on their rifles in a circle surrounding a large fire. Behind this group in dense masses were the murmuring backwoodsmen.

The captains wore civilian clothing of various kinds, and the black eyes of these tall vigorous figures averaging six feet high flashed first at the glowing coals and then at old Sam, who was the only composed person in the whole group.

Slowly he took a small knife from his vest pocket, opened it, brought forth a powerful piece of real Cavendish, cut off a quid, shoved it between his front teeth and his upper lip and passed the remainder to his neighbor, a powerful captain, whose upper part of the body was also covered with an Indian hunting shirt. The broad brim of a former extra fine beaver flopped down over his ears, and from the feet to the knees his muscular limbs were wrapped with thick, crimson-colored flannel as is the custom among the inhabitants of the western part of America and a very practical protection in Texas against the thorns of the mesquite trees. His ammunition pouch was made from the scalp of a pretty leopard skin. The eyes, being finished with red cloth, considerably enhanced the beauty of the pelt. It hung on the brown, untanned deerskin belt that lay close around the strong figure on account of the weight of the pouch. With a bitter expression the one described passed the black tobacco from hand to hand, but not one served himself, which was evidence of a very unusual mental disturbance.

After the tobacco had made the round, the old general put it back into his pocket and, whittling, continued the conference; he was so cool, so composed as a man is in the habit of being with a person whom he has met the first time in his life.

"I tell you," proceeded the General, "our situation is somewhat precarious — cannot deny it — but it is the only thing that will bring our people to reason. Santa Anna will destroy the colonies, but it is not Sam Houston's fault. Instead of coming together promptly, the militia remains nicely at home with the women, very comfortably at the chimney fire, thinking that a few volunteers can fight it out with ten thousand of these half-breeds. Missed it gentlemen, missed it. See it — the brave boys are gone, a shame for us, and the enemy is on our heels. Instead of four thousand of our men being here, there are thirteen hundred, gentlemen. The others are packing up, taking long pleasure rides to the Sabine. We cannot help it, comrades, we will have to retreat again into the timbers of the Brazos. We must move on, on, even today."

"Halt, General, those are idle words," cried one with a cap made of a wildcat skin, "Not a step from here—the enemy must soon be here, and then we will give him such a glorious whipping that it will be a pleasure for every right-thinking person to give it to the miserable vampires."

"To Battle! To Battle!" cried the crowd surrounding the conference. "Here for Texas or never!"

"Sam Houston is not of that opinion, my braves," answered the General, "nor is it his will. Sam will not risk the fate of the whole republic on the exigencies of a single battle here. Five-mile wide forests of the Brazos shall render us splendid service. Even if you are gallant and are willing to risk your lives, the interests of our country are not served if you are killed. No, my boys, we will yield this site to the grasshoppers as surely as Sam Houston is standing in his own boots."

"It is impossible for us to retreat further, General," said another. "Will not do, it will not do. We must fight. Why, General, our richest settlements lie between the Colorado and the Brazos. The old Austin would turn in his grave if he could hear the tramp of these murderous bands across the prairie. No, General, we must fight, must either win or die."

"Must either win or die!" came the muffled refrain from the two circles. But the old general whittled quietly on and seemed determined to win the victory in his own camp first.

"Boys," he addressed himself to the crowd, stood up, took another quid, closed his knife and began, "Boys, you want to fight—very praiseworthy. Your courage is in fact very praiseworthy. But suppose the enemy with his large amount of artillery should win, can you, will you, assume the responsibility? Can you assume the responsibility for having sought a battle before our somewhat tardy fellow citizens were in position to hasten to our reinforcement? Would you take it on your conscience if the Republic fell back under the Mexican yoke because an undisciplined crowd would not await a favorable moment for the battle? No. No, citizens, we must move back to the Brazos, where our men can tender good service with their rifles without risking much themselves. If we attack the five times stronger enemy here, we will have to storm him in the open prairie.

"I assuredly do not doubt what you call your courage, which, however, is pure foolhardiness. I am accountable to the Republic, to the whole people, for what I do. I can never consent to fight here. Once more, I call on you to follow me to San Felipe, and he who wishes the best for the Republic, be ready in one hour. We may expect the main force of the enemy any moment on the opposite bank, while a detachment of cavalry by no means negligible has already reached the Colorado above us. And General Urrea with practically two thousand cannot be far from here down toward the seacoast. And so, another time: for the densely wooded valley of the Brazos!"

The old general walked off to his tent, and the crowd, ill-tempered and mumbling discontent, also went back to the fires and began polishing the guns. But in one and one-half hours the Texan army vacated the camp on the Colorado.

Sam Houston had won, and on the next evening he arrived at San Felipe. He, however, did not stop there but marched up the river.

On the 30th of March the first enemy cavalry appeared near San Felipe, which lies directly on the Brazos. The inhabitants set fire to their stores and warehouses and fled across the river. Barely had they departed before the enemy moved in. He flew into a rage when he found only burning buildings instead of rich booty.

Houston now disappeared and his enemies could not determine his location until he appeared suddenly like the messenger of Nemesis on the arena of war and refuted the false and low-down accusations of the enemies of Texas that he was fleeing from fear. This could be done only by those who did not have the slightest conception of the General's character or by the armed or masked enemies of the Republic. But from both sides it sounded as convincing as when one would say that the Bengal tiger was fleeing from a dozen barking dogs.

It is still a puzzle to me how the General succeeded another time in persuading those independent spirits to retreat from the Brazos to the Buffalo Bayou. I am fully convinced that only a Sam Houston could do so—no other man in the Republic could.

The Amnesty

URREA SAT MUSING IN HIS TENT, great plans crossing through his mind. Santa Anna had risen so high. Why shouldn't Urrea, who needed to take just one more step to grasp the helm of the government by force, not be in position to bring the Mexicans under his banner? Were they not accustomed for centuries to be governed by the rod and the sword, just like another great body-politic of this kind comfortably holds its masses together with the lash? But he had done a foolish thing, the Señor saw that now. He should have protected Fannin's men against Santa Anna, and he would have won the sympathy of the Texans in the highest degree by such humane procedure. But everything was not lost yet. He could still do a little, he calculated, to redeem himself again with the Texans. Santa Anna had so often changed his color that he should rather be called the Mexican chameleon than the Napoleon of the West. Urrea, therefore, suddenly decided to become exceedingly humane and began to treat the Texan prisoners, approximately twenty-eight men—carpenters, who had been saved from death to build bridges—very well. Their rations were larger and better than those of the soldiers. I later became quartermaster at Matagorda, and there were more changes.

But a big, tall Yankee incognito suggested a singular plan to him. Doctor Harrison, in whose narrow-shouldered figure and Lord's-prayer face the gigantic and ever active spirit of the Yankee Nation lived, asserted that a truer Buckeye never traveled through the States than the Doctor Harrison standing before us. He said that his father, the old general Harrison, soon expected to become president of the Union; that his party aimed to take the field with the catchy slogan of Log Cabin and Hard Cider against the metallic silver system of Jackson, Van Buren and Company.

Urrea also was on the side of the apple cider drinkers and log cabiners, at least so long as he was a public servant. He pledged himself, as long as Harrison, Clay and Company would do so, to drink nothing but hard cider and, like the most menial son of Mexico, to live in a block house and to wear trousers and jacket of ordinary linen.

But after the victory he expected, just like the above-named firm, namely the rag factory of Harrison, Clay and Company, to consign the hard cider and log cabins to the workmen and country folks, the so-called democrats, who are characterized as locofocos[20] in the territory of Uncle Sam.

In other words, we noticed that General Urrea had plans that were to be pursued, if not at the present, at some time in the future. We will also see how the would-be-son of the old would-be-president showed the would-be-no-telling-what Urrea a Yankee trick by which the disguised doctor aimed to use both parties.

This hero was found by the Mexican cavalry in the valley of the Guadalupe River Valley and was at first cuffed about after regular Mexican fashion, but after a little while he succeeded in winning the favor of Urrea. He was in fact a very

---

[20] A faction of the Democratic Party.

peculiar individual, and up to the present time his appearance in the prairies has been a riddle.

That he was not the son of the old General Harrison has long been proven. But why he wandered around alone in the wild west and who he was is yet to be solved. That he it was who persuaded Urrea to issue a proclamation to the citizens of Texas in which a general amnesty was promised, we know.

That Urrea expected attractive results, in spite of Santa Anna's proclamation to the same effect that had been contemptuously rejected by the colonies, is also known to us; and it was later reported to us that the Yankee doctor was finally sent with a large bundle of Mexican magnanimity and love to the rebels, with which he presented the many offers, calling their attention to the large, confidence-inspiring seal of Urrea.

The Yankee speculated in every direction. If things would not go one way, they would probably go another, and words as sweet as honey flowed from the lips of the Doctor.

"Yes, gentlemen," he began, addressing himself to a group of young colonists who were the first ones that he met with his mission, "this Urrea is a big-hearted soul." He paused a moment to take a breath.

"Surely! I think he is," said a colonist.

"Fine pretenses that you parade before us," added another.

"I have a desire to swear allegiance to his flag," contributed a third.

"I think Jonathan Harrison must be making good profits—good business this—isn't it, Harrison?" asked another.

"Is not our honored friend one of those fellows that deal in wooden nutmegs?" asked a deep bass voice.

"Or a cypress-ham manufacturer?" another.

"Or does the gentleman come from the clock-makers craft, who make such pretty clocks that they can be hung on the wall only for ornamental purposes, those that we need not wind up as they indicate the time as well when they are run down as when they are wound up?"

"Yes!" interrupted a Mississippian, "Old Dan, our neighbor, had one of these would-be clocks. It would indicate the hour only when the hand was moved to the proper figure on the dial."

"Or, Jonathan Harrison, do you possibly belong to the factory that sells these shoes? Peculiar manufacturing, peculiar manufacturer, these Yankees did not walk an hour, gone are the heels—completely gone, Jack," said a young Kentuckian, who stood nearly seven feet tall, not counting the heels in the shoes that were so easily damaged.

Harrison was surprised that the wind now suddenly blew against him, while his well-thought-out speech seemed to have such good effect on the simple backwoodsmen at the beginning,

A few times he tried to interrupt them and give the situation another turn, but the strong voices of his former auditors would not give him an opportunity.

"Why," said one in the meeting, "suppose, boys, we let our honored friend here ride off in triumph?"

"Ride, Jack? Oh, I understand—ride on a rail."

"Hurrah for the rail!" they all cried, "let's see how the Yankee-delegate from Mexico can ride."

The Doctor made a very miserable face. Riding had never been his hobby, and now he experienced a distinct repulsion for this art, because it was usually followed with a tar and feather operation or at least with a few gentle dips in the

THE AMNESTY

next convenient stream or tank. Long he pled with and assured his executioners, and promised them that he would disappear at once if they would let him off this time. But all was of no avail. A strong eighteen-foot-long rail was brought up by two young athletes, while several hacked off cross-sticks with their Bowie knives on which the rail was to rest.

The Doctor, who now saw that no amount of pleading would save him from his ride, stepped up more boldly and said that he would just as soon ride on a wooden horse as on one put together of flesh and bones.

"Damn it, I don't give a damn for it, but you are low-down dogs to gang up on a well-meaning person like this. You want to fight for right and freedom, and yet you blame me for reading something to you from the enemy in which this child really was not in earnest. Damn you! The Doctor will fix you all yet—mark you that."

With every explosion of the Doctor the backwoodsmen would reply with a "Go it, Jonathan Harrison."

"That fellow has more spunk than I thought," said one in the laughing crowd. "Suppose we let him run—he may move off with his proclamation. Boys, run this off-breed Yankee across the Brazos—he will not proclaim any more. You can depend on it. Do it to please me, boys; I am a Yankee myself, y'know. I have never dealt in hams and clocks nor in wooden nutmegs."

During this time the Doctor had pushed himself off to the side, and now walked off with long strides through the tall grass, pondering deeply over the depravity of the human race and declaring that less business could be done with this rabble of miserable Texans than the ragged Mexicans.

He was large for a Yankee, and if he really was not one, as he said, he nevertheless had the genius for driving sharp bargains that really would have done honor to a "down-easter."

Through one of his tricks he got out of Urrea's imprisonment and by another one he evaded the unpleasantness of a lynch operation, by playing the bold and brave role when his pleadings would not help. He knew how to take the backwoodsmen on their weak side by his boldness.

The Doctor X, as we may call him, disappeared and no one ever heard who he was, what he was, where he went to, or from whence he came.

The March to Matagorda

WHEN IT CAME TO CULTIVATING THE SOIL, the Mexicans could not deny that the *carajo* Americanos were entirely different creatures from the Mexican planters. The plantation of the average Mexican (presupposing that he had one, which is only seldom the case) consists of a few hundred corn stalks among which a forest of weeds nestle, and only seldom does one see the yellow face of a squash shine through. A family's whole field can usually be covered with their blankets, and it is mainly the occupation of the wife to cultivate the field, to sow and to harvest. This is an old custom of the Mexicans that goes back to their Indian ancestry. With their conversion to Catholicism, they threw away the noble customs of the ancient Indians and took on the worst and most sinful habits of civilization.

The Mexican officers had not seen as much land in cultivation during a whole day on their great journeys as practically every planter here in Texas had already fenced in.

The cotton fields of a few plantations on the left side of the Navidad stretched practically for miles among the primitive forests that border the stream. It is a splendid region, and the plantation of Colonel Sutherland, where the army camped for the night, is especially favorably located in the bend of the river, whose course one can only surmise by the dark forests that everywhere enclose it. The residence of Colonel Sutherland was, like all others that I had encountered since my flight, deserted, and on the arrival of Urrea's troops, the poultry fled frightened into the forest or into the immense cotton fields, which was a great fortune for the feathered world, for otherwise not a trace of them would have remained in evidence very long.

On the second evening after we had left the Navidad, we arrived at the Colorado, whose swollen and red-colored waters pressed their way down to Matagorda Bay. The colonists had here also, as on the Guadalupe, either destroyed all boats or concealed them in the forests, and only after endless planning and trying did Urrea succeed, with the aid of the Texan prisoners, in getting the army across the river in four or five days, which the unnerved half-Indians would never have succeeded in doing with the river at high water.

The prisoners had expected to strike at least a few hundred Texans here to obstruct Urrea's passage, a work that one hundred men could have done. But we didn't then know that the Mexican armies had already crossed the Colorado fifty miles further up and were on their way to the Brazos. Consequently, it would have been foolhardiness to venture that far among the enemies. Meanwhile Urrea was much concerned.

For two days after we had crossed the stream, our course was down toward the coast along the luxuriant edge of the forests. We constantly had the stream only a few miles away to our right. It ran through a primeval forest more than a mile wide. From the timber great arms ran out in right angles and acute points into the immense prairie that extended on our left to the forests of Caney Creek and the San Bernard.

The further we penetrated into the colonies, the scarcer did the herds of cattle become, because the planters here had

had more time to take at least this part of their property to safety, although an immense number were still to be found in this immeasurable maze of nature.

A halt was made a mile this side of Matagorda, and General Urrea, who was usually the last one in breaking camp in the morning, galloped by us with his bodyguard of dragoons to determine the cause of the sudden halt. As he sped by me, he called out laughingly: "The Texans, my little Prussian!"

I had, in fact, hopes that the ironic call would be true. At least I expected that the citizens would give the enemy a fight before they would leave the town. But I was mistaken. After a halt for hours, the spies returned and reported that everything was safe. Later I learned that the Texans had placed a scarecrow with a musket in its arms on the flat top of a house, and this had the impudence to check Urrea's whole glorious division.

Since it was now known that not a person was in town, everybody went boldly and hurriedly forward, as large quantities of food and drink probably awaited them. The officers were already rejoicing over the booty that was to move off to the Rio Grande.

Matagorda

MATAGORDA IS A LITTLE TOWN of several hundred very lovely houses that are usually one-story and painted white. The dull blue or even flat red roofs and pretty green window frames of the generally new and elegant buildings present an appearance of neatness and the town has an atmosphere of friendliness that can be found only in the new world. The surrounding country is extraordinarily pretty. An immense green, treeless, undulating plain rolls away from behind the town toward the northwest until in the far distance it reaches the horizon, whose majestic arch seems to rest upon it. Great herds of deer here graze on the prolific meadows, and wolves and jackals chase about on the prairie in broad daylight without disturbing the other denizens of the wilderness. Before us waved and roared the mighty waters of Matagorda Bay, and as far as the eye could reach toward the northeast and southwest, we could see the dark basin moving in the wind and the muffled tumbling of the surf. Only a solitary, small stripe on the southeastern horizon, which would look more like a grey sheet of fog to the eye unaccustomed to the sea than a forty-two-mile-long peninsula, protects the mass of water before us, known by the name of Matagorda Bay, from the main bosom of the Gulf of Mexico, which is so terrible during a storm. Countless numbers of buffalo, redfish, sheepheads and other fish could be seen in the waters. Even the tumbler showed himself, and not infrequently could one see the fins of the greedy shark projecting out of the water. Oyster banks of the finest kinds reached out for miles in these waters, and flocks of pelicans, snipes, ducks, swans, coots and other varieties of the feathered species would sing and cry wildly along the coast as the wanderer walked along the sandy beach that the waves had built here. To the rear and somewhat to the west of the town flowed the Colorado, which was alive with fish, alligators, and turtles. A mile further down it mixed with the saltwater of the bay. Its dark forests extend up the valley in a northwesterly direction and project about six miles out into the great prairie. They then follow up the course of the stream that rushes down from the distant mountains in the west, and completely obstruct the view to the other side toward the Lavaca.

The first bend of the river forms a sharp angle of about fifty degrees with the bay, and not quite a mile from the point lies the town, whose outer edge is bordered with a bayou which, at the same time, cuts off a considerable part of the corner near the point. It empties into the bay but reaches within a few hundred yards of the Colorado.

The detached piece of land is low and swampy and is a favorite camping ground of the Caranchuas, who frequently pitch their camps here, as the fish and game here offer them food in abundance. But at the arrival of the troops the redskins had disappeared, as this general, whom they had aided in the battle against Fannin and from whom they could with justice ask for a part of the booty, instead of giving them justice, had six of the best warriors of this tribe hanged, and only after the hangmen had marched away were they permitted to rescue the bodies of their brothers and friends from the vultures and to bring them safely to the hunting grounds of their fathers.

It was about an hour before midnight when I made this round with Holzinger, who was in charge for the night. Pale as silver the moon floated over the dark forest from which the melancholy calls of the whippoorwill could be heard, and a wild chaos and muffled thunder—the hollow mumbling of the armored alligators—rolled over to us from the Colorado. Not a human voice was heard except the *quien vive* that the sentinels called out to us.

The quiet night in a camp during wartime always calls forth sentimental thoughts when one considers that any moment may be the end of one's life. This, combined with the beauty of nature about us, the muffled murmuring of the distant bay, the magic moon hanging on the blue vault, had made Holzinger first pensive and then talkative. The fine large plantations, the neat, pleasing houses that indicated a never-resting people in this splendid luxury, the budding industry of a young land, such as the people of the most densely populated part of Mexico could not imagine, made Holzinger rebellious against his own principles. He knew that he could only boldly trust me, that I was still for the independence of Texas with my whole soul, that I cherished sanguine hopes for our army that were so active in me that Holzinger himself began to believe in the ultimate victory of the Texans, in spite of the latest dispatches from Santa Anna, which really were not very comforting to us men of freedom. He reported that the old Tennessean had disappeared with his horde and that he had probably fled to the domains of the States. He had, therefore, dispatched six hundred men to Nacogdoches to constitute the garrison there.

The Colonel admitted that Texas deserved the name of Eldorado, as it is called in Mexico, and was charmed over the way the country looked. He considered Texas much more charming than the State of Vera Cruz, where his large but unimproved landed estates were, and said frankly, but in suppressed tones, that he would just as willingly serve the Texans as Santa Anna if they would give him the same rank that he held in the Mexican army and would give him reasonable compensation for his thirty leagues of land that he would naturally lose.

Hastily I seized the idea of depriving Santa Anna of a follower and began to explain to him the condition of my country. He was, however, aristocratically minded from the roots up, and my description changed his inclinations. He preferred to continue serving Santa Anna rather than to live with a people that would not respect him any more than any other carpenter. Since he had now become very talkative, which, by the way, was one of his weaknesses, he honored me with his confidence. He told me the story of his whole life, and I found correctly that he had had much misfortune, especially in family affairs. When his wife arrived from Germany, she immediately took passage for herself and her whole family with the exception of the eldest son on a returning vessel and left Mexico for Germany an hour after her arrival. Another woman in the city of Mexico, who was running a large millinery business and whom he fervently loved, ran off with the escort whom he had sent to bring her to the wedding, and nothing further was ever heard of the fugitives. Consequently, the Colonel was obliged to seek his happiness at some other place. However, he was always completely rejected in all of his amours, but, as he said, for his own benefit, as he now had prospects of becoming really happy. A high mining official, a nobleman from the Harz mountains, had promised him his foster daughter, a real angel. After we had returned to our house, he read her whole correspondence to me, as she had already written him several letters. Only a girl of highest education and finest feelings could have written such letters. The letters also of the foster mother of this angel indicated such a splendid person, such a refined spirit, that I inwardly regretted to see her thrown into the arms of a person of such inconsequential character.

I now knew his whole life, and I now stood a powerful step nearer to him than before. For an hour I had been only a listener, because I did not wish to call him out of his realm of fantasy, but as I was very sleepy, I had to let him know that I was human. Well he might have wondered that I could feel inclined to sleep with such pictorial portrayals of his imagination.

The next day was a noisy one. Long trains of loaded pack-mules carried the booty of the general and the officers away to Matamoras in order to have their share in safety in case of a bad turn, as they did not trust the quietness. The most valuable of the large magazines of my republican fellow-citizens of Matagorda were plundered in their order by the officers of the enemy. One circle after another received that permission and great quantities of wares wandered off to the Rio Grande.

Two days later Urrea moved with his division to the Brazos. A garrison of four hundred men remained with Holzinger at Matagorda to construct a fort. I decided to remain there also. Practically all the Texan prisoners remained there to work on the fortification. On the next morning, as was often the case, we witnessed a general infliction of corporal punishment upon the defenders of the fatherland because some of the men had presumed to steal sugar. But in order to avoid a misunderstanding, I must observe that they were not castigated for the stealing. That is an offense that is not taken so seriously if the thief is not so simple as to put his hands on the belongings of the officers or Catholic priests. Here this was the case. Sugar was a very rare article in Matagorda. And what would become of the official corps, if this article should give out? This offense required an exemplary punishment, and its infliction took place in the usual interesting manner for the spectators. The hands of the offender were well tied together and the loop thus formed was hung over a Mexican wonder, a six-foot-tall, carob-tree-like non-commissioned officer. Half negro and half Indian, this righteous citizen of Mexico, who, in spite of his height, had an indescribable aversion to the work of war, was lassoed like a buffalo and immediately brought along to Texas, where he now filled his honorable position.

It was, in fact, really amusing to see the little hero wiggle on the back of the bony man while another one, also a dignitary, strained his arms to whip a half dozen sticks to pieces on the back of the first one.

Another plot was nipped over a half-dozen wine bottles whose contents were being thoroughly enjoyed. Holzinger and several lieutenants almost fainted when they discovered the merry revel. Even the guard, who was supposed to protect the contents of the house, was sitting cleverly with his companions.

A crashing thunder of *carajos*, etc., tore the surprised drinking-bout out of its hilarity, and a terrible vengeance was to be taken on the thieves who had the temerity to drink wine. Wine, this heavenly gift, the Master certainly did not let grow for the plebeians.

But it soon developed that proceedings against this nobility were suspended. Soon the poor devils began to stoop far over and to make very unpleasant faces. A frightful vomiting set in, and suddenly awful cursing followed in all parts of the camp. Many provisions were thrown away as it was generally said that the damn Yankees had poisoned the food, and only with fear were small particles eaten.

As I examined the emptied bottles, it evidently was wine that they had drunk, and I could barely suppress my laughing when I read the words "Antimony Wine."[21] I, however, remained silent, as I calculated that it would be of considerable benefit to the Texans, since the Mexicans would eat only as much as was absolutely necessary.

Next morning the fellows were out of danger but very weak, and they swore never to touch another drop. That they had not kept their vow, however, I discovered on the fifth day when one of the patriots was so thoroughly befogged that he could not dance the fandango but tumbled to the floor probably five times in a few minutes.

---

[21] Wine laced with a small amount of the chemical element antimony as an emetic to induce vomiting.

San Jacinto

SANTA ANNA, WHO REGARDED THE WAR as practically finished, marched carelessly through the unfamiliar country. Fire and plundering accompanied him through the colonies. He had just pillaged and burnt Harrisburg, a little town on the Buffalo Bayou, when the Texans under General Houston marched up unobserved on the opposite side of the bayou with the positive determination to set a limit to the monster.

Houston's hopes to assemble a large army about him were not realized. As more plantations were left behind him, more strong arms were called from his army to take their families across the border to safety. The roads of the Republic were alive with caravans of women and children who were fleeing from the bloodthirsty enemy to the Sabine.

The Napoleon of the West did not know that Old Sam was close around him. Neither did he suspect that a backwoodsman had captured his courier to General Filisola, who was on the Brazos with approximately thirty-five hundred men. The courier and dispatches were brought into Houston's camp. The dispatches contained Santa Anna's campaign plans and indicated the route that he expected to take in order to destroy the last traces of the heretics.

Barely were the dispatches read before the plans of the Texans were formulated. "Now is the time or never!" cried all the men as with one voice. "The usurper or Texas must now fall. Not another step backwards. Forward! We are strong enough. We are men. We know what we are fighting for. Our God will be with us" and the like was heard throughout the volunteer army.

No man could have stemmed this tide, not even a Houston. But fortunately the Texas Oak this time agreed with the colonial army.

"Forward!" It thundered through the troops.

On the 19th of April he crossed Buffalo Bayou to occupy a favorable position near Lynchburg, which, according to his dispatches, Santa Anna intended to conquer.

The troops lay in a well-protected position in the forest near the bayou and behind a rise in the ground. They were not noticed by the enemy on their arrival on the 20th until they greeted him with a discharge of grapeshot from two six-pounders; whereupon he hastily drew back to await the arrival of General Cos with five hundred men and a twelve-pounder. To the surprise of the Texans, Cos arrived the next morning.

Deaf Smith had stymied Urrea's division for quite a while on the Brazos, especially at the arrival of the Mexicans at Brazoria, in that with only his rifle from the opposite bank, he prevented Urrea's whole division from getting water or watering their horses for several hours. He shot everyone down that his bullets could reach.

This ever-to-be-remembered patriot, in company with several volunteers, here passed around Santa Anna's troops, and eight miles from the place where the fate of the young republic was to be decided, destroyed a bridge on Houston's order, the only one that the Mexicans had to cross a stream that wended its way down through the prairie in case they were beaten by Houston.

Their retreat was cut off without the enemy knowing it. Santa Anna had taken position several hundred yards from Houston. His right wing rested on a prairie island, and the remainder of his troops stretched in a straight line down to the San Jacinto River, which a short distance further up receives the waters of the Buffalo Bayou.[22]

The army of the western Napoleon was busy cooking its afternoon coffee and roasting beef when Old Sam and his men suddenly came storming over the elevation that had hitherto concealed them. Mirabeau B. Lamar with sixty cavalry men attacked the left wing and the advancing artillery sent its grapeshot at the right wing. During the same time the whole center of the backwoodsmen advanced in a double quick time on the astonished Mexicans, who, however, let their copper bullets fly. But the advancing forces were not to be confused. Without firing a shot, they went directly to their goal across the open prairie. And at a distance of about twenty steps, when they could see the white of the enemies' eyes, they fired their first volley. They then turned their guns, and with the butts high in the sky, and with glittering Bowie knives, they charged forward with the battle cry of "Remember the Alamo!"

"Revenge, fearful revenge!" thundered on every side, and the destructive masses joyfully shouted a wild chaos of names—father, brother, friends, fellow countrymen. As the tiger thrusts his fangs into the lion killed in battle and tears

---

[22] In fact, the left wing of Santa Anna's army was away from the river and the right wing was closest to the river. To their rear was a marsh and a lake; ahead was a low ridge that separated the Mexicans from the Texans.

him to pieces, so the raging backwoodsmen now cut the enemy to pieces with their dripping Bowie knives, a hand wide and practically two feet long. Their pistols smashed the heads or the hearts of the Mexicans that were lying on their knees and begging for mercy, "No mercy—no mercy—death! Remember the Alamo! Fannin's blood is crying down from heaven!" shouted the raging ones to them, and stroke after stroke, shot after shot crashed down the enemy that was now fleeing in every direction. In vain Santa Anna shouted to his fleeing forces, in vain he struck down the first to flee, but everything was of no avail. The whole mass rolled away in confusion with death on their heels. There was no halting, no reflecting. Everything, everything stampeded frantically away, out into the endless prairie, and the cowardly fleeing ones fell scattered under the hands of the practically inhuman backwoodsmen. Several officers fled in full speed from the grim reaper and Santa Anna also seized his splendid warhorse and swept like a cyclone over the prairie toward the Brazos.

The tumult of battle rolled off toward the place where the bridge over the stream had been destroyed. An adjutant is the first to plunge into the flood that rushes to Galveston Bay—his noble animal struggles and pants, it is about to sink, the rider throws himself into the water, a good swimmer, he and the horse swim forward a distance. Again the horse staggers, it breathes heavily, it snorts, the eyes begin to pop out. It lets its limbs drop limply, and suddenly the dagger of the rider is thrust into the throat of the sinking horse. The noble steed once more lunges wildly upward, the blood rushes from the mouth, another time it frantically tries to reach the shore and another time it is about to sink, but solid bottom is reached, and trembling and panting it walks slowly to the shore. A minute of rest and the rider mounted the still panting horse and rode off slowly to the appearing forests in the southwest. Other officers stand on the bank and shudder—and hesitate—no one is willing to risk such a terrible battle. Now they see a single rider about a mile back speeding toward them, and still further in the distance one can see the dark masses of the fleeing infantry and their pursuers. The officers forget the battle with the waves and plunge in. They move forward, but only a short distance. The current washes them out into the bay, their horses weaken, the riders jump off like the adjutant, they pierce the already-dying horses. It does no good. Farther and farther they go out into the restless elements, in vain they fight against the wet death, the noble horses disappear, the riders still calling for help or cursing follow them, both a repast for the sharks.

A single rider sweeps up—it is our Napoleon himself. He wants to plunge into the floods, but he sees the disappearance of the officers. Shuddering, he turns his horse, he springs off, he lets his horse run, and he himself disappears from the bank into the prairie.

The floods had briefly hummed away over those that had disappeared when the black cloud of the panting infantry stormed in consternation to the wet grave. Not a shot was heard any more, only distressed and confused cries for help from the dwindled and unarmed foot-soldiers. They plunged into the water to escape the still thirsting Bowie knife. Many looked at the opposite bank and endeavored to reach it. Even those who had never known how to swim entrusted themselves to the water, but the waves closed in over them and carried them out into the bay to their companions.

The remainder soon stood in the water up to their necks, clinging to one another to keep the current from carrying them away. But from time to time those on the outer rim would disappear, tearing away a few of their companions to the halls of death.[23]

A few of the backwoodsmen stood on the bank and fired into the despairing mass with their pistols. Others went into the water with swinging rifle-butts, and still others rushed forward with their horrible, dripping knives in order to utterly destroy all that had any part in the murder of their father, brother or friend in the west.

But blood enough had been shed. A higher power wanted to save the wretches in order that they might tell their brown brothers beyond the Rio Grande the frightful story of the Battle of San Jacinto.

Orders were issued to discontinue the killing, but it was difficult to soften the raging colonists—they had made up their minds to stop only with the last Mexican. Several Texan officers who had just come up brought them again to reason, and "Pardon!" finally sounded from all lips. The Mexicans, more dead than alive, came out on the bank and fell trembling on their knees. They were, however, immediately dragged from this position so repulsive to a free man and sent to the camp under a light guard.

But imagine the disappointment of Houston's troops the next morning. The arch-enemy, the black murderer! Santa Anna was missing. They raged about, and as the thought that

---

[23] The scene at the destroyed bridge, with Mexican troops being swept from a surging bayou into the bay, is great drama but not great history. Most Mexican troops were pushed back across marshes into Peggy's Lake (aka McCormick's Lake), where they were sitting ducks for the Texans, but they would not have been swept into any bay. Other Mexican soldiers fled to the west below Buffalo Bayou, where they would have eventually come up against Sims Bayou more than ten miles to the west. That is where most current scholarship places Vince's Bridge, which was destroyed by Deaf Smith. The bayou is wide in its upper reaches and could be a challenge, but it is far from any bay. Santa Anna was probably captured at that location.

he had probably escaped passed through their angered minds, the tumult increased and the lives of the prisoners hung on a thread.

During this general disturbance a little troop rode into camp with a single prisoner, apparently a common soldier. But he had barely entered the camp before the prisoners noticed him and from all lips sounded a plaintive "Santa Anna." They clasped their hands and fell on their knees before their idol. Santa Anna it was indeed, the commander-in-chief himself, and those that brought him in were surprised at their fortunate capture. They had found him in the high prairie-grass where he had concealed himself, and he assured them on the way that he did not know anything about the flight of Santa Anna. He, however, tried to bribe them with a gold watch, his purse and a few other articles, which were contemptuously rejected in Texan-American fashion.

The rejoicing was now as unrestrained as the raging was before, and the happy backwoodsmen pledged the prisoners not only to keep their promised pardon, but also to treat them in real Yankee fashion, that is, in a humanitarian manner.

The prisoner, trembling from head to foot, was taken to General Houston, who had been wounded in the battle. He was, as one might well imagine, not in the best mood, but he received the prisoner in such a manner as to give him new courage.

The general listened to the insipid, miserable flattery of the Mexican without appearing to be much elated, as his wound was causing him great pain. Santa Anna, who had meanwhile gotten new courage by taking a powerful dose of opium, continued in his operations. He asked what would be done with him.

"What to do with you, to do with you?" said Houston sullenly. "No discussion about you now. First we'll drive all the Mexicans over the Rio Grande, then we will consider what kind of fate the murderer of our people, especially Fannin*s division, deserves."

A terrible tumult indicated the excitement outside of the tent. The troops unanimously demanded the death of the prisoner and then to hasten forward immediately to destroy the remainder of the enemy on the Brazos. Santa Anna, although he did not know what the confusion meant, suspected the true state of affairs and his opium courage left him again. This murderer, who had caused the death of thousands, who, instead of fostering the welfare of his fatherland when he reached the highest position of honor, hurled it into an abyss with the help of his accomplices, the Jesuits, to put the shackles of slavery anew on the splendid land, this characterless criminal trembled as he now realized that his miserable life was the cause of the tumult outside. He denied that Fannin had agreed to a capitulation, but maintained that he had surrendered at discretion. "Discretion? Ha! I would almost like to laugh when I hear of Mexican discretion, but the memory of my butchered comrades would rather cause the tears to flow from my eyes."

The fallen Napoleon spent the night in nervous restlessness and in constant fear of being murdered. Only the positiveness of Houston, who ever had the welfare of the Republic in mind, saved his life for the present.

As the captured president was anxious to know whether he would ever set foot on Mexican soil again or die here, he asked for pen and ink, with which he wrote dispatches to generals Urrea at Brazoria and Filisola, who was also on the Brazos but father up. These were to leave Texas speedily without risking a battle with the ferocious backwoodsmen.

The dispatches left with Houston's approval and with the resentment of the Texans for their destination. The discontented troops wanted to thank only their rifles for the independence of their land, and feared that an agreement would be made with the murderer that would justify him in making claims for his life, which, according to their opinion, could not be saved.

But immediately with the dispatches General Rusk, a young, vigorous, and well-liked officer, advanced. Sam Houston had given him the direct command of the Army, as his wounds did not permit him to accompany the advancing troops.

The loss of the enemy was: 630 killed, including one general, four colonels, two majors, seven captains and twelve lieutenants.

Two hundred eighty wounded, including eight major officers.

Seven hundred thirty prisoners, including General Santa Anna, General Cos for the second time, four colonels, six majors, and Santa Anna's private secretary.

Sixteen hundred muskets, three hundred sabers, two hundred pistols, several hundred horses and mules and twelve thousand piasters[24] were taken, which sum was renounced by the army in favor of the little navy of the Republic.

David Burnet, the president of the provisional government established by the National Convention, arrived a few days after the battle to confer with Houston about the disposition of Santa Anna.

---

[24] Ehrenberg says piasters, but pesos seem more likely

The Retreat

HOLZINGER'S DETACHMENT LYING AT MATAGORDA during this period busied itself in devouring and devastating the supplies and provisions, and in transporting the lighter and more valuable objects to the Guadalupe. All were of the opinion that the existence of the Republic of Texas had been only a dream, but for the master of Mexico and his instruments that he needed to lay the Federal Union of Mexico in shackles this was a happy dream, as their wishes to drive the colonists out of their fatherland, which had been contemplated for the longest, was now fulfilled and they apparently could now take possession of the beautiful, cultivated plantations with perfect right. In their imagination they were already selecting the houses and plantations where they expected to live later.

Don Juan Holzinger had his little place also. On the 19th of April, two days before the Battle of San Jacinto, a little sloop approached the harbor. It, however, did not seem to fully trust the situation and crossed the Bayou at a respectful distance to reconnoiter.

The Mexicans saw that the vessel would not venture up and they decided to entice it in by trickery. Not having a Texas flag, they ran up a white one, which seemed to work. The sloop approached, looked the situation over, and turned as if to cross the sand bars, but under the rather strong land breeze bore out to sea again. The officers had not expected this and had neglected to place their cannon in time. Consequently, the single ball that they fired after the ship fell into the waves far on this side.

In a short time, the sails disappeared on the distant southern horizon and nothing remained for us except the sullen faces and the *carajos* of the officers.

Holzinger now had the Texan prisoners work hastily on the construction of a boat with which he expected to soon examine the long peninsula that was separated from the mainland by a strip of boggy land. He promised himself much booty and aimed to use this boat to take it from Matagorda to safety at Matamoras.

Every afternoon at six o'clock the numerous bugles of the Mexicans sounded for roll call and thereupon for prayer, when all troops were required to uncover their renowned heads and to fall with grace on their knees. Here they prayed for the annihilation of the heretics in which, as I believe, we accursed Texans were especially mentioned as worthy objects to be taken off by the black gentleman.

Meanwhile the officers, who seemed to think that where so many organs were being strained in fervent prayer their voices would really not he particularly necessary, went about their usual business, that is, they did nothing and smoked *cigarritos*.

It was at this time on the 24th of April, as the troops as usual were lying on their knees and praying devotedly for our destruction, although a little woozy, as Santa Anna had just issued them ten percent of their wages, or who knows if they were not just kneeling down, when a tall man on a little Indian pony rushed wildly into the camp. The feet of the long fellow, who according to his uniform was a worthy sergeant of the central government, hung deep down into the grass. It looked, in fact, as if a six-footed animal was running along, which was more delusive because the movements of his feet harmonized with those of the horse. His hands also were in constant motion and the whip flew incessantly around the feet of the panting Indian pony. But this instrument did not seem to have enough effect, as he shouted and swore frightfully as he sat on the practically sinking animal. The long fear-inspiring beard hung in long cues from his lips, and his burning black eyes through the drawn-together eyebrows expressed a true picture of fear.

"*Presidente* dead, *Presidente* dead!" he shouted to the frightened lines of soldiers, and they stared after him as if he were a delegate from hell. This messenger with frightful news now trotted, spreading consternation, to the house where Holzinger's headquarters were and hastily reported that an adjutant and he were the only ones to have escaped the claws of the cannibals. At the same time, he had orders to retreat immediately, which that officer, the same one who had to shoot Fannin, did at once. In half of an hour this officer whipped away in full speed all by himself to escape the vengeance of the backwoodsmen, deserting soldiers, booty and everything else.

Holzinger, who had no less fear, now took the command, but only to bring his rich, extensively accumulated plunder to safety. On the following morning, when the boat was rolled from its scaffolding and found fit for service, he had his belongings, his booty, provisions and an excellent eighteen-pounder brought onto it. He then advised the troops that he would retreat by sea and directed them to take their former route back over the Colorado and admonished them to good behavior, and soon we had the pleasure of seeing the whole detachment hastily leave in unorganized little groups as if the diablos were already on their heels.

At sundown we also left, under full sail in our twenty-foot-long and twelve-foot-wide flat-bottomed frigate. At the mouth of the bayou we found a flat-bottomed boat about fourteen feet long and eight feet wide which we took in tow and freighted it with part of our cargo and crew, Holzinger, eight Mexicans and six Texan prisoners. On it we arranged our kitchen, namely, a large iron cooking stove plundered at Matagorda.

On account of the weak construction of our boats, we sailed along close to the shore. For several days we went along a low, dreary coast where not a single tree broke the monotony of the plain. But millions of sea fowl and countless herds of deer enlivened this desolate region, many parts of which are flooded by the bay when the high spring tide presses in from the main body of the Gulf of Mexico. The trip from Matagorda to Matamoras can be made by shallow draft vessels between banks because a chain of long, narrow islands forms a channel about one hundred miles long, composed of bays and lagoons. A pilot acquainted with these waters can land within a few miles of the Rio Grande within a few days, while a stranger to these waters would require weeks or even months to reach the same destination.

According to Holzinger's calculations and maps—all maps of Texas are wrong except those in Scherpf's[25] works— we should not have been far from Matamoras, disregarding the fact that we seldom set our sails because we usually had crosswinds that we could not use with our flat-bottomed

---

[25] Noted mapmaker and guide publisher G. A. Scherpf.

boats. On the third afternoon we arrived at a peninsula projecting far out into the bay. Around the point an immense body of water extended at right angles from our course and the bay far into the land. Not a trace of land was to be seen ahead of us and neither to the right nor to the left. If we should get out of the lagoons and out into the open gulf, we would be lost, as a single large wave would smash our boats and send us to destruction. With the seemingly endless stretches of water ahead of us and equally immense grasslands behind us, we were in a very precarious position. If we could have had a seagoing vessel, we could have rocked with the greatest pleasure on the raging billows of the gulf. But as it was, we could not risk it. Nothing but a slightly indented coastline was on Holzinger's map, and he could not explain from whence the immense water masses ahead of us and to the right came.

For our part, we Texans were very glad, and estimated correctly that we were still between land and, at that, not very far from Matagorda. As the land rose from ten to fifteen feet above the level of the sea, a person could see only a few miles. We, however, kept silent and hoped that our army would arrive at the southwestern harbor, which we had to pass, sooner than we could reach it with our boats.

In this way plan after plan rolled through the heads of four of the prisoners to attain freedom. I and a young Yankee, my confidential friend, were quietly working to get free, but we wanted to do so smartly and only when we had reached a better-looking region. I had enjoyed myself enough wandering around in the wilderness alone, and did not wish to risk it another time, at least not in these grasslands. We decided to spend the night on the point of land and had just prepared supper when one of the prisoners stepped to me and told me confidentially that they aimed to take possession of one of the boats during the night and return to Matagorda and that they had further agreed to kill the Mexicans if they should offer resistance. At the same time, he earnestly requested me not to tell the young Yankee anything about it. I shook my head, went to the others and told them that I would be willing to make the trip with them by land, but that under no conditions would I agree that either the Mexicans or Holzinger be murdered. Regardless of how cruel the enemy had been toward us, they should at least consider that Holzinger, even if only through selfish motives, had saved the lives of twenty-eight Texans, that the Mexicans had been very friendly toward them and that, even though they had been beguiled by their priests, they were still citizens of Texas. There were, in fact, several from San Antonio and one from Nacogdoches in the group, and I felt sorry for the miserable wretches that had been incited or drafted to take the field against us.

  The prisoners shook their heads disapprovingly, and I suspected nothing good. Consequently, I decided on my plan as the night set in and communicated it to my friend, the Yankee John Adams—I must here say to his honor that he did not have anything to do with the anti-slavery and the prohibition movements of the former president. He was a true-blue Yankee, a perfectly independent sort of a fellow, and even if he could not restrain himself from following his downeaster nature at times, his tricks were usually harmless. He had seen much of the world and knew a little about every trade.

  He could ride, hunt, and fish. He had kept school and had learned the carpenter's profession. He was an excellent architectural draftsman. He had sold matches and, in the back forests, medicine. At one time he also dealt in jewelry and nobody knows what else, until he finally, while serving as a supervisor in a tobacco factory in New York and selling tickets at the Bowery Theater at nights, came to the decision to enter the war in Texas with Colonel Miller.

Holzinger and his men slept in the little boat, while we quartered ourselves on the land; but this night Adams and I went unnoticed into the large boat, raised the anchor, which was nothing more than an anvil that anchored both boats, and drifted from the shore, unnoticed in the darkness. We were afloat but a short time when the foaming waves began to lash severely against the sides of our boat. In vain our anvil floated into the deep in order to anchor again; the chain did not reach to the bottom. The boat struck back and forth and the breaking waves threw their spray into our faces.

Black clouds were hurrying across the heavens; the already strong wind howled stronger and more furiously every minute over the spraying sea, and we rowed with all our might to regain the shore that we had just left, but in vain. Holzinger sprang up and, frightened at the storm that howled about us, stared outward. He was looking for the land but it had disappeared. In despair he cried "Up, up, you swains! Treason! We are lost!" Everybody sprang up immediately and howled in competition with the wind. "Shut up, you vagabonds, take hold of the oars, you dogs, if you do not want to swallow salt water in half of an hour," cried my companion to the despairing ones and then continued in a more friendly tone, "Must row hard, boys. The coast is not far away. See the black cloud in the west. That is a squall. If it hits us, you might as well pray your Ave Maria—damn us another time as you have done so often—before morning the sharks will have a splendid breakfast on your bony carcass."

The firm voice of the Yankee, who was rowing for life and death, somewhat quieted the frightened Mexicans, as they were of the opinion before that we had let them drift out into the bay without oars.

"Over here, Colonel Holzinger, with your people, everyone an oar in his hand, draw gallantly, quickly, quickly, if your life is dear to you. Only a short time and it may be too late forever! Look—you understand just as much about life on the water as John Adams understands your politics."

The Mexicans and even Holzinger yielded tremblingly to the orders that thundered from the lips of the Yankee so coldly, so piercingly and so deliberately.

"Hello, you softshell turtles, strike in hard with your oars! Time, boys, keep time. Mixed up too much, as if thrashing beans. Time, time. Reckon we won't get to the land if it keeps up like this. What, damn your bottoms, why do you move about in your seats when a little water spatters into your faces. Don't look that way—don't give a damn for it, it's refreshing."

"Holla, Polasky," he yelled over to me—he generally called me that because of the difficulty of pronouncing my name. "Take the helm away from that miserable Apache, or I will take it myself—reckon he fits better at a fandango than at the helm of a boat in a storm. Must worry myself to death with these—Halt! Halt, boys," he cried suddenly, interrupting himself. "The devil knows where the land is. Oars up, Mexicans, we must listen for the breakers."

Everybody instantly obeyed the Yankee dictator, and he stared with bulging eyes into the impenetrable darkness. But the raging squall, whistling in its approach, drowned the sound of the surf, and vainly we tried to get some sign of the direction. It whistled and hissed about us, but secretly my friend Adams noticed that the mighty waves of the bay were where we were being dashed back and forth. Two of the Mexicans were busy dipping out the water that was dashed in by the waves, and our prospects of being saved appeared to be ever more hopeless.

"Sir," said Holzinger smoothly, "wouldn't you consider it wise to throw the stove, the cannon and other heavy articles overboard?"

"Sir," the dictator replied, "Sir, I say, I figure I would not think it wise. I think it would be better to be perfectly still. John Adams knows what he has to do." A pause set in and another time the pilot appeared to listen with head stretched forward.

"Oars up! Up with your oars!" he called another time and everyone obeyed and was quiet.

"Calculate, calculate, land back of us," mumbled Adams to himself, but then he continued, louder, "Hallo, I say. Polasky, my boy, must turn around, favorably toward the land. I hear the surf."

He brought the helm into the proper position for the turn, and continued with his preemptory orders:

"Sails up! Up *Mexicanos*! Quickly! Quickly! We will soon have a calm, and after that we may row until tomorrow morning and still not get to the land."

The Mexicans didn't need to be told a second time, and in a few minutes the mast bowed under the pressure of the sails. The frigate now glided firm and straight over the bay; the storm died by degrees; the heavens began to brighten up; only a few single clouds now hastened along the horizon, but in front of us the storm roared like the ceaseless thunder of an earthquake. Something dark like land spread itself out before us, and between it and our boat boiled the whirling, foaming waves.

"Sir," cried the Colonel in greatest fear, "Land! Land! The surf! We must cast anchor!"

"Damn you and the surf, I say," the Yankee exploded, "keep yourself cool—entirely cool, Colonel Holzinger. Not a word. Calculate. I know how to look after my post. Calculate, you see."

A fearful, grinding jolt, a trembling of the whole boat, all spars bent themselves like the bows of the Comanches. A distressful cry among the Mexicans and a loud, meaningful laugh of the Yankee followed. The latter now quietly rolled up his blankets and went to the shore to sleep.

It was solid earth. The boat lay high and dry and the Mexicans took down the sails. I left to find a place to sleep.

When I awoke, the sun was standing high above the bay. The same solitary grasslands and the same masses of water lay about us, but inward on the land we discovered a dark streak that we momentarily took for a forest. Above the mass of water lying before us we also discovered dark cloudlike figures that likewise betrayed the presence of land.

Holzinger still could not comprehend how he had gotten out on the bay during the night, and what had become of the other four Texans. Neither could he explain to himself the dictatorial language of the Yankee of the previous night and he asked us about it.

"Well, sir, reckon I was right. Reckon so. The Colonel could see that the whole bunch did not understand a bit about seafaring, and I reckon I understood a little bit. Therefore, I took the helm. I had no particular desire to swallow salt water. Did better, sir, I reckon, than if I had stood up and howled along with the chorus. Reckon the sharks would have had a good breakfast of us."

The Colonel shuddered.

"Yes, sir, absolutism is necessary in such a ticklish predicament. I reckon sir, last night I wanted to knock everyone down that would not work. Did not want to make any distinction. The Colonel was very good, sir. You did very well last night. I was captain, and, sir, today I am your prisoner again. Do what you consider right."

After we had discussed everything, the Colonel was very well pleased with our precaution and praised John Adams quite a bit.

The weather was fair, the bay was quiet and a favorable east wind was blowing toward the land on the opposite side. Consequently, we immediately floated the boat, set sail and sped pleasantly through the small waves. On this trip we caught astonishingly many fish, and after eating we sailed into a dark bayou about thirty feet wide. The evergreen magnolias on both banks of the sparkling canal had overlapped in the middle, and the closely overlapping tops were closely interwoven with air plants and vines. In places the silvery festoons of Spanish moss, six to eight feet long, hung down to the surface of the water, and only in a few places could a ray of the burning sun shine through or a speck of the blue sky appear. The scattered penetrating rays illuminated the cool, evergreen arcade and the mossy festoons with bewitching beauty. We were often obliged to bend the waving moss to the side. We liked it so well here that we decided to spend the night and determined to reconnoiter the surrounding regions to find out, if possible, where we were. Holzinger did not doubt that we were nearer to Matamoras than to Matagorda; both of us hoped and believed the contrary.

After the night had set in and the fires had practically died down, the Yankee Adams and I walked off quietly but with long strides, leaving Holzinger and his men in the wilderness, and directed our steps northeastward toward the colonies that, in our opinion, could not be far away. We were convinced that the echo of peaceful industry would soon ring again through the primitive forests, and we felt that, with the splendid spring, the spring of the new Republic had also set in.

We traveled during the whole night, and at the break of day we arrived at a plantation on the Trespalacios. Flocks of fowls and grunting herds of hogs were the only inhabitants of deserted buildings that were full of implements and furniture and provided a few articles of food. Since we did not consider ourselves safe here from Holzinger, who would be sure to follow us, we resumed our journey after several hours of rest and swam across the little stream, because the boats here had been concealed and the bridge broken down. Before sundown, we arrived at several plantations on the left bank of the stream. They were located on a little prairie about two miles wide that ran toward the southeast between two densely forested little streams. Toward the north, however, we could discover no other boundary than the endless depth of the dark blue heavens. Between that and the far outlines of the rising prairie, the sun, bloody as the murder at Goliad, sank into the quiet depths of the ocean.[26]

We spent the night in a house in which we found an abundance of corn and a mill. As usual the trees around the house were alive with poultry. A keg of salted pork also stood in the pantry. Consequently, we proceeded at once to get some

---

[26] It is difficult to reconcile Ehrenberg's geography. If he and Adams walked overnight to the Trespalacios River, their boat must have never left Matagorda Bay. From the Trespalacios it is impossible to see the sun setting into the gulf, but perhaps he was only poetically assuming that an ocean lay out there somewhere.

of the chickens from the trees to fry, a process which my friend understood very well. He held a bit of burning sulfur fastened to a stick under their bills. Although several fluttered away shaking their heads, two hens and a cock fell down, whose age, however, must have extended into the indefinite past. Although we cut him into small pieces, the more we fried the tougher the meat became.

After we had spent several very comfortable days here, we decided one beautiful morning, as practically all mornings are in Texas, to go out into the neighborhood on an expedition of discovery and to find out, if possible, if the Mexicans on their retreat did not have the Colorado and this region behind them. That they would have to cross the Rio Grande was positive in our conviction, although we knew nothing outside of the destruction of Santa Anna. We knew the spirit of our people. "Victory or Death," was their watchword. And because they fought for the right, like their fathers, they were always successful, since a higher power watched protectively over the Anglo-Americans.

We had visited several very pretty plantations in which provisions in abundance were at hand, and the greatest order prevailed in the dwellings themselves, from which we concluded that no plundering enemy had entered this part of the Republic. But what part this really was still remained a puzzle for us, although we cared little. We believed that the Texans would be back as soon as the circumstances would permit. Until then we would be masters of the plantations.

When we came around a bend in the forest, we discovered in a majestic group of live oak trees the home of a settler who from appearances had only recently moved in. No field surrounded the house, but the neat improvements around gave an impression of good condition, and the large herds grazing in the distance could belong only to a man who would be among the richer class of people.

We stole up carefully like the Indians through the bushes along the edge of the forest, but neither saw nor heard anything other than that the house, like the others, had been deserted. Consequently, we more boldly yet cautiously approached the door, when suddenly a tenor voice of a man trilled the following stanza:

In Mexico none shall be free,
The people is too blind to see,
They cannot cheer the liberty,
O Yankee doodle dandy.

"Hello, John Hitchcock, old soul, what are you doing here?" shouted my visibly surprised Yankee friend to an approximately twenty-two-year-old slender Georgian who sat on the floor among piles of books.

"Hello!" exclaimed the child from Old Georgia. He sprang up to the side to grasp an axe standing nearby, looked at us and then rushed recklessly out and told us, between protracted questions and answers, how he had come out here.

"Boys, you know, twelve of us from Matagorda were obliged to go to the Colorado and had to build a boat for Urrea's division to cross over the stream. Well, we did it, but the copper faces, the Mexicans, my boys, wanted to take us along to Mexico. But John Hitchcock had no desire to go along. I took a long shot, came here yesterday, found everything comfortable, well-suited to amuse this child for a while. I have decided, boys, to remain here at least a week to enjoy the happiness of freedom. Then I will trot to Matagorda."

So the Mexicans already had the Colorado back of them; they must have had great haste.

That evening I shot a little, fat, two-year-old steer with my pistol, and for the first time in quite a while we enjoyed a tender steak. The remainder of the meat was cut after Mexican fashion in strips possibly twenty feet long and hung up under the live oak trees to be dried by the air and not by the sun.

During the night the great herds frightened us not a little when they stampeded up to the building. The house and the whole earth trembled, and we thought at the beginning that the whole enemy cavalry was sweeping across the prairie.

Away from the Free and Sovereign Prairie

BOOKS, BEEFSTEAKS, WARM CORNBREAD, great pans full of milk, maps and well-cooked hominy stood in loveliest variety on the table around which we three were seated most comfortably.

My friend Adams had just helped my friend Hitchcock to a piece of ox-heart fried chestnut brown.

"Well, John Hitchcock, here is as fine a piece as is barely to be had at Bishop's in New Orleans," said the Yankee representing the waiter.

"I must confess, John, you have improved yourself wonderfully in the art of cooking."

"Why, who would not?" answered John, "I have had to cook enough for the brown bums, and the worst of it was that I generally did not get any of it myself."

"Your own fault, Johnny, your own fault, must look out for yourself—be satisfied yourself—then the others," answered Adams, cutting the heart of the ox to pieces and taking a powerful draught of milk from the gourd cup.

"A long life to the old blind cow that furnishes us with milk at night and in the morning!" he continued. Whereupon John Hitchcock brought the milk-delivering Adams and his worthiness another milk toast, which we gallantly and cheerfully drank and then gave our attention to the other articles again.

"Perfectly at home, gentlemen? Perfectly comfortable, I hope?" cried a small person from a Comanche pony. A grey felt hat shaded the sun-tanned features, and the dangerous rifle lying across the saddle betrayed the backwoodsman.

We looked up in surprise and discovered the gentleman in front of the door who had just addressed us. Adams, who recovered from his surprise first, arose to examine the rider. But he still did not know what to say, and consequently he began, "Pretty weather, stranger!"

"Very pretty weather, sir," was the reply of the smiling felt-hat man.

"Reckon you come from the army, stranger?"

"Guessed it, sir, I come from General Rusk's camp."

"General Rusk, stranger? What kind of a general is that?" said friend Adams in astonishment.

"Well, I must confess, Adams," interrupted Hitchcock, "Rusk! Rusk! You don't know who Rusk is, the gallant Rusk! The attorney from Nacogdoches? Very ignorant, Adams, you don't even know our leading men."

"Rusk, sir, is a gallant young lawyer, who, since Houston is wounded, is driving the enemy out of the country in his stead," explained the stranger.

"Thank you, sir," said Adams, "reckon you could tell us much of our friends, provided you get off, come in. This house is an asylum for every Texan."

"I have noticed it, gentlemen," smiled the stranger again, dismounting from his horse, which Hitchcock immediately unsaddled and took to the river for water.

"Now, stranger, be seated and help yourself to our modest meal," I wanted to say, but the gentleman seemed not to need the invitation and moved his chair to the table without formalities, cut off a considerable piece of the heart and asked for a gourd of milk.

"Thunder!" mumbled Adams, looking at me, "What kind of a fellow is that?"

"Thunder," I replied, "a real Texan, I suppose." Adams shook his head, brought the requested milk and placed it beside the stranger.

"Now, sir," said the inquisitive Yankee, "what is the name of our guest, if we may ask?"

"Thomas Kelly, gentlemen, who is enjoying your steak very much," was the answer of the continually smiling backwoodsman.

"Reckon Mr. Kelly is correct—excellent beefsteaks—very fine fellow, that John," bragged Adams, "the best Guinea-negro could not do any better; but on the side, stranger, ah Mr. Kelly, I wanted to say," continued my friend, "reckon you are one of the colonists of Texas."

"Reckon, sir, you are correct," was the answer.

"And, Mr. Kelly, I am very curious," my friend excused himself, who in reality was showing more than American curiosity, "do you live somewhere in this region when you are at home?"

"At one time this was my home. Now it is yours, but in about eight days, gentlemen, I would be glad to have you give it back to me." Again his peculiar smile followed as we looked at him in surprise. "Yes," he continued, "Mrs. Kelly will soon be here and will be surprised at the good order of all of the things. She will especially enjoy the books. But, gentlemen," he said, "I have told you everything about me. Now you will not consider it impolite if I should ask for the names of the inhabitants of my property, who have evidently remained here during the whole of our retreat."

"A falsehood, Mr. Thomas Kelly," replied Adams. "We have been here only a few days—are prisoners, escaped from the Mexican camp. Here, sir," pointing to me, "is one of Fannin's men, and there," indicating the entering Hitchcock, "is one from Major Ward's division, and here, the speaker, sir, is John Adams, one of Colonel Miller's hundred Yankees, who completely lost their mother wit when they landed on the coast of Texas."[27]

"So," said Mr. Kelly, vigorously shaking hands with us another time. "Welcome! Welcome within my walls. You who fortunately escaped from the bloody catastrophe where your and my brothers were so shamefully murdered, are welcome, another time. Thomas Kelly will always gladly remember that he waited on one of Fannin's men on his flight from the Mexican hyenas." Another time out hands clasped one another, and he continued to speak to us: "But, my boys, do you know too that soon not a Mexican copper hide will be on this side of the Rio Grande? They are running home with all their might to their tortilla-making women."

"We really do not know," interrupted Adams, "but we reckon, sir, that you would do us a great favor if you would tell us what happened with the Texan advance after the splendid Battle of San Jacinto."

---

[27] Ehrenberg mentioned the episode earlier. Major William Parsons Miller recruited and led a battallion of seventy-five Tennessee volunteers. Coming ashore at Copano in March 1836, they were immediately captured by Urrea without resistance in unclear circumstances. Taken to Goliad, they were spared the fate of Fannin's men because they had surrendered without a fight. Ehrenberg may have mis-identified Hitchcock as being from Georgia.

"Indeed! Indeed, my brave boys, with the greatest pleasure for you as well as for myself I will repeat the miserable scenes that followed the twenty-first and the twenty-second. But a little more milk—I am very thirsty."

Adams filled the gourd again, and after the gentleman had drunk, he began: "You probably know, my boys, that after we had painted the grass of the San Jacinto prairie red with blood for vengeance and had captured Santa Anna, this characterless monstrosity sent off dispatches to General Filisola to please us, directing him to evacuate Texas.

"But almost simultaneously with the dispatches, the troops from San Jacinto were at the Brazos with their rifles. Rusk was, as already indicated, our leader. The opposite bank was clear of the enemy troops, and we crossed the Brazos to observe the movements of the enemy. Even before Santa Anna's orders reached the headquarters of General Filisola, he had sent couriers to all of the other detachments, ordering them to immediately unite with the main army and to retreat beyond the Colorado.

"There were six thousand of the enemy in the land, and we felt obliged to know something definite of their intentions before they united. Consequently, Rusk with three hundred cavalry rushed ahead and reached the enemy just as Filisola united with Urrea between two prongs of the Bernard,

"Now, boys, for two days in succession whole clouds fell from the skies. Possibly you know how it rains here once it begins, and you may also know the rich black soil of the Bernard, where the upper soil is over twenty-eight feet thick and not a stone to be found in the whole region. Every inch of it is just as rich as and healthier than the dense chills-and-fever forests of Illinois. Filisola was sitting in a highly unpleasant predicament in this region—the cannon over their axles in mud and the soldiers knee-deep in water. Sleeping was impossible and the squatters and Deaf Smith with his companions on their large American horses, for whom it is a small matter to travel through a country like this, drove all the cattle away from around them.

"A famine broke out among the Mexicans, and practically the whole army was shivering, especially when three hundred of our cavalrymen raced up to them as if it were the most beautiful weather in the world. To raise a defense was out of the question—it was but a matter of surrender. But Rusk would not consider the matter, as he did not want to have these five thousand dependents on his hands. On the contrary, forward was the word, forward over the Rio Grande. You get out from here the way you came in here, forward, or we will fire on you, was the answer of the Texans.

"It touched our hearts to see the wretches in such a condition, but we could do nothing for them, as we did not have anything for ourselves except the cattle that had been driven some distance away. When they saw that we did not want any prisoners, another delegate came and agreed with General Rusk to clear out of the Republic as speedily as possible, if they were given a little more time and would not be disturbed in their retreat. The retreat continued.

"All bonds of organization were severed, and not an army of soldiers but a starving mass, a confused mass of confused shadows, approached the Colorado. They had expected supplies and provisions to be landed at the various Texas ports, but our little fleet destroyed their hopes. On their renowned march through the colonies they needlessly destroyed the herds of cattle and unpardonably offended their confederates, the Indians. These wild hunters of the prairie, these never-forgiving redskins, now scalped the single stragglers who fell out behind the main army and those who dared to search through the country for herds of cattle. Even in broad daylight they would rush out of the timber in the river valleys, strike the rider from his horse with the tomahawk and, in the presence of the frightened army, rush off with the captured horse. Barely a gun was fired, as the stores had gotten wet and practically all ammunition had spoiled. Consequently, the redskins could carry on their work almost unhindered.

"Every night our three hundred cavalry camped near so that they could survey the whole Mexican camp. Our guards and scouts passed clear around and, under constant fear that our people would repeat the San Jacinto scene, the glorious army finally reached the Colorado. The crossing of this stream cost them three days and much of their baggage, which we found partly destroyed when we shortly thereafter crossed the river with man and mouse in three quarters of an hour."

"Thunder and lightning, stranger, how did you do that?" asked Adams.

"Well, sir, how did we proceed? We all swam across and the few who could not swim crossed over on the horses or in the boat that our people had built for Urrea, then we fastened long cables to the cannon and, like a steam winch, dragged them across the bed of the red waters without further ceremony. I left the army at the other bank of the river to see after my house and business. But Rusk is continuing to follow the shadow army in whose ranks things are getting worse every day. We had already left several living skeletons behind us who had laid themselves behind a bush or under a live oak tree with death before their eyes, to be possibly eaten alive by the wolves.

"But it is too horrible, boys, to describe all of these scenes that will be a great and frightful warning to the Mexicans, and I venture to say boldly that never, never again, will they rob and devastate our colonies."

"It will be well for the enemy if they do not," answered Hitchcock. "We will not proceed so kindly the next time."

"Reckon not, sir, in spite of the fact that our people in the face of hellish slaughter by the enemy have done honor to their descent from the great nation beyond the Mississippi. Santa Anna was their objective, they wanted the murderer and the fear of his escape made them rage. But as soon as he was safely in their hands, this horrible veil, unbecoming for a North American, dropped from their figures and unmistakably the blood of Uncle Sam followed quietly after the enemy.

"I have probably described the conduct of our people as too cruel, but the misery of the enemy was so great that we could not help them. Many of our fellows gave a miserable starving wretch the last bit of food that he had, although he had possibly murdered a brother or a friend on the western prairie. Their humanitarian acts induced the enemy to bless those whom they had been taught all of their lives to curse."

"It is great, sir, noble, and I am proud to belong to this nation," said Adams, and a pause set in.

Hitchcock now asked the stranger how far it was to Matagorda and which road to take to get there.

"Gentlemen," answered the planter, "this road here winding off toward the east will take you directly to the lower ford of the Colorado. The stream is ten miles from here and then there are just as many to the town."

"Sir, only twenty miles? Sir, that is impossible," interrupted Adams, "I figure, sir, that it is at least forty-five miles."

"You are completely off, sir," said the planter. "I am well acquainted here, completely at home in this region. Formerly when I still lived on the other side of the river, I chased about for days after the red thieves, the Indians. At that time, they were still rather bold and practically every week they stole an ox or a horse from me or one of my neighbors. But that time is past, and the countryman in Texas can now wear his scalp in safety."

A half hour after this scene we three defenders of liberal principles, loaded with a few provisions, were walking over the great, somewhat rising prairie toward the Colorado, where we aimed to spend the night. The few treetops that we could at first see projecting over the distant low elevations grew from minute to minute, and soon the primitive forest extending off toward the northwest lay before us. A few miles from the stream itself we walked in the densely wooded valley where we could not see for ten steps into the dense forests. The whole world was alive. Flocks of wild turkeys were crying in every direction, and the splendid wilderness resounded with the many varieties of beautiful woodpeckers, whose little art could be heard from almost every tree. The whippoorwill was already calling from the dark interior, although the sun had just hidden its fiery face, and the mockingbird was twittering his variations, composed of the melodies of all the other charming songsters of the forest.

A herd of stately deer walked across the road and looked curiously but not fearfully at our wandering trio. Many rabbits shot across our path and whole bunches of black and grey squirrels danced along the road in front of us, or merrily chased one another through the highest tips of the oak and pecan trees, or flew from one limb to another, or shot like lightning down the stately trunks whose species one could barely determine on account of the many air plants and vines that covered them. Everywhere gigantic grapevines hung down from the trees. And when one comes to the stream itself and looks up and down over the surface of the water, one sees nothing but a dense growth of plants that slant up out of the water. The banks themselves are bordered by weeping willows whose melancholy branches droop into the water.

Not a boat was to be found, but that was no obstruction to us. Without further consideration we swam across and landed on the other bank only slightly fatigued. The first thing that we saw on the other side was a few unrecognizable and decomposing corpses; we hurried past.

About a half mile from the stream we came to the border of the timber, and a devastated plantation lay before us. The dwelling had been burned down by the enemy and only a black spot indicated where it had stood. We gathered some half-burned fence rails and started two large fires, between which we arranged our beds.

The flames shot probably fifteen feet up into the raven-black sky. The glow of the heat extended high above the two fiery pyramids, and millions of insects, bugs, moths and butterflies swarmed out of the forest toward our camp and fell—a perfect rain—with singed wings upon us. Instead of getting protection from our fires, they worked to the contrary and we were obliged to retreat. A clear place in the open prairie exposed to the wind offered us a better place to sleep.

The Capture of the Rhine-Prussian

BARELY HAD THE SUN RISEN before we donned our boots and joyfully hurried down the edge of the forest to the little town of Matagorda. We shouted for delight: "Joy, joy, finally we are free; today we will see our countrymen again. The prairie is ours, the young republic is victorious, the new star radiating freedom is rising on the western horizon and the splendid park, the Eldorado, our Texas, our new, everlasting, precious fatherland, has been dedicated to the industry-loving people of the north, of the new world and of the old. The welcome immigrants will follow in, and the flower garden, the mottled savannas, will disappear before the plow, guided by the strong arm. But great fields of snowy cotton, the juicy sugar cane and the noble tobacco will in a short time charm the eye just as pleasantly. The orange, the lemon, the peach, the splendid magnolia, everything beautiful that the South produces will decorate the asylum of the countryman, and a king in his own house, on his soil, he would not exchange with the rulers of Europe."

We could barely speak for joy when we entered the neat little bay town for the second time. The scarecrow that bid Urrea's division halt was still standing on the roof of the one-story house, and the inhabitants, who had returned the day before, looked with pain upon their devastated property. They received us very cordially and did everything in their power to cause us to forget our former suffering.

The four volunteers that we had left on the beach on the night the storm almost delivered us over to the raging sea were here also and raged and stormed at us. But we laughed and received the applause of the inhabitants of Matagorda.

Barely had we been in town for an hour and told the story of our flight and indicated the place where we had left Holzinger before an expedition on horseback under the leadership of the Yankee left for Lavaca to cut off the Colonel on his way to Matamoras and bring back the Colonel, the booty and the eighteen pounder as, according to the old planters, he would have to pass through two more mighty bays before he would be forty miles from Matagorda. Meanwhile I remained in town.

Holzinger and his people, who could not sleep for fear, had soon discovered our flight, but instead of following us, they put out to sea, as they feared that we would follow them with the aid of the Texans. They labored with more than Mexican strength. Under considerable worry and not without danger they finally worked themselves out of the first bay. They thought that they were now finally in the Laguna del Madre that reaches down nearly to Matamoras. But, Oh horrors!

On the fourth day they discovered another endless mass of water. Since they did not dare to sail straight across, they were obliged as before to shove the boats around in the shallow water near the shore. As they were lying in a bayou a few days later, the Caranchuas paid them a visit, which was not at all agreeable to the Colonel and the half-Indians as they remembered that they had hung several warriors of this tribe near the Guadalupe. The redskins received many presents, and while they were sleeping off the effects of the whiskey, the boatmen stole away to find another endless bay after several days of wearisome labor. They believed it to be the gulf and would not venture out upon it.

But they could neither stay here nor turn back unless they wanted to be captured and, as they believed, shot. Their food supply also was running short. Consequently, they were obliged to go forward.

Slowly and warily they moved forward. Day passed after day without an important discovery being made. Completely exhausted, they were camping during the noon hour under several small groups of mesquite trees when suddenly a thundering "Surrender or I'll shoot!" frightened them up. It was a single backwoodsman who had stopped at a distance of forty yards with hammer cocked and gun in position. His voice was so positive and his rifle so threatening that the whole troop didn't hesitate a moment and surrendered unconditionally. The next minute the remainder of our Matagorda expedition rushed up, which was composed of five men. Three of them took charge of the boats and the prisoners with the exception of Holzinger. The Colonel was required to mount one of the horses. And after each of the colonists had tied one of the other horses with a lasso to his saddle, they went in a full gallop over the prairie to Matagorda.

On the third day after their departure, the land expedition returned; on the fourth the boats with the recaptured booty and the excellent cannon appeared. Our oarsmen had made the ten-day journey of the Mexicans in a little more than two days and had caught a lot of fish besides.

Adams and I had considerable trouble protecting Holzinger against mistreatment from several of the inhabitants of Matagorda of whose property he had the most valuable on his boat. Undoubtedly he would have been shot if we had not preached peace from morning until night among the embittered spirits. We brought forward his virtues: he had saved the lives of about twenty-eight men and it was to him alone due that they did not find ash piles in place of their houses on their return. But the four prisoners contradicted our first contention, although he really had saved them. They claimed, and with justice, that he saved their lives only because he needed their help in building bridges and boats, which his unnerved soldiers would never have been able to do, and that he intended to take them as slaves to his estates, which, in fact, was the case. They were to build him several houses and a steamboat. The robbed citizens contradicted the second contention, saying that this was no act of virtue on his part. On the contrary, they claimed, he had protected the buildings because if they were destroyed he would fear a catastrophe like the present one. And what would the owners then undoubtedly have demanded? "His death!" cried one, and "his death!" shouted another. "He is the miscreant who made Fannin so many sweet promises in order to induce him to surrender—his death!"

The prisoner seemed to be lost. But suddenly a brilliant idea passed through the head of the Yankee. He stepped to the front and asked for a hearing, which was granted him. He made an eloquent speech that I will here try reproduce in short outline:

"Citizens of a free republic!

"John Adams is no Cicero, to be sure, but he cannot avoid speaking. Yes, he feels compelled to thunder away when justice, the honor of the state and the laws are at stake, at risk of being trod under foot." He took a breath; the masses muttered. "Yes, gentlemen, I reckon you want to shoot this fellow. You are right—he deserves it. Adams thinks so also, but there is another nut, citizens. Is it right? Are we allowed to? I reckon not." He shook his head seriously.

"Reckon no one can forbid us to do it, John Adams, we are a free nation," cried the dubious crowd.

"Reckon our principles," continued Adams, "forbid us from doing so. Reckon, gentlemen, you know General Rusk's agreement with Filisola. Reckon, one article reads like this: free departure over the Rio Grande—isn't it so?"

A deathly stillness followed this question, and for a considerable time not a one of the reflecting crowd answered. They knew that he had spoken correctly. At last one called out: "Let him live, the rascal!" "Let him live!" several more called out.

"Well, people," continued the Yankee, "I see that you are reasonable—you say he shall live—must turn him over to the government. He will be treated honorably. He is our prisoner, has surrendered on our honor, our humanity."

"Halt, gentleman," cried one out of the crowd. Americans are addicted to disputing matters of politics and laws. "That fellow is free. We can't hold him. It's a lawful, definite agreement with Filisola."

"Hey, sir, you're going too far," interrupted John Adams. "The prisoner will be turned over to the government. The president can decide. He has violated the agreement. He has plundered—that is against the article where it says that all the property belonging to Texas citizens shall be turned over to our people uninjured and payment shall be made for that which has been taken away. By the way, people, we can't give up the nicely shining cannon until we know that Filisola has completely fulfilled the agreement."

"John Adams is right," shouted the masses. "Liberty and law forever!" was the cry, and Holzinger was saved. On the next morning he was taken away to Quintana, the seat of the government at that time.

Santa Anna

AFTER THE BRAZOS HAS LEFT THE HIGH PLATEAUS where it takes its rise and has worked its way through the forested lower regions, it suddenly enters a broad prairie about six miles from its mouth. The prairie extends all along the shoreline of the Republic and often extends twenty miles inland. Only in the southwest beyond the Guadalupe does one see occasional groups of cactus and mesquites and now and then an aloe, but eastward of this stream, the eye wanders ceaselessly over immense treeless meadows. Off in the west appears a pale streak, the forests, and to the south flow the immense waters.

The basin here into which the Brazos rushes thunders its mighty and highly dangerous waves against the sandy beach. Most of the time it splashes and froths its silken spray over the clay banks that enclose both sides of the stream at its entrance into this whirl. Not without danger and only guided by the skilled hand does the pilot boat shoot safely through this endless rushing together and whirling of the raging gulf. But not alone here, but the whole solitary beach, both upward and downward, trembles and groans under the approaching waves that break almost everywhere, as at the mouth of the river, in roaring surf. Woe to the wanderer who is seized by this wild surf. In a moment he disappears under the snowy sea, and far, far out in the quiet gulf his corpse may appear on the quiet waters again. Seldom does this restless sea lie before us, for the surf is thundering practically constantly. The only time when the traveler can find this coast practically quiet is when a strong land wind is battling directly against the foaming waves. But this is rarely the case. Then the gulf is roaring instead of the surf, and the storm blows the merchantman far out onto the bosom of the gulf.

At the mouth of the Brazos are two small villages, Velasco and its small log fort on the left side, and Quintana, then the seat of the government, on the right, exactly opposite each other. Both are competing for preference in trade. I would probably prefer the latter one on account of its safer harbor. For a width of a hundred yards or more, the shores here are bordered with layers of immense tree-trunks that were brought down by the Mississippi from its primitive forests thousands of miles away and thrust out into the bosom of the sea, which then deposited them along the low shores toward the left. In this respect is Texas especially favored, as not only good firewood can be found here but also excellent building timber.

It was Quintana where we arrived after a three-day journey with our prisoner, Holzinger, toward the end of the month of May. The Colonel was charmed by the beautiful landed estates that we passed, but he was also in constant fear of being murdered, although not a single incident had occurred that could have given him cause for this fear.

We rode to the residence of the President, Mr. David Burnet, who was living in the large warehouse of the firm of McKinney and Williams, and delivered the Colonel to the highest officer of the land. He received him in a friendly manner, and after we had made our report, a man of middle size, approximately five-feet-six-inches tall, with bowed head, stepped in. Apparently he was a Mexican of a very common type, but his pale features led us to assume that he had some Indian blood in his veins. His rather long, shining black hair lay flat on the well-proportioned head, and the sparkling black eyes rested humbly on the floor. But the hyena might as well try to imitate the dog of the chase as this man with the sinister expression could pretend to be humble. He stepped rather shyly through the door, his hands hung folded and limp before him, and he gazed constantly at the floor as if he feared the glances of the Texans.

"*Presidente, Señor Presidente, mi General Santa Anna!*" cried Holzinger to the fallen idol of blood and rushed toward him. Ho doubt he would have fallen on his knees before the fallen general had not he grasped him by the hands and greeted him with a double-meaning look. The features of Santa Anna seemed inclined to take on a friendlier expression when he saw before him such a willing tool of his former splendor and despotism, a thoroughbred aristocrat—or was it possibly a consolation to him not to suffer alone?

After the first greeting was over, questions and answers in Mexican proceeded rapidly, of which I could understand very little since my conversation 'til now had only dealt with the army, mustangs, the noble art of cooking and baking and other sentences from prosaic life. Consequently, I cannot give an account of the emotional language that took place between the hero and his subject. After a good meal I went over the river to Velasco.

"The war is at an end," was the report from the west, "although the enemy has not fulfilled all the terms of the agreement, his tattered columns have re-crossed the Rio Grande after the Comanches robbed and almost destroyed them on their way across the Tamaulipas Prairie between the Nueces and the Rio Grande. Many are lying scalped in the road and in the tall grass. The redskins have moved off to the mountains with all the horses and mules."

That was also the end of the renowned expedition that aimed to punish the congress of the United States and that probably had in mind to enslave all of the damned *Americanos*. O Gloria! A majestic old tree trunk on the Colorado heralds in large letters the triumphant crossing of Urrea's division, but only a little cut underneath it tells the traveler of the re-crossing of the General in retreat. Although there is abundance of room on the high trunk, no other escutcheon of this kind will ever appear on it.

The next day I asked for my discharge, which Mirabeau B. Lamar, minister of war at that time, immediately granted.

Volunteers from the States flowed in great number into the new republic. Although they came too late for the fighting, the government accepted their services for a definite time. The day following, one of the last in May, Mr. Burnet sent Santa Anna to one of the little warships that was lying at anchor outside of the surf. It was to take him to Vera Cruz.

Mr. Burnet's course certainly would not have been bad if one could have trusted Santa Anna. The captured Mexican president still had power if he were set free, as his term of office did not expire until the fall, but if we kept him in prison until then we could not expect any support from him on the treaty of independence that Mr. Burnet had entered into with him. The people of the two towns, General Green's volunteer brigade that had just arrived from the States and the minister of war, with his elegant power of speech as leader, were determined to prevent his departure. Even the navy promised that they would under no circumstances take him to Vera Cruz. All of Texas at this moment demanded his death with the possible exception of a few politicians who thought more of the welfare of their country than the gratification of the passions of their hearts. But the latter were obliged to yield to the general voice. Santa Anna, who was cherishing the wish to be free soon, was brought back. When this order was disclosed to him, he requested, battling with despair, to be shot on the ship, as he feared that he would be hanged on the land. But the officers assured him that he was under the sacred protection of the laws and that the next congress would decide his case.

After the longboat in which the prisoner sat had made its way from the fleet through the surf, it cut over to the Velasco side where all the inhabitants, militia and travelers had assembled. The trembling president, who accidentally sat under the flying colors of the Republic, drew his hat far down as he sat crumpled up in the boat. He bowed constantly to the spectators on the shore—a revolting spectacle. A deathly fear marked his features, and he dropped exhausted into the stern of the boat after it had passed the Texans.

But this picture of humiliation did more to save the fallen one than all the speeches of Houston or Burnet could have done. It reminded the deeply offended ones that he was now their prisoner, the prisoner of a civilized people. Without incident he reoccupied his room with our president and under the noble treatment of Mr. Burnet he finally adjusted himself to his fate.

Holzinger received his freedom and messengers left at once for Matagorda to turn over his private property to him on his arrival, but the Colonel did not dare to go near the town. And ignoring our encouragement, he forfeited his several hundred dollars' worth of effects, among which were several very splendid uniforms. The following day he went with the *Pennsylvania* to New Orleans. He had orders from Santa Anna for the Mexican consul there to purchase for Santa Anna a silver coffee service and all the other necessary accessories to fit up an elegant table, a number of delicacies and, finally, a negro cook, as the plain manner of living and art of cooking of the backwoodsmen did not appeal to the taste of this fine gentleman. But the very respectable consul conducted himself entirely without propriety and would not advance the crushed president a single dollar. Consequently, Holzinger had to travel on without completing his mission. He did not go to Mexico but pursued matters pertaining to his heart. New York was his aim. But here also he found the portals of his happiness closed. His ideas of marriage were "blown up" as our people say, and he returned with a raging hatred against the Yankees and their breed such as had never burned in his breast before, to the particularly dear Mexico. "Mexico, Santa Anna, and the Catholic priests forever," is now, as formerly, the motto of Don John Holzinger.

Santa Anna's Attempted Flight

"ISN'T IT A PASSABLE COUNTRY, this Texas, stranger?" asked a slender young backwoodsman of his companion who was also riding along the road.

"Excellent, sir, charming. I have traveled much, but such a paradise as yours, sir, I have never seen," responded the other, apparently a gentleman from the old world. "To be sure," he continued, "it was worthwhile to fight for such a land. Who would not risk the utmost for such a home as this? No, this strip from Bastrop up to Waterloo is incomparable. I wish that my poor countrymen could have only a single look at this heavenly park—I am convinced that they would have another opinion of the splendid lands beyond the Atlantic Ocean. All letters are of no value, sir, as they will not believe us. They all rely on the papers. There it stands, it says. See famine in America, revolution, fire, murder, etc. Stay in the homeland. You have your bread here, what further do you want? If one reads the quoted article, he sees at once that it usually is one of the misleading articles from the _New York Herald,_ but all contradictions are in vain—they will not help—we on this side are all barbarians, sir. You know, sir, what kind of articles usually fill the political sheets before the elections, such as: 'Dissolution is certain if H....s party wins.' 'Revolution if Van Buren-Jackson principles are put into force.' 'Destruction of the

Southern States if X's tariff bill passes the House,' and others as misleading. I will not say anything of the countless articles that are written only because of jealousy between town and town or state and state, much less of the senseless wit with which the editors have to fill their columns or play upon local conditions. No, sir, all talking is in vain and the only remedy is to print the defense also. Then, sir, it may go—it is in print. That is the only thing that will shake up the firm, well-learnt ideas."

"Well, stranger," interrupted the backwoodsman, it is not necessary for you to tell me of that. I reckon I know what the northerner says of the southerner. I am something of a northerner myself, sir. I am a Hoosier and proud of it, sir. But I had to laugh, sir, when I made a little trip to the City of Brotherly Love a few years ago. Sir, you should have seen the worthy old Quakers, how they warned me against hell—New Orleans. I had the pleasure also, sir, of seeing the shrewd, pious shopkeepers compete with the down-easterner in trying to hang their wares on the neck of the simple backwoodsman. But, sir, we Hoosiers have a little wit also. The Quakers could not get the best of this child. But I must admit that I was a little afraid of New Orleans, sir.

"Not really afraid, but I thought, sir, a little precaution is better than a calculation too late as to how I should have done it. The old foxes had told me how the Spaniards in New Orleans fought with long knives during broad daylight in the open streets and in the marketplace, how the French parleyvoos relieved every honest northerner or westerner of his money, how people would disappear in the mud in the streets, how two hundred people died daily of the yellow fever and no telling what else. I figured, therefore, sir, what I should do. First I went over to Chestnut Street and bought me a twelve-inch-long knife from a respectable Quaker which this pious shopkeeper kept on sale for the benefit of those who were traveling to the South. In regard to my money, sir, I did not need to be afraid. In order to prevent the yellow fever, I bought thirty boxes of Dr. Brantreth's Universal Pills. Now I seated myself on the *Eliza*, a real Baltimore schooner, sir. You may judge for yourself—in eleven days we were in the mouth of the Mississippi and sailed up that powerful stream. The banks on each side, sir, consist for the first forty or forty-five miles of immense drift logs, alligators, reeds, marsh, mosquitoes and snail colonies, and a little further up bears, panthers and wolves hold forth. But on the next day, sir, we passed an altogether different strip of land. Sugar plantations miles long lay like a chain on both sides of the mammoth stream compared to which our Ohio is only a small brook. The land, sir, at this time lay lower than the water level, which was held in its bed by levees from twenty to thirty feet wide. But, sir, when a man has had nothing under him for ten or twelve days but the rolling waves and has seen nothing over him but the endless blue, he would like to jump overboard for joy and swim ashore to the beautiful residence of the plantation owner, to which is joined a group of negro huts like a small town, each with a little garden, together with the magazine and the refinery."

The stranger interrupted the speaker, asking why a small garden was with each little house.

"Why, sir," continued the backwoodsman, "do you not know that each black man has his little piece of ground—raises sweet potatoes, corn, cabbage, red pepper, cauliflower, turnips and no telling what else. You know, we Americans are satisfied with good beefsteak, ham and eggs, cornbread together with tea, coffee or milk; but the French in New Orleans mix together everything that can be found in the house and make their excellent gumbos, kickshaws and other dishes from them. The Spaniards will not be outdone and throw in a few handfuls of fiery red pepper besides. Those, sir, are dishes that no honest man of our type can eat."

"But what do the negroes do with all the vegetables?" asked the wanderer.

"Why," said the Hoosier, reflecting a little, "I reckon they take them to New Orleans and sell them. 'Tis their grog money, sir. But," he continued in his account, "one night the captain who was towing us cried through his megaphone: Look out on the *Eliza*, look out, turn you loose! And before we had time to do anything we crashed into a brig from Havana and splintered up its back-board, or star-board, or lay-board side, as they call it, for which our captain had to pay every cent of damages. The next day, sir, as I wandered up from the landing, with my big knife always handy, I saw neither Spaniards who wanted to fight nor any that seemed to show any desire to. On the contrary they cried in competition with their parrots and monkeys: 'Here the best oranges, here the best bananas, gentlemen, here the best of everything, sir!' and so forth, and then in French, and then in Spanish and Italian. These black and brown and yellow people make a hellish noise. Even the filthy Chocktaws that bring weeds and roots of the forest to the town for sale were not missing; but with none of them does one see knife, dagger or pistols.

"After I had wandered about for a while, I came to the American quarters, called a municipality, and met a large number of my countrymen, who were carrying long knives like mine. We soon, however, discovered that the many frightful stories that we had heard were absolutely untrue, and we had no other use for our knives than to pitch for quarters with them on the large sugar and tobacco barrels.

"Of yellow fever no one had heard anything for two years, and my Brantreth pills were capital thrown away. Couldn't sell them, could not even induce one of my countrymen to take them for nothing. You see, sir, the false reports have their advantages too; if it isn't for one, it is for the other. Discarded speculations, sir, idle speculations. In order to keep me as a customer, because I annually bought many wares for my father, the old Quaker shopkeeper warned me against New Orleans. He feared I would buy there in the future, which, in fact, I did, sir, and . . . ."

"Hey there, gentlemen! Hey there! Good morning to you. I suppose you are freighting for Waterloo, are you not? Take me along—the best way to idle away the time is in good company, and it is also comfortable on a country hike where the redskins still roam about at times."

The two travelers looked around and beheld a rider with narrow shoulders, about five feet eight inches high. White and blue striped trousers, a shirt with short sleeves, half boots and a sagging Kentucky felt hat from which the good rain had washed all the starch decorated the stranger's figure. After the customary salutations of which, I must admit, there were only a few, and a few trivial remarks, "male talk," the stranger asked in English, with a nasal tone: "I reckon, gentlemen, this is the Waterloo road on which we are now traveling?"

"Perfectly correct, sir," was the reply of the backwoodsman.

"I suppose, gentlemen, that it isn't very far any more to the town?" asked the apparently very talkative stranger again.

"A few miles, sir," was the laconic answer.

"Well, sir, you have different kind of miles in Texas. Are they horse-miles or ordinary miles that you mean?"

"Certainly, they are our horse-miles, mister, but you need not be afraid—we will soon be in sight of the Colorado chain of hills and at its foot lies the little hill town."

The forest now opened itself and several miles toward the northwest the dark mountains were piling up, out of which the Colorado flowed into the plains. The two sides of the road as it still continued in the forest were bordered with gigantic pecan trees, oaks, cypress and other varieties of trees, but little of their ancient stems was to be seen. Immense masses of interwoven grapevines rose from near the road and reached to the tops of the gigantic trees, and often garlands of the same growth thirty or forty feet long hung down over the center of the road so that the traveler was not infrequently obliged to cut off these and other vine growths.

Little of the green was to be seen, as a cover of large black grapes concealed the fresh vegetative growths from the traveler, and the European, reveling in the charm of the scenery, rode on through the natural alley.

"I suppose, gentlemen, you know of Santa Anna's trick?" said the stranger after a pause.

"What, sir? What kind of a trick?" asked the two together, starting up out of their musings. "We don't know anything of Santa Anna, stranger, except that the fellow is being treated altogether too well and that he is making us a lot of unnecessary cost."

"That fellow should be treated differently," added the backwoodsman, "or they should run him home to the padres, so that we would at last be rid of him—he lives like the Pope in Rome"

"Don't reckon that's so, sir," said the stranger, "the gentleman is presently decorated with ornaments—shackled in irons."

"By thunder, is it true, stranger?" asked the backwoodsman, "How does it come? What has happened to David Burnet? Has he taken the staggers? Or has he lost his mind?"

"None of them, gentlemen, but Santa Anna has again acted in Santa Anna style. I will tell you about it if you want to hear it. You no doubt know, gentlemen, that this fellow was taken to Columbia last June because the government was transferred there. To make it short, I must say that this gentleman had developed a plan for some time to poison his guards and run away—had gotten some poison from some free Mexicans that were standing around, and last week business was to pick up. But his secretary, gentlemen, a very sly fellow, who probably suspected that nothing good would come from it, betrayed the matter to the last detail. You can imagine how raging Burnet was—had him placed in irons at once and liberated the secretary. This will probably be the end of him. According to my opinion he is a dead man. The Congress will soon pass on him, gentlemen; I must admit that I would not like to be in his shoes."

The European could not speak for astonishment, but the backwoodsman was perfectly cool and swore that it would have made little difference to him if the prisoner had escaped. He added that the nation held David responsible for Santa Anna, and if he let him escape, he would have to settle with the enraged nation the best he could.

The stranger was on the point of objecting to the indifference of the backwoodsman, when he was distracted by the appearance of the charming little town.

The conversation now turned to the army of the Republic, which, as the stranger stated, consisted of nearly three thousand volunteers from the States, and if the Mexicans should ever again cross the Rio Grande, the people could easily raise an army of ten thousand men. Also the next presidential election was taken under consideration, and it developed that the three travelers were thorough Houston men and that they did not wish to have anything to do with David Burnet, who, in other respects, was a perfect gentleman.

Old Sam had the votes of the traveling clover leaf and he also had those of the nation.

Conclusion

AGAIN THE NORTHWEST STORM IS HOWLING down over the plains from the Rocky Mountains, and again the redskin and the buffalo are fleeing ahead of it down to the mild climate of the free young Republic of Texas.

The star of the hope of the West is sparkling merrily at the tip of the pole of liberty. Just as boldly as the flag of liberty is defying the northwest storm, it is also defying the political hurricanes. The confusion of the elections is over. Old Sam is at the helm. He, the careful pilot, who had safely guided the frail craft through the foaming, thundering, breaking surf, the voice of the people elected as their pilot after the brig had passed over dangerous shoals and banks and is now cutting through the gently rocking waves.

The old general or the new president, as one likes, at once took charge of the holy power entrusted to him and sent Santa Anna home. This gentleman, as he still had power, recognized the independence of Texas and agreed to obtain the same recognition. Will he execute his pledges?

"Suppose, never," mumbled the backwoodsman, "Old Sam damned dictatorial."

The old general took his own course; he knew what should be done. He understood the backwoodsmen and they understood him.

But the old oak had deluded itself. As soon as the Mexican was out of the trap and had finished a trip through the States to Washington to make a similar recognition there, he returned home. His presidential term had expired and he had no inclination to take a seat on the decaying chair again. He rather declared to the world that his lifetime power was over, that he could not do anything and, consequently, could not fulfill his pledges.

Old Sam laughed and said that he had half-way known this in advance, but that he wanted to spill no more blood and wanted to build the nation on noble foundations.

Meanwhile the citizens have forgotten about this long ago, and the roads are alive with immigration caravans. The forests are groaning under blows of the ax and felled forests appear on all sides. Day and sunlight is finally penetrating into the regions of the primitive forests. Numerous houses of the industrious settlers are springing up at the rim of the prairies and everything is pointing to an enormous crop next year. Never, no never, did Texas see such activity.

Since there is nothing to be feared from the enemy, three thousand volunteers have been discharged and the old worn-out Mexican machinery trembles when the patriot Deaf Smith with his rangers undertakes an excursion toward the Rio Grande. This gentleman, I must observe, is now captain of a ranger corps that is guarding the desolate region between the Nueces and the Rio Grande. It is very dangerous to get within range of his ever well-loaded rifle, as he shoots without making many formalities about it if he does not get a satisfactory reply to his three-fold "Who goes there?" Not everyone knows that it is necessary to speak very loud to communicate with him.

Conclusion

As already stated, Mexico has not recognized our independence but better yet, the most powerful and most liberal nations have done so. Even the holy cornerstone, the bull-slinging state-holder of Christ has sent down his gracious benedictions from the seven hills. O, lucky Texans! Are not all of these proofs that Texas can defend herself against her miserable enemies?

Yes, the sons of Uncle Sam have again proven to the world that they possess common sense and that they know how to defend liberty, that to attain it everything else must step into the background, that for the highest gift of universal blessing, blood and money must be freely poured out—in a word, that the people must possess patriotism, real patriotism, not the evaporating kind. Deeply, deeply, it must touch the heart, and clear and true it must express itself on the fortunes of the fatherland. Not even that soil on which we first saw the light of day is entitled to the conception of fatherland if we are crushed in its grinding machine. No, only in the country where I myself am a cog in the wheel can I say that this is my fatherland.

For it, my life!

For such a fatherland the deep inward patriotism clutches the lance. When demons, heartless and soulless creatures, endeavor to cheat the people out of their national consciousness and try to reintroduce the old golden times with their hypocrisy and robbery, then this godly spirit will not remain with blank words and vain protestations, but, on the contrary, it will step forward to vigorous action.

The countrymen and the merchants, the workmen and the manufacturers, the soldiers and the officers, the servants of the people, all, all are citizens of the State, everyone is a part of the mighty machine. Everyone must help bear the burdens of the land, and everyone must, therefore, have equal rights before the laws. No monopoly, no preference, no caste, no meaningless forms, no selfishness in that which pertains to all, and no shackles for the press! No shackles of thought! None for the tongue that speaks the truth!

These are the principles of the Texans. For these, yes, for these we would gladly sacrifice our lives, and another time I cry:

Liberty! Law! And Texas forever!